NOLO Products & Services

Books & Software

Get in-depth information. Nolo publishes hundreds of great books and software programs for consumers and business owners. Order a copy—or download an ebook version instantly—at Nolo.com.

Legal Encyclopedia

Free at Nolo.com. Here are more than 1,400 free articles and answers to common questions about everyday legal issues including wills, bankruptcy, small business formation, divorce, patents, employment and much more.

Plain-English Legal Dictionary

Free at Nolo.com. Stumped by jargon? Look it up in America's most up-to-date source for definitions of legal terms.

Online Legal Documents

Create documents at your computer. Go to Nolo.com to make a will or living trust, form an LLC or corporation or obtain a trademark or provisional patent. For simpler matters, download one of our hundreds of high-quality legal forms, including bills of sale, promissory notes, nondisclosure agreements and many more.

Lawyer Directory

Find an attorney at Nolo.com. Nolo's consumer-friendly lawyer directory provides in-depth profiles of lawyers all over America. From fees and experience to legal philosophy, education and special expertise, you'll find all the information you need to pick the right lawyer. Every lawyer listed has pledged to work diligently and respectfully with clients.

Free Legal Updates

Keep up to date. Check for free updates at Nolo.com. Under "Products," find this book and click "Legal Updates." You can also sign up for our free e-newsletters at Nolo.com/newsletters.

1st edition

The Legal Answer Book for Families

Attorney Emily Doskow & Marcia Stewart

FIRST EDITION	FEBRUARY 2011
Editor	MARY RANDOLPH
Cover Design	SUSAN PUTNEY
Book Design	TERRI HEARSH
Proofreading	SUSAN CARLSON GREENE
Index	THÉRÈSE SHERE
Printing	DELTA PRINTING SOLUTIONS, INC.

Doskow, Emily.
    The legal answer book for families / by Emily Doskow and Marcia Stewart. -- 1st ed.
        p. cm.
    Summary: "Provides a clear and concise overview of laws that affect personal relationships and families and answers everyday legal questions that nearly every family encounters at some point. This book includes an appendix of detailed information for all 50 states"--Provided by publisher.
    ISBN-13: 978-1-4133-1373-4 (pbk.)
    ISBN-10: 1-4133-1373-6 (pbk.)
    ISBN-13: 978-1-4133-1374-1 (e-book)
    ISBN-10: 1-4133-1374-4 (e-book)
    1. Domestic relations--United States. I. Stewart, Marcia. II. Title.
    KF505.Z9D67 2010
    346.7301'5--dc22

                          2010042816

Please note

We believe accurate, plain-English legal information should help you solve many of your own legal problems. But this text is not a substitute for personalized advice from a knowledgeable lawyer. If you want the help of a trained professional—and we'll always point out situations in which we think that's a good idea—consult an attorney licensed to practice in your state.

Acknowledgments

We couldn't have written this book without our editor Mary Randolph. Every page reflects Mary's outstanding editing and writing skills and great ideas. Special thanks to Emily Alschbach for her invaluable help assembling the appendix of 50-state rules and resources. Thanks also go to Nolo editors and authors Janet Portman (for help with material on juvenile justice and education issues), Ilona Bray (for contributing material on immigration issues affecting families and children), and Diana Fitzpatrick (for her advice on family-related tax issues). And big thanks to Terri Hearsh in Nolo's Production department for her great design and eye for detail, and to Jennifer Balaco, Desiree Stephens, Wendy Jacobson, and Nolo's other marketing staff for their support and enthusiasm for this book.

Table of Contents

Appendixes

Your Family Legal Companion

Questions about our families and the law pop up all the time. Where can I get a copy of my child's birth certificate? If I don't have a will, do my stepchildren inherit from me? How much child support will I have to pay if I get divorced?

Finding the answers isn't always easy, even in the age of instant online information. Laws affecting couples, children, and families vary from state to state. Online resources are often out of date or too general. Sure, lawyers can tell us, but obviously it's not practical to dash off to a lawyer every time something comes up.

That's why we wrote this book. Use it to find quick answers to a wide variety of practical questions you might have about how the law (federal, state, and local) affects you and your family. We'll tell you what kinds of legal matters you can handle on your own—and when it makes sense to hire a lawyer.

You'll learn basic legal rules, and from there you can go right to specific information for your state. The two appendixes at the end of the book provide detailed information about state laws on a myriad of family law topics. Appendix A covers marriage, divorce, child custody, and child support. Appendix B covers adoption, children, and elder care. In addition to state laws, these appendixes include carefully chosen lists of websites, government agencies, and nonprofit organizations that offer the best information on specific topics.

This book is for people in any kind of family. If you have children or are thinking of having or adopting them, or are getting married or divorced (or thinking of doing so), you're bound to have legal and financial questions. If you're planning for your own senior years or helping a parent plan, questions about government benefits are almost inevitable. If you're with a same-sex partner, the laws seem to be changing every week—here, you'll find out the latest developments (and information about how to stay up to date). In other words, whether you have a question about a newborn or a teenager, a house full of kids or an empty nest, a parent or a spouse, this book has something for you. It's the ultimate resource for commonly asked questions about creating and protecting families.

Marriage

We think of marriage as a romantic institution, but it's also a legal arrangement—a contract, really, with terms written by the state. Most people enter into that contract with no real idea of what those terms are. Most people planning to get married haven't considered how a prenuptial agreement works, and most newlyweds (or not-so-newlyweds) don't know what marriage means in terms of sharing a spouse's property, income, and debts. Things get even murkier if your fiance is from another country or you're in a same-sex relationship. Here are some of the basics about marriage and marriage-like relationships.

STATE RULES AND RESOURCES

The Marriage section of each state's listing in Appendix A contains:

- your state's rules on marriage requirements, such as blood tests, waiting periods before marriage, and the like; same-sex marriages and domestic partnerships; common law marriages, and more, and
- links to relevant government and nonprofit agencies, including courts that handle family matters.

The Legal Rights and Benefits of Marriage

Married couples receive numerous rights and benefits under both federal and state law. These include:

- income tax benefits, such as the ability to transfer property between spouses with no tax consequences
- inheritance rights to a deceased spouse's property (see Chapter 8 for more on this)
- government benefits, such as Social Security spousal retirement and death benefits
- employment benefits, such as obtaining health insurance through your spouse's employer and the right to take medical leave to care for a spouse who becomes ill
- the right to make medical decisions if your spouse is incapacitated and to make decisions about body disposal and organ donation
- financial support, including equitable property division and the right to seek alimony in a divorce

- the ability to sponsor your spouse for a green card
- the right to leave your spouse unlimited amounts of money not subject to the federal estate tax
- protection from having to testify against your spouse in a court proceeding, and
- consumer benefits, such as family rates for health, homeowners', auto, and other types of insurance.

These are just some of the many benefits that come with marriage. Some of them—the ones that are governed by state law—also apply to same-sex couples who are legally married or are in domestic partnerships or civil unions in marriage-equivalent states. But because of the federal Defense of Marriage Act (DOMA), the federal rules and benefits relating to marriage don't apply to same-sex couples.

Getting Married

Whether you're planning a wedding in a church or another religious venue, at city hall, on the beach, or in Las Vegas, you must follow the same basic rules.

Who Can Get Married

Only opposite-sex couples may get married in all but six U.S. jurisdictions. The exceptions are discussed below, in "Same-Sex Marriage."

Other rules vary slightly from state to state, but here are the essentials:

- Each person must be at least the age of consent, which is usually 18. Younger people may be able to marry with their parents' consent.
- The intended spouses cannot be too closely related, such as siblings, aunts or uncles, or nieces or nephews or, in some states, first cousins.
- Both people must have the mental capacity to understand what they are doing and its consequences.
- The parties must be sober at the time of the marriage.
- Neither spouse can be married to someone else.
- The couple must get a marriage license.

You do not need to be a legal resident of a state to be married there, although there is usually a residency requirement for divorce.

Three's a Crowd: Adultery, Bigamy, and Polygamy

Adultery, consensual sexual relations by a married person with someone other than the person's spouse, is illegal in some states. In states that still allow fault grounds for divorce, adultery is always sufficient grounds for a divorce. In addition, some states factor in adultery when dividing property between divorcing spouses, and adultery may find its way into custody proceedings.

Bigamy means having two spouses at the same time; polygamy is having more than two. A marriage in which one of the parties is already legally married is bigamous and usually therefore void. In most states, if the bigamy was intentional, it is also a crime. Polygamy is a crime in all states.

Marriage Licenses and Certificates

A marriage *license* is the piece of paper that authorizes you to get married before the fact, while a marriage *certificate* is the document that proves you are married once the wedding ceremony is over. Following are the typical steps couples take to get married.

Get the license from the appropriate city or county official, such as the county clerk, in the state where you want to be married. Before you go into the county office, find out what documents you might need to bring—you'll need some kind of identification, and you might also need to bring a birth certificate or divorce decree. Also, find out any requirements for witnesses. You might be able to make an appointment, which should cut down on standing-in-line time.

There's a fee for the license (usually $25 to $100, depending on the state and county).

Licenses are good for 30 days to one year, depending on the state. If your license expires before you get married, you can apply for a new one.

 STATE RULES AND RESOURCES

Where to find state license requirements. See your state page in Appendix A for license requirements, including blood tests (discussed below).

Have a ceremony. Depending on the state, there may be a short waiting period (usually just a few days) between getting a license and getting married.

Get the marriage certificate. Most states require both spouses, the person who officiated, and one or two witnesses to sign the marriage certificate; often this is done just after the ceremony. Then the person who performed the ceremony must file the certificate with the appropriate county office (for example, the county clerk's office) where you live. A few weeks after getting the marriage certificate, the county sends the newlyweds a certified copy of the marriage certificate.

Will It Hurt to Get Married? Required Blood Tests

A few states require premarriage blood tests to check for sexually transmitted diseases (STDs) in both partners, and to see whether or not the bride to be has immunity to rubella, which can cause problems during pregnancy. The tests may also disclose the presence of genetic disorders, such as sickle-cell anemia or Tay-Sachs disease. No states require HIV tests, but some give out information about HIV and AIDS. In most states, blood tests aren't required for people over 50 or if someone is pregnant or sterile.

If either partner tests positive for an STD, what then happens depends on the state. Some states may refuse to issue a marriage license.

Marriage Ceremonies

A wedding ceremony may be nonreligious (civil) or religious. Civil ceremonies must be performed by a judge, justice of the peace, or court clerk who has legal authority to perform marriages, or by a person given temporary authority by a judge or court clerk. Religious ceremonies must be conducted by a clergy member—for example, a priest, minister, or rabbi. Some states have programs —like California's "deputy for a day" system—that allow a nonclergy friend or relative to officiate at a wedding. There's also the Universal Life Church, which will ordain anyone over the Internet for a fee, but has occasionally run into legal problems over the validity of the ordinations (and therefore the marriages performed by the Universal Life minister).

Usually, no special words are required as long as the spouses acknowledge their intention to marry each other—once you've included that, you can design whatever type of ceremony you want.

Who Keeps the Ring?

If an engagement ends, the former sweethearts may well disagree about who should get to keep the engagement ring.

Most courts consider the gift of an engagement ring a conditional gift, which isn't final until the wedding actually takes place. If there's no wedding, then the giver has the right to get the ring back.

But, some courts delve into the reasons the engagement was broken. So, a man who gave his fiancée a ring but then called off the wedding, especially if the bride to be stood ready to go ahead, might not get the ring back. But, if she precipitated the breakup by being unfaithful, a court might order her to return the ring.

Changing Your Name After Marriage

Though many people do so, no law requires you to change your name just because you get married.

A spouse who wants to take the other spouse's name should promptly and consistently begin to use that name. A court procedure isn't required, but it still takes some time and effort to change your name.

Some institutions will accept your marriage license as proof of your name change. However, others prefer to see a government-issued form of identification in your new name, so it's a good idea to change your name with the Social Security Administration (SSA) first. Visit www.ssa.gov to download the required application form, or call SSA at 800-772-1213. Then mail or take the completed application—along with your marriage license and proof of your identity—to a local Social Security office. A few weeks later, you will receive your new Social Security card and you can begin to change your name with other institutions.

The big bureaucracies will take the longest to process your request, so, next, you'll want to get the ball rolling with the local office of your state motor vehicle agency (usually called DMV), the U.S. passport office, and the tax agencies. Then you can dive into the long list of other businesses and organizations in your life—banks, insurance agencies, health care practitioners, the voter registration office, employers, clubs, utilities, publications, and so on. Some of these may require that you fill out forms and provide proof of your new name, but others may simply change your name over the phone at your request. Finally, don't forget to update your personal documents, such as your will, living trust, or health care directive.

If this seems overwhelming, there are online businesses that can help. They collect your information and then provide already completed forms and letters for you to send to the SSA, DMV, passport office, banks, and utilities. This can save a good deal of time and may be worth the money. Just double-check to make sure they're using the most current government forms and instructions, and ask about how they keep your private information secure.

Creating a New Name

If you and your spouse both want to take a new name, such as a hyphenated version of your last names or a brand-new name, you'll need a court order. There are some restrictions on the new name you may choose:

- You cannot choose a name with fraudulent intent—for example, to avoid paying debts, keep from getting sued, or get away with a crime.
- Your new name cannot interfere with the rights of others—for example, you can't take the name of a famous person with the intent to mislead.
- You cannot use a name that would be intentionally confusing, such as a number or punctuation.
- You cannot choose a name that is a racial slur.
- You cannot choose a name that includes threatening or obscene words or words likely to incite violence.

RESOURCE

For more information on changing your name, see www.nolo.com/legal-encyclopedia/name-change. If you live in California, you can use *How to Change Your Name in California*, by Lisa Sedano and Emily Doskow (Nolo). See www.nolo.com for a sample chapter and full table of contents.

Sharing a Spouse's Debts, Property, and Income

How you will share and, if you divorce, divide the debts, property, and income that you and your spouse accrue after marriage depends mostly on where you live—specifically, whether your state follows community property rules or the common law (also known as equitable distribution) system of dealing with marital property. (Chapter 2 explains how these rules play out in divorce cases, and Chapter 8 explains their relevance for estate planning.)

Common Law Property States

The majority of states (all but the community property states listed below) follow "common law" property rules. In these states, debts incurred by one spouse in that spouse's name alone are usually that spouse's debts alone. However, a debt is owed by both spouses if it was:

- for a family necessity, such as food or shelter for the family or tuition for the kids, or
- jointly undertaken—for example, if both spouses' names are on an account or on the title to a house.

All other debts, such as a business debt from one spouse's business, are considered the separate debt of the owner spouse—and generally a creditor cannot go after the income or property of the other spouse to collect.

Property also generally belongs to the spouse who earns it or whose name is on the title document. All these are separate property:

- income earned by one spouse, if it's kept separate (if it's mixed with the other spouse's money, it can be nearly impossible to tell what belongs to whom)

- property bought with one spouse's separate income or funds, unless the title to the property (such as a car) is put in both spouses' names
- gifts and inheritances received by one spouse, and
- property owned by one spouse before marriage (and kept separate).

Community Property States

In community property states, all of the income earned and property acquired, as well as all debts incurred, belong to both spouses together. (Together, the spouses are called "the community.") Couples who prefer to keep some or all of their debts and income separate can do so by signing a prenuptial agreement (discussed below).

Community Property States			
Alaska*	Idaho	New Mexico	Washington
Arizona	Louisiana	Texas	Wisconsin
California	Nevada		
* In Alaska, spouses can sign an agreement making specific assets community property.			

Most debts incurred by one spouse during the marriage are owed by both spouses, even if only one spouse signed the paperwork for the debt. Debts incurred before marriage, such as a student loan, don't automatically become joint debts. However, a creditor can come after community property funds if the person who owes the debt fails to pay it. For example, if your spouse defaults on a student loan, the lender can try to collect from your joint accounts, even if you earned most of the money that's in those accounts.

All income earned by either spouse during marriage, as well as property bought with that income, is community property, owned equally by the spouses. Even if the spouse who earns income keeps the money in a separate account, that money still belongs to the other spouse too. However, money and property that the spouses owned before marriage is considered separate property as long as it's kept in the name of the person who owned it and not mixed up with the community money. It's common, however, for spouses to mix their money together once they marry, making it nearly impossible to tell what might still be separate property.

Gifts and inheritances received by one spouse are the separate property of that spouse.

When one spouse owns a business that was started before the marriage, the business is considered that spouse's separate property—but the income generated by the business is community property, and the community often acquires an interest in the business itself because of increases in its value or because the nonowner spouse contributed work or ideas to it.

How Marriage Affects Your Credit— and How to Avoid Problems

Many couples assume that a new, merged credit record is created when they marry. But, in fact, every credit record is tied to a single Social Security number. That means that your credit record, and any credit report you get, stays separate from your spouse's.

Both credit records do, however:
- list accounts that you and your spouse open jointly
- list accounts with one of you named as cosigner, and
- reflect the addition of a spouse to an existing account as either a joint account holder or an authorized user.

How One Spouse's Credit Report Affects the Other's

Lenders use credit reports and scores to decide whether to lend you money and how high an interest rate to charge. Some employers, landlords, and insurance companies also take into account an applicant's credit history when making a decision.

When you and your spouse apply jointly for credit, a rental home, or insurance, both of your credit histories will be considered. If either one of you has unfavorable information in your credit report, it will hurt your chances of getting credit—or at least getting it at a good rate.

Ways to Hold Credit

When you're married, you have four choices when it comes to applying for credit:

- Apply individually.
- Apply jointly.
- Make one spouse a cosigner for the other.
- Make one spouse an authorized user but not a joint account holder.

Which one is best? It depends on the circumstances. Here are some factors to consider.

Individual Credit

One way to avoid trouble is to apply for credit individually—that is, without your spouse. Of course, this strategy works only if your income and assets alone are substantial enough to qualify you for the credit. Qualifying on one income can be particularly difficult when applying for a large loan, such as a mortgage.

If you live in a community property state, as a practical matter it may be difficult to get a large loan on your own; lenders generally insist that couples apply together, because both spouses are responsible for the debt no matter who applies for it. If your spouse's credit record is bad, the lender may be reluctant to lend to you in the belief that your spouse's bad financial habits will make you less likely to be able to pay off the debt.

If you live in a common law state and you take out a loan in your own name using only your own credit record, you're the only person responsible for paying it back. If you don't pay the loan, you're the only one whose credit will be damaged.

In either case, if your name is the only one that appears on the loan documents, only your credit will be damaged if you do not make payments.

Joint Accounts

If you and your spouse are joint account holders, you are both liable for the debt. If you open a new account, each of you is legally responsible for repaying the entire debt. (And remember, if you live in a community property state, you may be liable even if your name isn't on the account.)

If one spouse adds the other to an existing account, the credit history—positive or negative—of the person with the existing account will affect that of the spouse who is added to the account. For example, if you have a positive credit history and add your spouse as a joint account holder to your existing account, your positive credit history will be factored into your spouse's score. If you have poor credit and add your spouse, your spouse's credit score will be harmed.

Adding your spouse to your account as a joint account holder will not affect your credit score unless your spouse uses much or all of your available credit.

Cosigners

Someone who cosigns for a debt becomes fully responsible for that debt if the primary borrower does not pay. Usually, lenders require a cosigner only if they're concerned that the borrower won't be able to pay. If your spouse has bad credit and a lender wants a cosigner, do it only if you are prepared to make payments if necessary.

Remember that if you are in a community property state, you are probably going to be liable for your spouse's debts even if you are not a cosigner.

Authorized User

If one spouse has poor credit, an alternative to applying for credit jointly is to designate that spouse as an authorized user on the other spouse's credit account. That way the less-qualified spouse can use the credit but is not liable for the debt (again, unless you're in a community property state).

Making one spouse an authorized user will not affect the account holder's credit score unless the authorized user uses much or all of the available credit—using up a large percentage of one's available credit has a negative affect on a person's credit rating. And, if the more solvent spouse decides later to remove the other from the account, it is much easier than if both were joint account holders.

If one spouse becomes an authorized user on the other's account, the account will appear on the authorized user's credit report. It may or may not affect his or her credit score. The latest version of the FICO scoring formula—the most widely used credit scoring system—does not factor authorized user status into scores. Older versions do, however, and many creditors still use them.

Level With Each Other Before Marriage

Experts recommend that couples review their credit reports together before getting married or taking on joint financial liabilities. If you're already married, a review is still a good idea. You can get a yearly free copy of your credit report from each of the three credit reporting bureaus—Equifax, Experian, and TransUnion—at www.annualcreditreport.com.

Check the reports for derogatory information such as:

- late payments and past-due amounts
- high balances
- collection accounts and charge-offs
- bankruptcy
- tax liens
- unpaid student loans, and
- foreclosures.

Although bad credit can be the result of extenuating circumstances, such as extensive medical bills, it also can result from poor money management. If your spouse's credit report reveals high balances, unpaid debts, or other negative history, you'd be well advised to keep your finances separate for the time being—until you've had a chance to discuss the reason for the credit issues and observe your spouse's financial habits. That means not opening new accounts jointly, not adding your partner to your existing accounts or being added to your partner's accounts, and not sharing a checking account.

How to Improve a Spouse's Bad Credit Record

Bad credit is not an insurmountable problem, but it can take time to turn things around. If you have excellent credit, you can help your spouse by:

- adding your spouse to one or more of your existing accounts (do this only if you are convinced your spouse will not charge up your balance)

- helping to pay down your spouse's balances, particularly if they are closer to the credit limit than yours are
- transferring your spouse's debt to one of your lower-interest accounts
- taking over bill paying if your spouse has spending or money management problems
- setting financial goals together, and
- checking your credit reports annually.

RESOURCE

More about maintaining good credit and repairing bad credit. See *Credit Repair*, by Robin Leonard (Nolo). Also, the Bankruptcy section of Nolo. com includes lots of useful articles on debt and credit, including the basics of credit reports, and the Personal Finance & Retirement section includes articles on budgeting and money management.

Prenuptial Agreements

A prenuptial or premarital agreement ("prenup") is a written contract created by a couple in anticipation of getting married, for the purpose of defining each person's financial rights and responsibilities. Typically, a prenup lists each person's property and debts and specifies what each person's property rights will be if the couple divorces. Without a prenup, state law controls how property is divided at divorce.

What You Can Do With a Prenup

Prenups have commonly been used by very wealthy people to protect assets, but couples of more modest means are increasingly turning to them. Prenups can be used to:

- keep finances separate and clarify financial rights and responsibilities during marriage by stating who owns income earned and property acquired during marriage
- clarify ownership of and interests in a spouse's business
- create a plan for how property will be divided in the event of divorce
- decide on (in most states) alimony or spousal support in case of divorce

- state intentions regarding an estate plan and waive inheritance rights
- get protection from the other spouse's debts, and
- reach other financial agreements, such as how you will buy a house together, start a business, put each other through college, or set aside money for savings.

What You Can't Do With a Prenup

While state laws vary, in general, you cannot use a prenup to:
- restrict child support, custody, or visitation rights
- encourage divorce (by appearing to offer a financial incentive for one spouse to end the marriage), or
- make rules about nonfinancial matters, such as having and raising children, or how you'll share household chores.

In a few states, you can't use a prenup to give up the right to alimony.

Lawyers and Prenups

To get started, an engaged couple should evaluate their circumstances, agree on what they want their prenuptial agreement to cover, and even start writing a draft of it. Most states require (or least suggest) that each person have an independent lawyer review the agreement, and it's a good idea whether your state requires it or not. Having two independent lawyers involved will help you craft a lasting agreement that both of you understand, and will help avoid court fights should you end up in an acrimonious divorce. In particular, if one spouse has much less money or assets than the other, the lower-earning spouse must have an attorney; otherwise, if there's ever a lawsuit over the prenup, the court may set it aside because the weaker party didn't have good advice.

If you make a prenup, be sure to follow through by making your estate plan. For example, if you are using a prenup to waive inheritance rights, make sure that your will and other estate planning documents actually transfer property as you intend. The prenup itself isn't enough to make sure your wishes are carried out.

Information about finding and working with an attorney is in Chapter 9.

RESOURCE

Help with prenuptial agreements. Before you visit a lawyer, you can decide essential terms and begin drafting your own prenuptial agreement, using Nolo's *Prenuptial Agreements: How to Write a Fair & Lasting Contract*, by Katherine E. Stoner and Shae Irving. This book includes a summary of each state's prenuptial laws. See www.nolo.com for a sample chapter and full table of contents.

Green Cards for Fiancés or Spouses

If you are a U.S. citizen or permanent resident, and you are engaged or married to a citizen of another country, your fiancé or spouse may be eligible for a green card. However, many people believe, wrongly, that they can just bring their fiancé or spouse to the United States or (if the immigrant is already here) to an office of U.S. Citizenship and Immigration Services (USCIS) and the immigrant will be given an instant green card or even U.S. citizenship—a belief that has led to sad cases of people being sent right home again.

The reality is that your fiancé or spouse will have to go through a multistep application process. It's your job to start the process, by submitting to USCIS either a fiancé visa petition (which can be used whether you are married or engaged) or an immigrant visa petition.

A fiancé or spouse who is currently overseas won't be allowed to enter the United States until both the visa petition and subsequent applications have been approved.

If your fiancé or spouse is already in the United States, the process gets even more complicated. A very recent entry by the immigrant on a tourist visa with the intention of applying for a green card could be considered visa fraud and disqualify your spouse for a green card. Completing the application process at a USCIS office within the United States is not permitted for some immigrants, depending on whether you (the petitioning spouse) are a U.S. citizen and whether your immigrant spouse entered the United States with a visa or illegally. That leads to further problems, because if your spouse has no choice but to leave the United States to complete the application process, but has lived in the United States illegally, your spouse may face a penalty and be forced to spend years outside the United States before returning.

Even if everything goes right, be prepared for a long wait. Every type of visa application involves several stages, including application forms, a medical examination, fingerprinting, various approvals, and an interview with a U.S. government official.

> ⚠ CAUTION
>
> **If you're not yet a U.S. citizen.** If you have U.S. permanent residence (a green card), you cannot bring your fiancé to the United States until you're married. Even then, your spouse will have to spend some years on a waiting list before entering the country. Work on getting U.S. citizenship to speed things up.

Eligibility for Fiancé and Marriage Visas

The basic requirements for the fiancé visa and the marriage visa are different.

Fiancé Visas

To qualify for a fiancé visa, the immigrant must:
- intend to marry a U.S. citizen of the opposite sex
- have met the citizen in person within the last two years, and
- be legally able to marry.

Also, the immigrant must be living in another country—someone who is already in the United States isn't eligible for a fiancé visa.

As part of the fiancé visa application process, you'll have to prove your intention to marry. That means providing a selection of documents, such as copies of your love letters and emails, phone bills, and wedding ceremony contracts for services such as catering and flowers. You'll also have to prove that you've met within the last two years, by submitting copies of plane tickets, hotel bills, or any other relevant documents.

Marriage-Based Visas (Green Cards)

To be eligible for an immigrant visa or a green card based on marriage, the immigrant must be legally married (it doesn't matter in what country) to a U.S. citizen or permanent resident of the opposite sex. Neither the immigrant nor the U.S. spouse can be married to someone else.

In the application process, you'll have to prove all of these things. Legal marriage is usually the easiest to prove, simply by providing a copy of your marriage certificate. Do your best to get your marriage certificate from the most official source possible, such as a government office. Unless it's all that's available in the country where you were married, USCIS will reject a certificate from a ship's captain or another nongovernmental place.

A binational marriage must be the real thing, not just a sham to get a green card. You'll have to prove that your marriage is for real by providing copies of documents such as joint bank statements, children's birth certificates, photos of the wedding and honeymoon, correspondence that demonstrates an intimate relationship, and more. Also, near the end of the application process, you'll have to attend an interview, either at an overseas U.S. consulate or (in the rare case where the immigrant is in the United States and eligible to complete the green card application process here) at a USCIS office. Similar to what you've seen in the movies, an interviewing officer who suspects fraud may separate you and your spouse and ask you detailed personal questions about your marriage and your life together.

Inadmissibility

To qualify for any type of visa, an immigrant must show that he or she is not "inadmissible." A person who can't show a means of support in the United States outside of public assistance, who has a criminal record or associations with a terrorist organization, who has committed visa fraud or repeatedly entered the United States illegally and been removed, or who has a communicable disease like tuberculosis would not be admitted to the United States. Inadmissibility is a major stumbling block for many immigrants, though waivers are available in some cases.

What's Next in the Green Card Application Process?

How and where an immigrant actually applies for a green card depends on a number of factors. These can include who the immigrant is marrying, whether or not the immigrant is in the United States already, and, if so, whether the person got here legally. In some cases, particularly where inadmissibility may be an issue, hiring an experienced immigration attorney is well worth the cost.

RESOURCE
More on fiancé and marriage visas.

The Immigration section of www.nolo.com includes many useful articles on U.S. green cards, visas, and citizenship, including eligibility and sponsorship requirements, interviews, exams, and bringing your spouse to the United States.

Fiancé & Marriage Visas: A Couple's Guide to U.S. Immigration, by Ilona Bray (Nolo), can help you complete the application forms, assemble the appropriate documents, and have a successful interview. See www.nolo.com for a sample chapter and full table of contents.

Same-Sex Marriage

In the last two decades, the legal landscape for same-sex couples has changed in extraordinary ways. Legal marriage is now available to any same-sex couple willing to travel to a marriage equality state—but the marriage won't be recognized by the federal government or, in some cases, by the couple's home state. In short, for same-sex couples, marriage is a lot more complicated than just saying "I do."

States That Allow Same-Sex Marriages

Five states and the District of Columbia now allow a same-sex couple to get married and enjoy all of the benefits of marriage under their laws.

States Where Same-Sex Couples Can Marry		
Connecticut	Iowa	New Hampshire
District of Columbia	Massachusetts	Vermont

While these marriages are legal for all purposes in the state where they are entered into, the federal government does not recognize any same-sex marriages, and many states refuse such recognition as well (see "Non-Recognition Issues," below).

All of the states that allow same-sex marriage recognize same-sex marriages—as well as civil unions and domestic partnerships—performed elsewhere. In addition, although they don't allow same-sex marriage or an equivalent themselves, both New York and Maryland do recognize same-sex marriages performed elsewhere. In these states, as long as you were legally married in a state or country that allows same-sex marriage, you will be treated like any other married couple: You can file a joint state tax return, provide health and retirement benefits for your spouse if you work for the state government, and enjoy numerous other rights that come with marriage under state laws, including divorce, child custody, property division, family leave benefits, and medical rights such as hospital visitation.

Same-Sex Marriage in California

The law is particularly unsettled in California. Same-sex couples cannot currently marry in California, even though a federal judge ruled in August 2010 that the state's ban on same-sex marriages violates the federal constitution. That ruling is currently being appealed to a federal court of appeals and may well end up in the U.S. Supreme Court.

In May of 2008, the California Supreme Court ruled that limiting marriage to persons of the opposite sex violates the California Constitution. Same-sex marriage became legal for a few months—until November of 2008, when voters passed Proposition 8, which once again limited marriage in California to opposite-sex couples. Between May and November, approximately 18,000 same-sex couples wed in California. Under California law, they are still legally married. The state also recognizes the marriages of same-sex couples who wed in other states and countries that allow it.

Non-Recognition Issues

The federal government does not recognize the marriages of same-sex couples who wed in states or in foreign countries (Canada and England, for example) where such marriages are legal and valid. Under the Federal Defense of Marriage Act (DOMA), these couples receive none of the marriage benefits provided by federal law. Forty states have passed their own DOMA statutes or constitutional amendments expressly limiting marriage to a man and a woman, and none of those DOMA states (except California) recognize same-sex marriages, although some of them do recognize domestic partnerships or civil unions.

This means that same-sex couples who marry or register as domestic partners in states that offer these options cannot take advantage of the hundreds of federal laws that confer rights, benefits, and protections to married heterosexual couples—such as Social Security spousal survivor and retirement benefits, the ability to file joint tax returns, and special estate planning benefits. They can take advantage only of state-recognized rights and responsibilities of marriage, such as joint tax filing and the ability to inherit from a spouse even without a will.

Non-recognition also means that a couple can travel to a marriage equality state, get legally married, and then return home to their non-recognition state and find that their marriage has very little meaning where they live. In at least two states, judges have refused to grant divorces to married same-sex couples because the state where the couple sought the divorce did not recognize the marriage itself. This leaves the couple in the position of having to either stay married or move to a state where the marriage is recognized and establish residency (which can take as long as six months to a year) in order to file for divorce there.

Domestic Partnerships and Civil Unions

A number of states have established for same-sex couples legal relationships that are the functional equivalent of marriage but are called something else—either domestic partnerships or civil unions. The term "domestic partners" is somewhat confusing, because it is used to describe legal marriage-equivalent relationships; legal relationships that only provide partial marital rights; and unmarried couples, of the same or opposite sex, who live together in a family relationship, and in some cases are recognized by local governments, businesses, colleges, and universities.

Marriage-Equivalent Relationships

California, Nevada, Oregon, and Washington State offer domestic partnership status that is the functional equivalent of marriage; New Jersey and

Illinois do the same but call the relationship a civil union. Some of these states limit domestic partnership registration to same-sex couples, but some include opposite-sex couples in which one partner is 62 or older. (This is to avoid affecting Social Security benefits, which can sometimes be reduced when the person receiving benefits gets married.)

No license is required to enter a domestic partnership or civil union—usually it's just a matter of filing a notarized form with a state office like the secretary of state. Ending a domestic partnership or civil union in a marriage-equivalent state usually requires that the partners go through the same court procedures that opposite-sex couples must use. There may be an abbreviated process for couples who haven't been registered for very long and don't own any property, but not many people qualify for that. Couples living in a non-recognition state generally need some legal advice on how to terminate their domestic partnership or civil union. (Chapter 2, "Divorce," provides more detail on ending a same-sex marriage or domestic partnership.)

Limited Rights and Benefits

A few states offer some limited rights and benefits to same-sex couples who register. Colorado, Hawaii, Maine, and Wisconsin all provide for some form of legal relationship, but the rights that come along with the relationship are a far cry from the marital rights provided in the marriage equality and marriage equivalent states.

In addition to these state-level rights and benefits, some public and private entities may offer domestic partners benefits such as:
- health, dental, and vision insurance
- sick and bereavement leave
- accident and life insurance
- death benefits
- parental leave (for a child you coparent)
- housing rights and tuition reduction (at universities), and
- use of recreational facilities.

> **RESOURCE**
>
> **Helpful resources on same-sex marriage, domestic partnerships, and civil unions.**

For details on laws in your state, including municipalities and other entities offering domestic partnership benefits, see the "In Your State" section of www. lambdalegal.org, or call 866-542-8336. Also, see the National Center for Lesbian Rights (www.nclrights.org, phone 800-528-6257), a national lesbian and gay legal organization that provides education, resources, and support.

Making It Legal: A Guide to Same-Sex Marriage, Domestic Partnerships & Civil Unions, by Frederick Hertz with Emily Doskow, fully explains same-sex relationship laws, reviews key issues that influence the decision to marry, and offers practical guidance. You can see a sample chapter and the full table of contents at www.nolo.com.

The Lesbian and Gay Couples section of www.nolo.com (under Divorce & Family Law) contains a wide range of articles that discuss issues affecting gay and lesbian couples.

Chapter 9 of this book provides advice on finding and working with attorneys. You'll want to see an experienced lawyer for advice about your marriage or domestic partnership (especially if you got married in a state that recognizes same-sex marriages but live in a state that doesn't), advice on legally ending your relationship, or other legal questions.

Common Law Marriage

In 15 states and the District of Columbia, heterosexual couples can become legally married without a license or ceremony (see the Marriage section of your state page in Appendix A for details). This type of marriage is called a common law marriage. Contrary to popular belief, a common law marriage is not created when two people simply live together for a certain number of years. To have a valid common law marriage (in states that recognize it), the couple must do all of the following:

- live together for a significant period of time (not defined in any state)
- hold themselves out as a married couple—typically this means using the same last name, referring to the other as "my husband" or "my wife," and filing a joint tax return, and
- intend to be married.

Common law marriages are not that common—they're actually fairly unusual. When one exists, the spouses receive the same legal treatment given to formally married couples, including the requirement that they go through a legal divorce to end the marriage.

Living Together

Many laws control the property ownership rights of married couples. In most states, no such laws exist for the many unmarried couples who live together, except for the handful of states with marriage-like domestic partnerships or civil unions. If you and your partner (gay or straight) are unmarried, you must take steps to protect your relationship and define your property rights. You will also face special concerns if you are raising children together.

Palimony

"Palimony" is a word coined by journalists—not lawyers—to describe the division of property or the alimony-like support paid by one unmarried partner to the other after a breakup. Members of unmarried couples are not legally entitled to such payments unless they have an agreement. In the famous 1976 case of *Marvin v. Marvin*, the California Supreme Court ruled that a person who cohabitated and later sued for support could argue that an *implied* contract existed between the partners. To avoid argument, it's best to have a written agreement about any payments to be made if the relationship ends.

Preparing a Written Property Agreement

If you want to legally establish how you will own property during your relationship, as well as what will happen if you separate or if one of you dies, you must put your intentions, desires, and expectations in writing. Your agreement will be called a "nonmarital agreement" or "living together contract." (Or, if you are planning for what happens when you die, you'll need to make a will.)

Almost all states now enforce written contracts between unmarried partners. And the longer you live together, the more important it is to write a contract making it clear who owns what. Otherwise, you might face a serious (and potentially expensive) battle if you split up and can't agree on how to divide what you've acquired.

A written property agreement is particularly important if you buy a house together. It should cover all of the following:

- **How you will take title to the property.** Your options vary from state to state. Many states let you hold title as "joint tenants with rights of survivorship," meaning that when one partner dies, the other automatically inherits the whole house. Or you might want to hold title as "tenants in common," so that each owner can choose who gets that partner's share by making a will or trust.
- **How much of the house each partner owns.** If you're joint tenants, then in most states, you must own equal shares.
- **What happens to the house if you break up.** Will one of you buy out the other, or will you sell the house and divide the proceeds? If you don't agree on who can buy the other out, how will you decide who gets first choice?

How Marriage Affects a Living Together Agreement

If you and a longtime partner make a property agreement while you are unmarried, will it be enforceable after you get married? Probably not. To be enforceable, premarital contracts must be made in contemplation of marriage. So, unless your living together contract is made shortly before your marriage, when you both plan to be married, a court will disregard it. It's best to review your contract and rewrite it as a premarital agreement.

Inheriting From an Unmarried Partner

If your unmarried partner dies, will you inherit? Not automatically. Your rights depend on whether your late partner made a will, trust, joint tenancy agreement, or some other estate planning document to leave property to you. (See Chapter 8 for more on this.)

Making Medical Decisions for an Unmarried Partner

If you are injured or incapacitated, your partner will not be allowed to make medical or financial decisions on your behalf unless you have executed the appropriate documents. To give your partner the right to make medical decisions for you, you must sign a form called a "durable power of attorney" (sometimes included in a "health care directive"). Without a durable power of attorney, the fate of a severely ill or injured person could be in the hands of a biological relative who won't honor the wishes of the ill or injured person. It is far better to prepare the necessary paperwork so the loving and knowing partner will be the decision maker. If you want your partner to be able to make financial decisions for you—when you become incapacitated or even for a short time because you're out of the country or otherwise unavailable—you need to execute another type of power of attorney, one that covers financial matters. (For more information about durable powers of attorney, see Chapter 7.)

Paternity, Custody, and Adoption

Unmarried same-sex couples who have children together need to take special steps when it comes to children. Unmarried heterosexual couples, on the other hand, aren't generally treated any differently than married straight couples from a legal perspective. Later chapters explain how you can head off problems over custody (covered in Chapter 3) and adoption (see Chapter 5).

Changing Your Name

Some unmarried couples want to share a last name. If you don't have a marriage certificate, you will need a court order (this is usually fairly simple) to change your name. For more information, see www.nolo.com/legal-encyclopedia/name-change.

Handling Housing Discrimination

In most states, landlords may legally refuse to rent to an unmarried couple. About 20 states ban discrimination on the basis of marital status, and most of them protect married couples only. Federal law does not protect unmarried couples from housing discrimination. Housing discrimination based on sexual orientation, however, is prohibited in some states and cities. Many of these laws also protect unmarried heterosexual couples.

Where Housing Discrimination Based on Sexual Orientation Is Prohibited		
States		**Cities**
California	New Hampshire	Atlanta
Connecticut	New Jersey	Chicago
District of Columbia	New Mexico	Detroit
Hawaii	New York	Miami
Maryland	Rhode Island	New York
Massachusetts	Vermont	Pittsburgh
Minnesota	Wisconsin	St. Louis
		Seattle

RESOURCE

For unmarried couples.

Living Together: A Legal Guide for Unmarried Couples, by Ralph Warner, Toni Ihara, & Frederick Hertz (Nolo), explains the legal rules that apply to unmarried couples and includes sample contracts about jointly owned property. See www.nolo.com for a sample chapter and full table of contents.

The U.S. Department of Housing and Urban Development (HUD), at www.hud. gov, offers advice on fighting housing discrimination.

A Legal Guide for Lesbian and Gay Couples, by Denis Clifford, Frederick Hertz, and Emily Doskow (Nolo), sets out the law on everything from medical and financial issues to parenting and estate planning and contains useful sample agreements. See www.nolo.com for a sample chapter and full table of contents.

The Alternatives to Marriage Project, www.unmarried.org, is a national organization that provides resources, support, and advocacy for unmarried people living together.

The Renters' & Tenants' Rights section of www.nolo.com (under Real Estate & Rental Property) has many useful articles about housing.

The National Center for Lesbian Rights (www.nclrights.org, phone 800-528-6257) is a national lesbian and gay legal organization that provides education, resources, and support.

Divorce

D ivorce is the legal termination of a marriage. Couples separate, divide their property (everything from the house to the retirement accounts), and, if necessary, make arrangements for sharing time with their children and dealing with issues of child custody and support.

Although states use different rules for dividing property and dealing with children of a marriage, the basic procedures of divorce follow the same general pattern everywhere. The process is always both paperwork heavy and emotionally challenging, but couples can now take advantage of increasingly available services like mediation and collaborative divorce. Those who do usually end up feeling less damaged by the process than those who are determined to fight everything out in court. And many lawyers are choosing to embrace a less adversarial model, encouraging divorcing couples to resolve financial and family issues as amicably as possible.

 STATE RULES AND RESOURCES
The Divorce section of each state's listing in Appendix A contains:
- your state's rules on grounds for divorce (fault and no-fault), length of separation required, state residency requirements, and how property is divided, and
- links to state resources for divorce information and forms you can fill out yourself, including courts that handle divorces .

Separation or Divorce

Separation simply means that you are living apart from your spouse. You're still legally married until you get a judgment of divorce from a court.

There are three kinds of separation: trial, permanent, and legal. In most states, all three have the potential to affect your legal rights regarding property ownership.

Trial Separation

You and your spouse may choose to live apart for a trial period while you decide between divorce or reconciliation. Your living arrangements don't change the legal rules that control the ownership of property. For example, if you live in a community property state, money you earn still belongs equally to you and your spouse. And if you are in a common law state, a debt you incur on your own probably isn't your spouse's responsibility. (Chapter 1 discusses marital property rights and Appendix A includes rules in your state.)

If you and your spouse are hoping to reconcile, it's a good idea to write an informal agreement about some issues that will surely come up while you are separated. For example, will you continue to share a joint bank account? Who will stay in the family home? If you have young children, how and when will each of you spend time with them?

If you decide there's no going back, your trial separation turns into a permanent one.

Permanent Separation

When you live apart from your spouse without intending to reconcile, but you are not divorced, you are considered permanently separated. In most states, living apart can change property rights between spouses: If you don't intend to get back together, then assets and debts acquired during the separation belong only to the spouse who acquires them. Once you are permanently separated, you are no longer responsible for any debts that your spouse incurs. Similarly, you're no longer entitled to any share of property or income that your spouse acquires or earns.

Legal Separation

In some (not all) states, you can get a legal separation by filing a request in court. People choose legal separation instead of divorce because of religious beliefs, a desire to keep the family together legally for the sake of children, the need for one spouse to keep the health insurance benefits that would be lost with a divorce, or simple aversion to divorcing despite the desire to live separate lives.

If you're legally separated, you're no longer married, but you're not divorced either, and you can't remarry. The court's order granting the legal separation includes orders about property division, alimony, and child custody and support, just as a divorce would. In states where legal separation isn't allowed, you have to choose either divorce or an informal separation with agreements between you and your spouse about how you deal with your marital property.

Domestic Violence

If you're in danger of physical abuse at home, get out and get help as soon as you possibly can. Many communities have women's shelters where women and children who are victims of domestic violence can stay until the crisis passes or until they find a permanent home. To find shelters and related services, consult the local police, welfare department, neighborhood resource center, or women's center.

You may also want to get a temporary restraining order (TRO) from a court. A TRO orders the violent partner to leave you alone. It may require, for example, that the perpetrator stay away from the family home, your workplace or school, your children's school, and other places you frequent, such as a gym, friend's house, or church.

In many places, the court staff will make it easy for you to get a TRO. In many states, the court clerk will hand you a package of forms and help you fill them out. In other areas, nonlawyers may be available to help you with paperwork. When you've completed your forms, you'll go before a judge to show evidence of the abuse, such as hospital or police records or photographs. You can also bring in a witness, such as a friend or relative, to testify to the abuse. Judges often issue TROs after normal business hours.

Useful resources include:
- National Coalition Against Domestic Violence (NCADV), 303-839-1852, www.ncadv.org. Provides information and resources, including links to relevant state agencies
- National Domestic Violence Hotline, 800-799-SAFE (7233), www.ndvh.org. Provides information to callers—gay or straight.
- Women's Law Initiative, www.womenslaw.org. Provides state-by-state information and resources on domestic violence.

Annulment

Like a divorce, an annulment granted by a court ends a marriage. But, unlike a divorce, when you get an annulment, it's as though you were never married, at least in some ways. Although you need to divide your property just like other divorcing couples, you are legally entitled to call yourself "single" after the annulment, rather than checking the box for "divorced" wherever that comes up.

Religion is the most common reason for choosing annulment over divorce. In particular, the Roman Catholic Church doesn't sanction divorce or subsequent remarriage, but does allow someone whose first marriage was annulled to remarry in the church. But even if you get a religious annulment, in order to end your marital relationship in the eyes of the state, you must obtain a civil annulment through the courts.

Although most annulments take place very soon after the wedding, some couples seek annulments after they have been married for many years. In that case, the court considers all of the same issues as in a divorce: Property is divided, and support and custody decisions are made. Children of a marriage that has been annulled are still legally considered "legitimate" children of the marriage.

In most places, you can get a civil annulment for one of the following reasons:

- **Fraud or misrepresentation.** For example, one spouse lied about something that was important to the other in getting married, like the ability to have children.
- **No consummation of the marriage.** If one spouse is physically unable to have sexual intercourse, and the other spouse didn't know it when they got married, that's a ground for annulment.
- **Incest, bigamy, or underage party.** The spouses are related by blood so that their marriage is illegal under the laws of the state where they married, or one of them is married to someone else, or one of them is under the age of consent and didn't receive a parent's approval.
- **Unsound mind.** One or both of the spouses was impaired by alcohol or drugs at the time of the wedding or didn't have the mental capacity to understand what was happening.
- **Force.** One of the parties was forced into getting married.

Divorce and Family Court Proceedings

Every divorce case goes through some sort of court proceeding. Even if you and your spouse agree about how you will divide your property and handle custody, visitation, and support issues, a judge must still grant your divorce (or dissolution, as it's called in some places).

In most states, divorce cases—whether contested or not—are handled by a special court or a specific department, called "family court," "domestic relations court," or "divorce court." Most states have fill-in-the-blank forms for divorce cases, available from the local courthouse or court. See your state page in Appendix A for details on finding your state court forms.

Where Can You Get Divorced? State Residency Requirements

All states except Alaska, South Dakota, Washington, and (unless you have been living out of state before your divorce) Massachusetts require a spouse to be a resident of the state for a certain length of time, commonly six weeks to one year, before filing for a divorce there. If you file for divorce, you must show proof of having lived in the state for the required length of time. See your state's page in Appendix A for your state's residency requirement.

If one spouse meets a state residency requirement, a divorce obtained in that state is valid even if the other spouse lives somewhere else, as long as there was jurisdiction over the nonresident spouse. The court gets jurisdiction if the nonresident spouse:

- is personally given (served with) the divorce documents
- consents to jurisdiction by showing up at a court date or signing an affidavit of service, acknowledging receipt of the filed legal documents, or
- abides by the court's rulings—for example, by paying court-ordered child support.

If jurisdiction was proper, the courts of all states will recognize the divorce and any decisions the court makes regarding property division, alimony, custody, and child support.

SEE AN EXPERT

International divorces. If you receive documents from another country, consult an attorney about whether your state court or the foreign court governs the issues. This depends on many factors, such as the country involved, where the parties lived and for how long, and whether children are involved.

Kinds of Divorce

There's not just one way to divorce. Most states offer different paths, depending largely on whether or not you and your spouse can agree on financial and custody matters or need a judge to decide these issues for you. There are also legal differences; some states allow you to prove fault, and some don't.

Court websites often provide great information on the procedure you'll need to follow and the paperwork you'll need to submit. Check your court website, which you can find on your state page in Appendix A or by entering the name of your county and the words "superior court" or "family court" into a search engine.

Summary Divorce

In many states, an expedited divorce procedure is available to a minority of couples who haven't been married for very long (usually five years or less), don't own much property, don't have children, and don't have significant joint debts. Both spouses need to agree to the divorce, and you must file court papers jointly.

A summary (sometimes called simplified) divorce involves a lot less paperwork than other types of divorce—a few forms are often all it takes. You can probably get the forms you need from the local family court. For this reason, summary divorces are usually easy to do yourself, without the help of a lawyer.

Uncontested Divorce

In an uncontested divorce, you and your spouse work together to agree on the terms of your divorce and file court papers cooperatively to make the divorce happen. There will be no formal trial, and you probably won't have to ever appear in court. Instead, you file court forms, such as a petition, and a "marital settlement agreement" (MSA) that details your agreements about how you want to divide property and debts and any support payments. Custody arrangements for your children will either be in the MSA or in a parenting agreement that's attached to your MSA or stands alone as a separate agreement. Your settlement, and your final divorce, will have to be approved by a judge. That shouldn't be any problem unless it's clear that the terms are completely unfair to one spouse or that one person was under duress.

Many courts provide plain-English information and simplified forms to make it relatively easy to handle an uncontested divorce without a lawyer. But you may want to ask a lawyer to look over your paperwork and, perhaps, to help draft or review your settlement agreement. Some other experts who might be useful include:

- a counselor or a mediator to help you come to agreement on property and custody issues
- an actuary to value retirement benefits you or your spouse have through work
- an accountant to help you figure out the tax consequences of spousal support or property division
- a lawyer to prepare the special court order (called a Qualified Domestic Relations Order, or QDRO) you'll need to divide retirement benefits
- an appraiser to determine the market value of your house, or
- an accountant or actuary to help value an investment like a small business or a pension.

If you and your spouse both stay on top of all the tasks you need to take care of, you should be able to finalize your divorce as soon as the waiting period (every state has one) is over. (Waiting periods generally range from three to six months.)

Default Divorce

The court will grant a divorce by "default" if you file for divorce and your spouse doesn't respond. The divorce is granted even though your spouse doesn't participate in the court proceedings at all. A default divorce might happen, for example, if your spouse has left for parts unknown and can't be found.

Fault and No-Fault Divorce

"No-fault" describes any divorce where the spouse suing for divorce does not have to prove that the other spouse did something wrong. Every state offers the option of no-fault divorce—and in many states, no-fault is the only option. See the Divorce section of your state's page in Appendix A.

In a no-fault divorce, instead of proving that one spouse is to blame, you merely tell the court that you and your spouse have "irreconcilable differences" or have suffered an "irremediable breakdown" of your relationship or give some other reason recognized by the state. In some states, you must also have lived apart for a specified period of time.

In some states, you have a choice of using fault or no-fault grounds for divorce. Traditional grounds in a fault divorce are cruelty (inflicting unnecessary emotional or physical pain), adultery, or desertion. Some people choose a fault divorce because they don't want to wait out the period of separation required by their state's laws for a no-fault divorce. And in some states, a spouse who proves the other's fault may receive a greater share of the marital property or more alimony or get custody of the children. Even if you choose no-fault, some state courts still use fault as a factor in a no-fault divorce, when setting alimony, dividing property, or deciding custody—for example, a spouse who has deserted the family might receive a lesser share of the assets.

Mediated Divorce

In a mediation, you and your spouse jointly hire a trained, neutral third party, called a mediator—often a lawyer—to help you negotiate and reach a settlement. Mediation is often used in divorce cases to work out financial issues and property division, and some jurisdictions may require parents to work with a court-appointed mediator to try and work out a mutually agreeable custody or visitation schedule before the judge will hear the case.

(Chapter 3 discusses mediation in child custody cases.) A divorcing couple may also work with a private mediator to negotiate financial disputes over property and support (spousal and child). When you reach an agreement with an opposing party through mediation, you can make it legally binding by writing down your decisions in the form of an enforceable contract. The attorneys for one or both parties will usually finalize and approve the agreement. You may also want to consult with a lawyer before starting mediation to discuss the legal consequences of possible settlement terms.

Mediating instead of litigating will nearly always be less costly (and quicker) than fighting over an issue in court and minimize negative effects on children. Mediation sessions are usually scheduled quickly, and most sessions last only a few hours or a day, depending on the type of case. In contrast, lawsuits often take many months, or even years, to resolve. Private divorce mediation, where a couple aims to settle all the issues in their divorce—property division and alimony, as well as child custody, visitation, and support—may require half a dozen or more mediation sessions spread over several weeks or months.

Another advantage of mediation is confidentiality. With very few exceptions (for example, where a criminal act or child abuse is involved), what you say during mediation cannot legally be revealed outside the mediation proceedings or used later in a court of law. A number of studies show that people who have freely arrived at their own solutions through mediation are significantly more likely to follow through.

RESOURCE

Private divorce mediations are usually handled by sole practitioners or small, local mediation groups. A good online source of information is www.mediate. com, 541-345-1629. Before choosing a mediator, get referrals and interview them like you would a lawyer. *Divorce Without Court: A Guide to Mediation & Collaborative Divorce*, by Katherine E. Stoner (Nolo), provides divorcing couples with all the information they need to work with a neutral third party to resolve differences and find solutions. See www.nolo.com for a sample chapter and full table of contents.

> ### Will Divorce Mediation Work for You?
>
> You are most likely to have a successful mediation if all or most of the following statements are true:
> - The decision to divorce is mutual.
> - You have no desire to reconcile.
> - You want to stay on good terms with your spouse—either because you have children together or because of your own values.
> - You don't blame your spouse for your separation.
> - You understand the financial reality with which you are working.
> - Your spouse has not lied to you about anything important.
> - You can disagree with your spouse without saying or doing things you later regret.
> - You are not easily intimidated by your spouse.
> - Physical violence is not an issue in your relationship.
> - Alcohol or drug abuse is not an issue in your relationship.
> - You feel that your spouse is a good parent—and you want to work out a custody arrangement that is in the best interests of your child.

Collaborative Divorce

In a collaborative divorce, you and your spouse each hire a lawyer—but not just any lawyer. You want ones who have been trained to work cooperatively and who agree to try to settle your case without going to court—and if you aren't able to do that, the lawyers agree to bow out and you must hire new lawyers for the court proceeding. So, although each of you has a lawyer who is on your side, much of the work is done in cooperation. Each of you agrees to disclose all the information that's necessary for fair negotiations and to meet with each other and both lawyers to discuss settlement. Often other professionals—usually an accountant, actuary, and a therapist—are involved in the process.

Contested Divorce

If you and your spouse argue so much over property or child custody that you can't come to an agreement and, instead, take these issues to the judge, you have what's called a contested divorce. The judge, court clerks, and the attorneys (yours and your spouse's) will be the main players in your divorce case.

A divorce trial itself may be short (just a day or so), but the process is hard, painful, and likely to take years. In addition to the huge emotional toll on you and your family, a contested divorce, even one that ends in a settlement rather than a trial, can cost each spouse many tens of thousands of dollars.

Will You Need a Lawyer?

If your divorce is simple and uncontested, you might decide to do it yourself and not hire a lawyer at all. Or, you can use a lawyer as a mediator or a collaborative representative or to handle only specific parts of your divorce. For example, a consulting lawyer can explain your rights and the legal procedures you're dealing with, provide referrals to other professionals like actuaries or appraisers, or give you advice about one particular aspect of your divorce (such as alimony or custody) or documents (such as your marital settlement agreement).

On the other hand, if you can't work out issues involving children, property, and money with your spouse, especially if your spouse is being dishonest or vindictive, you will want to hire your own attorney. You'll definitely want to do so if there is a problem with abuse (spousal, child, sexual, or substance). A lawyer can help you get the arrangement you need to protect yourself and your children, such as getting a temporary order to keep your spouse away or for custody of your children, or filing a request in court for child support.

Even if you have a fairly good relationship with your ex, you may want to hire your own lawyer if a lot of property and assets are involved in your divorce—particularly if you have not been the main breadwinner or if you have a prenuptial agreement. For example, you may be especially concerned that you get your fair share of retirement accounts or that your spouse could be hiding assets.

Chapter 9 provides advice on finding and working with attorneys.

Divorce for Same-Sex Couples

Thirteen states offer some form of relationship recognition for same-sex couples, each state having different rules—and, of course, the rules are changing rapidly. In addition, some cities and counties offer local registration, with varying benefits. (See Chapter 1 for details.) And the only things more confusing than the mishmash of rules for forming same-sex marriages, civil unions, and domestic partnerships are the rules for ending those relationships.

Terminating a Marriage, State Domestic Partnership, or Civil Union

To terminate a legal same-sex marriage or marriage-equivalent state registration, you must go through the same divorce process in court that opposite-sex married couples do. If you don't legally end the relationship, your legal obligations, which are generally the same as those of married couples, will continue. For example, you could be on the hook for your ex-partner's credit card debts, could be ordered to share some of your savings with your ex, and could find yourself paying spousal support. Just as is true for opposite-sex married couples, there is a streamlined procedure for same-sex couples who haven't been together long and don't have kids or own property, but most people don't qualify.

Terminating a state registration or marriage can be complicated. If you live in a state that doesn't recognize same-sex relationships and you went elsewhere to marry or register, the local court may refuse to grant a divorce. If you have multiple registrations from different states, the judge may be even more reluctant to end all of them. You may need to go back to the state where you registered or married and complete the process there—but most states have residency requirements, some as long as a year.

Because this area of law is confusing and changing quickly, you're best off finding a local divorce lawyer experienced in same-sex divorces to help you through the process.

> **RESOURCE**
>
> **Attorneys experienced in same-sex divorces.** Contact the National Center for Lesbian Rights at www.nclrights.org or call 800-528-6257 for information and referrals.

Terminating a Local Partnership Registration

If you and a partner registered with the city or county, or with your employer, you don't need to go to court to terminate that relationship. You should still end the registration, but if you don't, you're not likely to run into a lot of financial consequences. Local registrations are easy to end, as are registrations with your employer that you entered for insurance purposes. Each city, county, and business has a termination form, and you simply have to get it, fill it out, and send it in.

Property, Custody, and Support

Every divorcing couple must consider how property and debts will be divided and whether one spouse will pay spousal support to the other. If you have minor children, you'll also need to make decisions about support and parenting time. You and your spouse will either need to work out these three big issues or, if you just can't do it, turn them over to a judge to decide. Even if you work out your agreements, the judge will have to approve them (see Chapters 3 and 4 for details).

Dividing Assets and Property

"Marital property" is the collection of assets you and your spouse have earned or acquired during your marriage, including your savings, house, investments, cars, pension plans, and the like. Marital debts are obligations you took on together during your married life.

In general, both the property and the debts belong to both of you, and part of the divorce process will be to divide them up between you. If you prepared a prenuptial agreement (discussed in Chapter 1), some of these decisions may have already been made. And assets or debts that either of you had before your marriage, or that you acquired after the permanent separation, are called separate property or debts. Some property that one spouse acquired during marriage (such as a car bought with separate income with title held in one spouse's name alone) may also be separate property, depending on state law. Generally, when you divorce, each of you will keep your separate property and be responsible for your separate debts, but, in some states, separate property can be divided at divorce.

If you and your spouse can agree on how to divide your assets and property, the court will simply approve your agreement. The terms will go into a court judgment or a document called a marital settlement agreement.

If you can't agree, the court will divide things for you. The nine community property states (listed in Chapter 1) divide marital property equally. The rest (known as common law property states) use a system of "equitable distribution," to divide property in a way that the court thinks is fair, but that isn't always equal. For example, two-thirds of the assets may go to the lower wage earner and one-third to the other spouse. See the Divorce section of your state page in Appendix A for details on how property is divided.

Who Stays in the House

If children are involved, the parent who provides their primary care usually remains in the marital home with them. If you don't have children and the house is the separate property of just one spouse, that spouse has the legal right to ask the other to leave.

If, however, you own the house together, this question gets tricky, particularly if you have children and share equally in their care. Neither of you has a greater legal right than the other to stay in the house. If you and your spouse don't come to a decision, the court will decide for you during divorce proceedings. Or, if you need a quick decision, you can ask for a temporary court order on the issue. That will require a short hearing before a judge. Temporary orders are usually valid until the court holds another hearing or the spouses arrive at their own settlement through negotiation or mediation.

Working Out Child Custody Arrangements

You and your spouse (or the court if you can't reach agreement) will need to decide whether you'll share custody of your children equally, or whether one parent will be the primary custodial parent. Custody means both the right to have a child live with you (physical custody) and the right to make decisions about the child's welfare and education (legal custody). (Chapter 3 covers these issues in detail.)

Child Support

Chances are that one parent will pay child support to the other, to make sure that the kids are always taken care of. Each state has guidelines for calculating child support, based on the amount of time each parent spends with the children and the amount each parent earns, as well as factors such as who pays for the children's health insurance or child care. (Chapter 4 addresses child support.)

Alimony

In some divorces, courts award alimony, also called spousal support, to one party. A support award is especially likely after a long marriage or if one spouse gave up career plans to support the other spouse or care for kids.

How Alimony Amount and Duration Are Determined

Divorcing spouses can agree on the amount and length of time alimony will be paid. But if you can't agree, a court will set the terms for you. Just keep in mind that having a court make the decision means there will be a trial, and that will cost you a lot of time and money.

The spouse who is ordered to pay alimony will usually have to pay a certain amount each month. Alimony continues for a set period of time that's defined in a judgment or settlement agreement, or until a certain event occurs, such as:

- the other spouse remarries
- the children no longer need a full-time parent at home

- a judge determines that after a reasonable period of time, the spouse receiving alimony has not made a sufficient effort to become at least partially self-supporting
- some other significant event—such as retirement—occurs, convincing a judge to modify the amount paid, or
- one of the spouses dies.

Taxes and Alimony

Alimony or spousal support is tax deductible for the person who makes the payments and taxable to the recipient. See Chapter 4 for tax-related issues regarding child support.

If a Spouse Refuses to Pay Court-Ordered Alimony

If you secure an alimony order but your spouse refuses to make the required payments, take immediate legal action to enforce the order in court. Orders to pay monthly alimony have the same force as any other court order and, if handled properly, can be enforced with the very real possibility of obtaining regular payments. If necessary, a court may jail a stubborn ex-spouse to show that it means business.

Pets and Divorce

Legally, pets are property, and courts generally treat them as such at divorce, awarding them to one spouse as part of the property division. Recently, however, some judges have ordered shared ownership of pets, most often dogs.

Estate Planning After Divorce

During and after your divorce, it's important to take a close look at who you've named, in wills or retirement plans, to inherit your property. It's very common, for example, for people to forget to change the beneficiary designation on a 401(k) plan—and as a result, for a big chunk of money to go to a former spouse when that wasn't the person's intention at all.

You should also review documents such as advance medical directives and powers of attorney, to be sure your documents still reflect your wishes. Here are some other estate planning tasks to consider:

- You may want to negotiate with your spouse to receive or provide death benefits from life insurance, a retirement plan, a will, or a trust, especially if your spouse is going to be paying child or spousal support and you want to be sure you are protected in the event of your ex's untimely death.
- Your divorce settlement can include a requirement that one or both spouses establish trusts to provide for such costs as grandchildren's education or financial support for adult children.

See Chapter 8 for more on estate planning.

Changing Your Name After Divorce

If you took your spouse's name when you married, you may decide to keep it so that you have the same surname as your children or for another reason. Or you may decide not to keep your spouse's name. In most states, you can request that the judge handling your divorce make a formal order restoring your former or birth name. If your divorce decree contains such an order, that's all the paperwork you'll need. In some states, you can even have a completed divorce case reopened to provide for a name change. You'll probably want to get certified copies of the order as proof of the name change—check with the court clerk for details. Once you have the necessary documentation, you can use it to have your name changed on your identification and personal records.

If your divorce papers don't show your name change, you can usually still resume your former name without much fuss, especially if it's your birth name and you have a birth certificate to prove it. In many states, you can simply begin using your former name consistently and have it changed on all your personal records. However, if you run into problems because you've used your married name for many years, you might want to do a formal name change back to your original name so that it's very clear that it's your legal name.

RESOURCE

More information on changing your name. See www.nolo.com/legal-encyclopedia/name-change.

Changing Your Child's Name After Divorce

Traditionally, courts ruled that a father had an automatic right to have his child keep his last name if he continued to actively perform his parental role. But this is no longer true. Now a child's name may be changed by court petition if a judge concludes it is in the best interest of the child to do so. When deciding whether or not to grant a name change request, courts consider many factors, including:

- how long the current name has been used
- the strength of the child's relationship with the parent who wants the name change, and
- the child's need to identify with a new family unit (if the change involves remarriage).

The courts must balance these factors against the strength and importance of the relationship of the child to the person whose surname he or she shares. Most judges won't change a child's name without a very good reason.

Keep in mind that even if your children's last name changes, it won't change the rights or duties of either parent regarding custody, visitation, child support, or inheritance rights.

 RESOURCE

Helpful divorce books and websites.

- *Nolo's Essential Guide to Divorce*, by Emily Doskow (Nolo), is a thorough 50-state guide to the ins and outs of divorce, from how to handle key issues (alimony, child custody, and support) to drafting a marital settlement agreement and dividing property to working with lawyers and mediators. You can see the full table of contents and a sample chapter of this and other Nolo books at www.nolo.com.
- *Divorce After 50: Your Guide to the Unique Legal & Financial Challenges*, by Janice Green (Nolo), provides in-depth information on all key issues that older couples face.

- *Divorce Without Court: A Guide to Mediation & Collaborative Divorce*, by Katherine E. Stoner (Nolo), provides divorcing couples with all the information they need to work with a neutral third party to resolve differences and find solutions, or to participate in a collaborative process.
- *Divorce & Money: How to Make the Best Financial Decisions During Divorce*, by Violet Woodhouse with Dale Fetherling (Nolo), explains the financial aspects of divorce.
- *Building a Parenting Agreement That Works: Child Custody Agreements Step by Step*, by Mimi Lyster Zemmelman (Nolo), walks you through the process of creating a complete parenting plan for your kids after your divorce.
- *Being a Great Divorced Father: Real-Life Advice From a Dad Who's Been There*, by Paul Mandelstein (Nolo), is a guide for divorced dads on how to stay connected to the kids and maintain a positive relationship with the ex.

For state-specific information and advice, useful articles, support groups, forms and worksheets, and referrals to divorce professionals, see these websites:

- www.divorcenet.com
- www.divorcesupport.com
- www.divorceinfo.com
- www.divorcecentral.com, and
- www.womenslaw.org.

Child Custody

Whon parents split up, a key concern is always how they will share care of their children. In an ideal world, the parents, thinking only of what's best for their children, would discuss parenting arrangements and come up with a plan that ensured the children would have a stable environment and significant contact with both parents.

In reality, of course, that doesn't always happen. In many divorces, the questions of custody rights and parenting time turns into a huge battle involving lawyers, court-ordered custody evaluators, and huge amounts of time, money, and emotional stress—and the result is a court-imposed custody arrangement that no one is happy with. And who suffers the most from the escalation of acrimony and the waste of money? The children.

Fortunately, many courts are doing everything they can to steer parents toward a reasonably amicable negotiation over parenting issues. Most courts now require parents who are in conflict over parenting issues to attend mediation sessions with a family court employee or private mediator (a trained, neutral third party) to work something out that's truly in the best interests of the children. Only if that process doesn't work are the parents allowed to bring their conflict to court.

 STATE RULES AND RESOURCES

The Child Custody section of each state's listing in Appendix A contains:

- your state's guidelines on child custody, and
- links to state resources related to child custody, including courts that handle custody matters.

Temporary Custody

When parents separate, they should come up with a temporary parenting agreement. It should cover the basics: who will stay in the family home, where the kids will stay when, and how much child support will be paid. (See Chapter 4 for details on child support.) It's a good idea to write down these agreements and include in the written agreement a statement that the arrangements are just temporary and that no one's agreeing to any permanent state of affairs. That way, you can take your time making a more long-term agreement, without worrying that agreeing to one thing now is going to bind you to it forever.

If parents can't agree on how to share time with the kids or who should have what type of custody, even on a temporary basis, the court will likely send them to mediation, where a trained mediator will try to get them to come to terms on temporary arrangements. (See the discussion of mediation below.) If that fails as well, the court will come up with a temporary custody arrangement that will be in place until the divorce is final. That process may take several hearings in court, which translates into a lot of money in lawyers' fees and an inevitable increase in bad feelings between the spouses.

A temporary custody agreement will remain in place until the judge approves a final judgment that includes permanent custody arrangements.

CAUTION

If you must take the kids and get out, get to court quickly. Family law judges frown on a parent who removes the children from the home without seeking the court's approval. A parent who must leave the family home quickly, perhaps because of domestic violence, should take the children along and, as quickly as possible, file a request in family court for temporary custody and child support. If you delay, the judge might order that the children be returned to the family home pending future proceedings to determine physical custody.

When Parents Decide on Custody: Parenting Agreements

Only a court can issue a custody order—but if parents can come up with their own custody and visitation agreement that works for the children, the court will be happy to approve it—meaning it will become a court order.

A parenting agreement is a detailed written agreement between divorcing parents that describes how they will deal with children's living arrangements, custodial time, holiday schedules, vacation, religion, travel, education, and other related issues. More and more, courts are encouraging the use of parenting agreements during divorce proceedings. If parents discuss and agree upon how to deal with issues affecting their children—rather than having the judge rule on those issues—they are more likely to stick to the terms of the agreement.

Parents may negotiate and write down a parenting agreement themselves, or seek the help of a child custody mediator, therapist, or another specialist. Once the agreement is complete, the judge must review it. As long as your parenting plan is reasonable, the court will approve it, perhaps as part of your final settlement agreement, and it will become an enforceable order. In other words, if your ex doesn't comply with its terms, you can return to court and ask the judge to order your former spouse to do so.

RESOURCE

More about making parenting agreements. *Building a Parenting Agreement That Works: Child Custody Agreements Step by Step,* by Mimi Lyster Zemmelman (Nolo), provides sample language and forms to create your own parenting agreement. You can see a full table of contents and a sample chapter at www.nolo.com.

Physical and Legal Custody

There are two types of custody: physical and legal. Physical custody means actually taking care of the children day to day—in other words, the child lives with the parent. Legal custody involves making decisions about a child's upbringing, such as medical care, education, and religion. Courts generally believe that it's best for children to have both parents responsible for legal decisions and, when possible, for both parents to share physical custody as well. That's why "joint custody," where parents share legal and physical custody, has become so common—and in some states the two types of custody are both encompassed in a custody award to one parent. However, it is possible in the majority of states for parents to share legal custody but for one parent to have sole or primary physical custody while the other parent has visitation rights.

Joint Custody

Parents with joint custody usually work out a schedule according to their work schedules, housing arrangements, and the children's needs. Kids may spend roughly equal amounts of time with both parents, or one parent may have significantly more parenting time—joint custody doesn't have to be exactly equal.

Joint physical custody works best if parents live fairly near each other, letting children maintain a normal routine. A common pattern is for children to split the week between each parent's home, although many other arrangements are possible, such as having the children spend weekends and holidays with one parent and weekdays with the other. There is even a joint custody arrangement called "bird's nest" custody, where the children remain in the family home and the parents take turns moving in and out, spending their out time in separate housing of their own. There's less disruption for the kids, but more hassle and expense for the parents.

Courts in every state are willing to order joint *legal* custody. In some states, courts automatically award joint legal custody unless the children's best interests—or a parent's health or safety—would be compromised. Many courts, however, are reluctant to order joint *physical* custody unless both parents agree to it and appear to be sufficiently able to communicate and cooperate with each other to make it work.

Sole Custody

In some cases, one parent may be granted sole physical custody. This could be because the other parent has moved away, is otherwise unavailable, or is abusive or neglectful. Except in cases of serious abuse, the noncustodial parent is usually given rights to regular visits with the children. (Visitation is discussed below.) Likewise, unless the noncustodial parent is abusive or the parents are completely unable to get along enough to make decisions together, the parents still share legal custody.

RESOURCE

Useful book on shared custody arrangements. *Mom's House, Dad's House: Making Two Homes for Your Child,* by Isolina Ricci (Fireside) is a highly praised classic on making shared custody work for parents and children.

Split Custody

When a court grants custody of one child to one parent and another child to the other parent, it's called split custody. It's rare, but can happen if the court concludes it's in the best interest of the child. For example, when one parent moves after a divorce, a high school student might prefer to stay behind with the other parent in order to finish the last year of high school.

Visitation (Shared Parenting)

The term "visitation" is still widely used, but many professionals in the field of divorce and parenting—and many divorced parents themselves—feel that the word doesn't accurately describe the relationship between children and a noncustodial parent. Parents whose time with their kids is more limited are still parents, and when they are with their children, they are parenting, not visiting. Because the term is still commonly used, we'll use visitation here interchangeably with the terms "parenting time" or "shared parenting."

A court may award primary physical custody to one parent and give the other shared parenting time that is not considered joint custody. The parents then either work out a parenting schedule themselves or, if they can't agree, follow the schedule set by the court. To avoid arguments over missed visits and inconvenience, many courts encourage parents to work out a detailed parenting agreement that sets a parenting schedule and outlines details such as how vacations will be planned and how parents will deal with things like parent-teacher nights and sporting events. In extreme cases, a court may order supervised visitation or deny a parent any right to spend time with the kids.

Reasonable Visitation

Courts commonly give the noncustodial parent the right to "reasonable" visitation, leaving it to the parents to work out a precise schedule of time and place. This gives the parents flexibility to take into consideration both the parents' and the children's schedules. Practically speaking, however, a parent with sole physical custody has more control over the dates, times, and duration of visits. That parent isn't legally obligated to agree to any particular schedule, but judges do take note of cooperation. If you are uncooperative merely to vex your ex, it can backfire when you need to ask the court for something in the future.

For the reasonable visitation approach to succeed, parents need to cooperate and communicate frequently. If you suspect that a loosely defined schedule won't work, insist on a fixed one. If you've already agreed to reasonable visitation and it isn't working out—for example, one parent is consistently late, skips scheduled visits, or doesn't provide enough information about where the kids are and what they are doing—you can go back to court and ask that the arrangement be changed.

Fixed Visitation

Sometimes courts set up a detailed visitation schedule, including the times and places for visitation with the noncustodial parent—for example, every other weekend. A court will be inclined to order a fixed schedule if the hostility between the parents is so severe that the regular contact between them may be detrimental to the child. A fixed visitation schedule can still be generous, but it removes opportunities for one party to control the other's time and gives the children predictability in an often unsettling period.

Supervised Visitation

When a noncustodial parent has a history of violent or destructive behavior, especially toward the child, or past problems with drugs and alcohol, the court may require that visits between that parent and the child be supervised. This means that an adult (other than the custodial parent) must be present at all times. The adult may be someone the parents agree on or someone appointed by the court. No matter how the supervising adult is chosen, the court must approve the person.

Grandparent Visitation

All states have some laws allowing grandparents to ask a court for the legal right to maintain a relationship with their grandchildren. But state laws vary greatly when it comes to the crucial details, such as who can visit and under what circumstances.

Approximately 20 states have "restrictive" visitation statutes, meaning that grandparents can get a court order for visitation only if the child's parents are divorcing or if one or both parents have died. States with more permissive visitation laws allow courts to consider a visitation request even without the death of a parent or the dissolution of the family, as long as visitation would serve the best interests of the child. The children's welfare is always the highest priority, although the courts also give great deference to a parent's decision to limit visitation with grandparents, and in most places, when parents agree that they don't want the grandparents to visit the kids, that's usually the end of the story.

Stepparents' and Others' Visitation Rights

In most states, someone who has helped to raise a child but has no legal relationship to the child—a stepparent, for example—has few legal rights to seek custody or even visitation. If you have been actively involved in a child's life but are not a legal parent, try to work out an arrangement with the child's custodial parent to continue that role. If that's not possible, check your state laws on visitation rights or consult a family law attorney.

Custody Decisions When Spouses Are in Different States

If parents live in different states, which state's courts are in charge of custody decisions? These questions are determined by laws called the Uniform Child Custody Jurisdiction Act (UCCJA) or the Uniform Child Custody Jurisdiction and Enforcement Act (UCCJEA), one of which has been adopted by every state and the District of Columbia.

In general, a state may make a custody decision about a child only if one of these tests is met (in order of preference):

- The state is the child's home state. This means the child has lived in the state for the last six months or was living there but is absent because a parent took the child to another state. A parent who wrongfully removes or retains a child in order to create a home state will be denied custody.

- The child has significant connections in the state with people such as teachers, doctors, and grandparents. A parent who wrongfully removes or keeps a child in order to establish these significant connections will be denied custody.
- The child is in the state and either has been abandoned or is in danger of being abused or neglected if sent back to the a previous home state.
- No other state can meet one of the first three tests, or a state that can meet at least one has declined to make a custody decision.

If a state cannot meet one of these tests, the courts of that state cannot make a custody award, even if the child is present in the state. If more than one state meets one of the tests, any of them may make a custody decision; to decide which one, judges in the different states will confer and make a decision. Once a state makes a custody award, other states must stay out of the dispute.

How Courts Rule on Custody: The Best Interests of the Child

If divorcing parents agree on a parenting plan that appears reasonable, the judge will usually approve it. But if parents are fighting and the court must make parenting decisions, almost all states require judges to base custody decisions on the best interests of the child. Laws in nearly every state provide guidelines on this standard, although judges have a lot of discretion in interpreting them.

Courts commonly consider:
- the child's age, sex, and mental and physical health
- each parent's mental and physical health
- each parent's lifestyle (such as a new live-in relationship) and other social factors, including whether the child is exposed to secondhand smoke or drug use in the home and whether there is any history of child or spousal abuse
- the emotional bond between each parent and the child, as well as each parent's ability to give the child guidance
- each parent's ability to provide food, shelter, clothing, and medical care

- the child's established living pattern (school, home, community, and religious institution)
- the quality of the child's education in the current situation
- the child's preference, if the child is old enough to weigh the alternatives (children's opinions are usually considered once they reach the age of 12 or so), and
- the ability and willingness of each parent to foster healthy communication and contact between the child and the other parent.

In some states, conservative judges will also consider factors like sexual orientation and whether a parent is cohabiting with a new partner, whether of the same or the opposite sex. (There's more about sexual orientation and same-sex parents below.)

If none of these factors clearly favors one parent, most courts tend to focus on which parent is likely to provide the children a more stable environment, and which parent will better foster the child's relationship with the other parent. With younger children, this may mean awarding custody to the parent who has been the child's primary caregiver. With older children, this may mean giving custody to the parent who is best able to foster continuity in education, neighborhood life, religious institutions, and peer relationships.

Custody of Embryos

Couples using in vitro fertilization in hopes of having children often create multiple embryos, which are frozen until they are implanted. If the couple later divorces, custody disputes may arise over the extra embryos—for example, the wife might want to use the embryos in an attempt to become pregnant, but the husband might object. After a number of these disputes were seen in courts, fertility clinics began getting wise and including a provision in contracts stating which partner would get custody of the embryos if a couple split up. If there is no such agreement, the divorce court will decide. Some give custody to mothers who want to raise children from the embryos, even over the husband's objection—but also sometimes allow the husband to opt out of paying child support. Other courts base the decision on whose genetic material went into making the embryo.

Expert Help

Often, judges need help in making custody decisions and determining what's in the child's best interests. Depending on state law and local custom, judges may:

- require the parents to meet with a mediator, who will then make a recommendation (see the discussion of mediation below)
- appoint an investigator or custody evaluator (often a mental health professional or social worker) to visit the parents' homes and talk with the parents and, if appropriate, the children, or
- appoint an attorney to represent the child, in cases where the conflict is so extreme that it's clear neither parent is capable of considering the child's needs and another adult must step in to advise the judge on best interests.

Court Preference for Awarding Custody to Mothers

In the past, it was very common for courts to award custody of children of "tender years" (five and under) to the mother when parents divorced. This rule has been rejected in most states, or relegated to the role of tie-breaker if two fit parents request custody of their preschool children. In most states, courts determine custody based only on the children's best interests, without regard to the sex of the parent.

Even without a court order, many divorcing parents with young children agree that the mother will have sole or at least primary physical custody, with the father spending time with the children according to a reasonable schedule, generally increasing as the children get older.

When a Parent Moves Away

A parent who moves out and leaves the children with the other parent may have trouble getting custody switched back at a later date. Even when a parent leaves to avoid a dangerous or highly unpleasant situation, leaving the children there sends a message to the court that the other parent is a suitable choice for physical custody. Also, assuming the children stay in the home where the parents lived as a family, continue in the same school, and participate in their usual activities, a judge may be reluctant to move them, if only to avoid disrupting the children's routines.

Religion and Child Custody

Even when they are married, parents of different faiths don't always agree on whose religion the children will follow. When parents separate, things can get even more complicated. Courts that are called upon to resolve disputes about the religious upbringing of children have a difficult job in trying to balance the competing concerns of:

- a parent's First Amendment right to the free exercise of religion, as well as the right to raise children as the parent sees fit (as long as the choices do not endanger the child), and
- the best interests of the child.

There is no uniform national law on the subject, and the U.S. Supreme Court has not decided a case involving religious upbringing and custody. Instead, the law varies from state to state and even from court to court. Some courts allow each parent to practice that parent's religion during custodial time; others believe it's better for children to have a consistent religious education and allow the parent with primary custody to make the decisions, prohibiting the other parent from interfering.

Sexual Orientation and Child Custody

Only the District of Columbia has a law on its books stating that a parent's sexual orientation cannot be the sole factor in making a custody or visitation award. In a few states—including Alaska, California, New Mexico, and Pennsylvania—courts have ruled that a parent's homosexuality, in and of itself, cannot be grounds for an automatic denial of custody or visitation rights. In many other states, courts have ruled that judges can deny custody or visitation because of a parent's sexual orientation only if they find that the parent's sexual orientation would harm the child.

In reality, however, a lesbian or gay parent can still face a difficult struggle when trying to gain custody in many courtrooms, especially if that parent lives with a partner. This is because judges, when considering the best interests of the child, may be motivated by their own or community prejudices and may find reasons other than the lesbian or gay parent's sexual orientation to deny custody or appropriate visitation. Any LGBT parent who is involved in a contested custody battle should contact an experienced attorney for help.

Custody by Someone Other Than a Parent

Sometimes neither parent can safely assume custody of the children, perhaps because of substance abuse or a mental health problem. In these situations, a court will give custody of the children to someone other than a parent—often, a grandparent—who becomes the child's legal guardian. If relatives aren't available, the child may be sent to a foster home or public facility.

Same-Sex Parents and Custody

For parents of the same sex who are married or registered in a marriage-equivalent state (see Chapter 1 regarding same-sex relationships), issues of custody will be pretty much the same as for opposite-sex couples. The court will respect both parents' rights and make custody and visitation decisions on the basis of the child's best interests.

However, it's more complicated when only one parent in a same-sex couple has legal rights. This is a fairly common occurrence—sometimes one partner adopts as a single person to avoid homophobic adoption rules; sometimes a lesbian mom gives birth in a state where the couple's relationship isn't recognized so that the her partner isn't considered a legal parent; sometimes a couple gets together after a child is born and the second parent isn't a legal parent. The courts are all over the map on the custody and visitation rights of the second parent in these cases. In some states, courts have held that a person who has established a psychological parent-child relationship with a partner's biological child is entitled to visitation and, in some cases, to legal status as a parent. In other places, courts have shut out nonbiological parents entirely based on the absence of a genetic or legal relationship with the child. The law is certainly not settled, and the best course of action is usually to try to mediate an agreement rather than going to court and fighting over kids you have raised together. There's more about mediation below.

> **SEE AN EXPERT**
>
> **Get expert help for custody questions.** If you are involved in a custody case and concerned about bias against you because you are gay or lesbian, consult an attorney. You can get attorney names from the National Center for Lesbian Rights (www.nclrights.org, phone 800-528-6257) or the Lambda Legal Defense and Education Fund (www.lambdalegal.org, phone 866-542-8336).

> **RESOURCE**
>
> **Help for gay and lesbian parents.** *A Legal Guide for Lesbian and Gay Couples*, by Denis Clifford, Frederick Hertz, and Emily Doskow (Nolo), has advice on negotiating custody arrangements. *Making It Legal: A Guide to Same-Sex Marriage, Domestic Partnerships & Civil Unions* by Frederick Hertz with Emily Doskow (Nolo), explains the law in different states and covers parenting issues. You can see the full table of contents and a sample chapter for each book at www.nolo.com.

Mediating Child Custody and Visitation Disputes

Mediation can often help divorcing parents resolve parenting arrangements with a minimum of hard feelings and expense. It's a nonadversarial process during which a neutral person, the mediator, meets with the parents to help them negotiate custody and visitation issues. Mediators are very skilled at getting parents—even those with a lot of bitterness over the divorce—to cooperate and work out a parenting plan for the sake of their children.

Most states require mediation in custody and visitation disputes, and others allow courts to order mediation. Whenever mediation is required by the court, the court will direct the parents to a mediator—in some places, the services will be free to the parents, but in many courts parents must pay if they can. Parents can also find and pay a private mediator themselves—either a family law attorney, a therapist with expertise in custody disputes, or even a nonlawyer mediator from a community mediation service.

A mediator does not have power to impose a solution on divorcing parents, but instead helps them reach an agreement. If the attempt fails and parents still can't agree on custody, the court will decide. In some states, the mediator can report to the judge about the mediation process and can make a recommendation about what the judge should decide, but most states consider discussions in mediation sessions to be confidential, meaning the mediator can't talk to the judge about them and can't be asked to testify in court.

Mediation is superior to litigation for resolving custody and visitation disputes for several reasons:

- **It's less expensive.** If you go to trial over custody issues, you'll end up paying lawyers (and possibly, expert witnesses) huge amounts. A custody trial could easily cost $10,000 to $20,000.
- **It's faster.** Mediation usually produces a settlement after five to ten hours of mediation over a week or two. Child custody litigation can drag on for months or even years.
- **It's easier on everyone.** Mediation enhances communication between parents and makes it much more likely that they will be able to cooperate on child-raising issues after the divorce. Experts who have studied the effects of divorce on children universally conclude that children suffer far less when divorcing or separating parents cooperate.

RESOURCE

Good mediation resources:

- Both www.mediate.com and www.acrnet.org (the website of a national mediation organization called the Association for Conflict Resolution) can help you find a mediator in your area.
- *Divorce Without Court: A Guide to Mediation & Collaborative Divorce*, by Katherine E. Stoner (Nolo), is a useful guide to mediation in divorce cases. See www.nolo.com for a full table of contents and sample chapter.

Changing Custody and Visitation Orders

After a court issues a final divorce decree or another order establishing a parenting plan, it's always possible to modify the order if circumstances change. However, parents can't just come in and ask for a change because they don't like the current arrangement; there has to be some significant change in either the parent's situation or the children's in order to get a court to agree to modify existing arrangements. (See below for examples.)

If the parents agree on a change to their existing parenting schedule, they can agree to a modification. If they included a provision in their final judgment to this effect, then they can just write down their new agreement, sign it, and consider it a part of the judgment just as if a judge had reviewed it. However, not all final judgments contain such a provision. If there isn't one, the parents can go into court—generally the same court that decided the original divorce and custody plan—and ask the court to approve their new agreement. This will ensure that if one parent later reneges on the agreement, the other person will be able to enforce it. If both parents agree, courts will approve their modification agreement unless the court concludes it isn't in the best interests of the child.

If a parent wants to change an existing court order and the other parent won't agree to the change, the parent who wants the change must submit a written request to the court that issued the order, showing a significant change in circumstances. This requirement encourages stability and helps prevent the court from becoming overburdened with modification requests. Here are some examples of a substantial change in circumstances.

Geographic move. If either parent wants to move a significant distance from where the children live, the court may have to make a custody decision. Custodial parents generally have the advantage in these situations, but if the other parent argues that the move will seriously disrupt the stability of the child's life, the court might modify a custody or visitation order and switch custody to the parent who's remaining where the child currently lives. In other states, the court will carefully examine the best interests of the child— looking at factors such as switching schools and distance from relatives— and decide which parent should have custody.

Change in lifestyle. If substantial changes in a parent's lifestyle threaten or harm the child, the other parent can often succeed in changing custody or visitation rights. If, for example, a custodial parent begins working at night and leaving a nine-year-old child alone, the other parent may succeed in getting a change in custody. Similarly, if a noncustodial parent begins drinking heavily or abusing drugs, the custodial parent may request modification of the visitation order—asking, for example, that visits occur only when the parent is sober, or in the presence of another adult. What constitutes a lifestyle change sufficiently detrimental to warrant a change in custody or visitation rights varies tremendously depending on the state and the particular judge deciding the case. A change in lifestyle may also be a positive one—for example, a judge may increase parenting time for a former alcoholic who has been sober for a substantial period of time.

Parents can't make it work. If parents share legal custody but one parent excludes the other from decision making, the left-out parent can go back to court and ask the judge to enforce the custody agreement or even change custody to give the offending parent fewer rights. And if parents return to court over and over again because they are unable to communicate effectively or to make any decisions together without conflict, a court is likely to change joint legal custody to sole custody, granting the sole decision-making power to the parent who has proved most capable of acting in the child's best interests.

Custodial Interference

In most states, it's a crime for one parent to take a child from the other with the intent to interfere with that parent's physical custody of the child. This crime is commonly referred to as "custodial interference." The police will become involved to get the child returned and arrest the parent who took the child. In most states, the parent deprived of custody may also sue the other person for money damages.

It's even more serious if a parent without physical custody (whether the parent has visitation rights or not) removes a child from—or refuses to return a child to—the parent with physical custody. This is kidnapping or child concealment—a felony in more than 40 states.

In many states, it's also a felony to take a child out of state with the intent of interfering with a parent's custody. Many states, however, recognize good-cause defenses—for example, if a mother took a child to prevent imminent bodily harm to herself or to the child. In addition, some states let a parent take a child out of state if the parent is requesting custody in court and has notified the court or police of the child's location.

> **RESOURCE**
> **International custody disputes.** The International Child Abductions Remedies Act is a federal law that covers child custody disputes involving other countries. See the Office of Children's Issues in the U.S. State Department (http://travel.state.gov/abduction/abduction_580.html) for details on international parental child abduction.

Custody Issues Involving Unmarried Parents

Parents who are not married have the same parental rights as those who are. The concept of "illegitimacy" has pretty much gone by the wayside, and all children are considered legitimate whether their parents are married or not. When an opposite-sex married couple with children breaks up, they are subject to the same laws as married parents relating to their parenting arrangements. They will use a slightly different procedure to get the matter before the court: It will not be a divorce, but a parentage action in which they legally establish the parent-child relationship and then ask the court to make—or affirm—decisions about shared parenting.

Unmarried couples of the same sex deal with different issues. See "Same-Sex Parents and Custody," above.

Surrogacy and Custody

As more and more couples face infertility issues, the use of surrogacy has become more popular. In the most common type of surrogacy arrangement, a gestational surrogate agrees to implantation in her womb of an embryo that was created from genetic material from either the intended parents or egg and sperm donors. In other words, the surrogate herself has no genetic connection to the resulting child, but carries the child to term on behalf of the intended parents. (In a so-called "traditional" surrogacy, the surrogate's own eggs are used, but this results in the surrogate being considered a legal parent in most states, which creates legal complications. Thus, traditional surrogacy is much less common.)

Typically, the surrogate receives a fee for her gestational services, along with reimbursement for all medical and other expenses associated with the pregnancy. It is, of course, illegal to sell either a child or genetic material, so the surrogacy contract must make clear that the payment is for services and expenses, not for the surrogate giving up the child. Surrogacy contracts are lengthy and complex, and surrogacy is not legal everywhere.

In places where surrogacy is legal and a valid contract is in place, the contract will usually be enforced by the courts even if the surrogate tries to break the contract and keep the baby.

RESOURCE

More on state surrogacy laws. For details on the laws in your state, see the website of the Human Rights Campaign at www.hrc.org (search for "surrogacy laws") or call 1-800-777-4723. You'll also find useful information on surrogacy at the National Infertility Association website www.resolve.com (click on "Family Building Options," then "Surrogacy"), or call 703-556-7172.

RESOURCE

Custody resources in your state:

- Your local superior court website may include detailed information on custody rules and procedures; many do. To find it, see your state page in Appendix A; you can go to your state's court website and look for a link, or you can enter your county's name and the words "superior court" or "family court" in any search engine.
- The site www.womenslaw.org offers excellent plain-English explanations of state custody rules.
- *Nolo's Essential Guide to Divorce*, by Emily Doskow (Nolo), contains strategic advice on working out custody arrangements, whether or not the divorce is contested. See www.nolo.com for a full table of contents and sample chapter.

Child Support

Divorce doesn't affect parents' obligation to support their children—every parent has that obligation from the moment a child is born until the child turns 18, and sometimes longer. Part of the divorce process will be a determination of whether support will be paid, by whom, and how much; generally, all of these things are determined by state guidelines.

Unfortunately, too many parents simply don't make good on their child support obligations. Some don't have the money, but some choose not to make payments for a variety of their own reasons—none of which will get them off the hook, legally. Parents who truly can't make their payments, perhaps because they're out of work, can always go back to court and ask for a change in the amount in light of their changed circumstances.

It is the children, of course, who suffer the most when child support is inadequate or nonexistent. Recognizing this, the trend in all states is to increase child support levels and implement new ways to enforce child support obligations.

STATE RULES AND RESOURCES
The Child Support section of each state's listing in Appendix A contains:
- your state's guidelines on child support, and
- links to state resources related to child support, including state child support enforcement agency and child support calculators and courts that handle child support matters.

Who Must Pay Child Support

All parents—biological or adoptive, married or not—have a duty to support their children. You're not obligated to support stepchildren (the children of your spouse) unless you legally adopt them.

What does support mean? Parents aren't legally obligated to provide their children material goods beyond food, shelter, clothing, and whatever education is required by state law. Courts don't intervene in how parents support their children unless children are being abused or neglected. However, when couples separate or divorce, courts will step in with orders about what parents must do to support the children. Or, if a single mother applies for financial assistance from a social services agency, the agency will do everything possible to get reimbursement from the children's father and to establish a child support order so that he's responsible for paying support instead of the government having to do it.

Divorcing Parents

Many divorcing parents work out temporary support payments while the divorce is pending, based on their family budgets, the parents' incomes, and the temporary parenting arrangement. Almost all judges and divorce lawyers use special software to calculate child support using state guidelines, which are usually too mathematically complex to allow for calculations by hand. Parents can work with a lawyer or mediator, use Internet calculators to get a ballpark idea of their state's guidelines for child support (discussed below), or simply work out what they think is fair. It's to both parents' advantage to write down the temporary support agreement and have the court approve it and enter it as an order. The receiving parent can then feel secure that the court can enforce payments if the paying parent bails out, and the paying parent can be secure in the amount that's agreed to, at least until it's time to enter a longer term order.

Parents who can't come to an agreement about support will find themselves in front of a judge—and that is an enormous waste of money and time, because the judge will simply order guideline support, which the parents could have figured out for themselves or had a lawyer or mediator calculate for them for a much lower cost than a contested hearing.

Child support guidelines use a formula to calculate support based on each parent's percentage of time spent with the children, each parent's income, which parent takes dependent exemptions and what each parent's filing status is, which parent pays for the children's health insurance and child care, and other financial factors. When a couple finalizes their divorce, they'll either agree to continue the temporary support amount that was being paid while the divorce was pending or settle on a permanent amount going forward. "Permanent" doesn't mean it can never be changed, just that it's part of the final judgment of divorce. (See "Modifying Child Support Payments," below.)

Mothers and fathers have an equal duty to support their children and an equal right to receive child support from the other parent if circumstances warrant it. A father with physical custody of a child has the right to ask the other parent for child support, just as a mother with physical custody does.

Unmarried Parents

If you're a parent, you're responsible for supporting your child whether or not you were ever married to the child's other parent, and whether or not a court ever ordered you to support the child. It's just part of being a parent. The court will use the same guidelines for unmarried parents as for married ones.

If a child is born to married parents, the husband is presumed to be the child's father. But if the mother is unmarried when a child is born, it may not be clear, legally, who the father is. Many unmarried fathers acknowledge paternity by signing a voluntary declaration of paternity at the time of the child's birth or soon after. Some states require such a statement of paternity before they will add an unmarried father's name to a child's birth certificate. It's also possible for a man who never married the child's mother to be presumed to be the father if he welcomes the child into his home and openly holds the child out as his own.

If a man believed to be a child's father resists taking responsibility, either the mother—or the state, on behalf of an agency paying support to an unwed mother—can file a paternity action to prove that he is the father, and if he is, the next step will be an action for child support. Sometimes the government catches up with the father many years later, and he is required to pay thousands of dollars in back support that he never knew he owed.

Establishing Paternity

A paternity lawsuit, to determine the identity of the father of a child born outside of marriage, may be brought either by the mother or by the father himself if the mother is denying his paternity. Paternity is usually proved by genetic testing. Once it's established, the father has all the rights and obligations of parenthood, including the duty to support the child and the right to ask a court for custody or visitation.

RESOURCE

Information on birth certificates and paternity statements. Contact your state's health department or bureau of vital statistics. See Chapter 6 for details.

How Child Support Obligations Are Calculated

Each state has guidelines for calculating child support, based on the parents' incomes and expenses and the amount of time each parent spends with the children. These guidelines (a requirement of the federal Child Support Enforcement Act), vary considerably from state to state. In addition, guidelines in some states give judges considerable leeway in setting the actual amount. But an increasing number of states impose strict guidelines that leave judges very little latitude.

RESOURCE

State guidelines and information on child support rules.
- www.alllaw.com/calculators/Childsupport offers child support calculators for each state. Parents can go online and get a ballpark idea of what guideline support would be in their state.
- www.ncsea.org, the website of the National Child Support Enforcement Association, has contact information for every state child support enforcement agency. See your state sheet in Appendix A for your agency, or call 703-506-2880.
- www.supportguidelines.com provides an extensive list of links to state and federal laws and agencies.

Factors That Affect Child Support Payments

Most state guidelines use similar factors to determine who pays child support, and how much. These factors usually include:
- each parent's net income
- the time the children spend with each parent
- the number, ages, and needs of the children—including health insurance, education, daycare, and special needs
- the family's predivorce standard of living, and
- hardship factors that affect a parent's ability to pay support (see below).

It's very common for parents to agree on child support after doing some research online or having a brief consultation with an attorney, because there's not all that much leeway in the guidelines. In other words, it's not really worth it to fight about it because the guidelines dictate a result and courts don't deviate from that result very often. If parents aren't able to reach a compromise and bring their dispute to the judge, courts often require each divorcing spouse to fill out a financial statement that gives a complete picture of the parents' financial situations. Even when parents do agree, each parent must detail monthly income and expenses for the court, so that the judge can evaluate whether the amount of support is appropriate.

How Courts Evaluate a Parent's Ability to Pay Child Support

The numbers used to calculate guideline support start with each parent's net income. Net income is gross income from all sources—such as wages, investment income, rental income from real estate, or public benefits—minus mandatory deductions, such as income taxes, Social Security tax, union dues, and health care costs.

When figuring net income, most courts don't consider voluntary deductions from a parent's paycheck, such as 401(k) contributions, or loan or credit card payments deducted automatically. Nor do they give credit for wage attachments, which generally mean that a portion of the person's wages are being withheld to pay off a debt or, possibly, to pay support for children from another marriage. (However, in some states, courts do allow a deduction for the amount of child support paid for other children.)

When calculating guideline support, most courts do not deduct reasonable expenses for the necessities of life—for example, rent, mortgage, food, clothing, and health care, and they almost never include expenses such as tuition, eating in restaurants, or entertainment. The idea is that parents' support of their children should have a higher priority than personal expenses. If expenses for necessities are particularly high for some reason, parents must ask the court to deviate from guideline support and take those factors into account. Otherwise, it's assumed that guideline support takes basic living expenses into account.

In most states, the judge is authorized to examine a parent's ability to earn as well as what the parent is actually earning, and to impute income and order child support payments based on the ability to make more income. Say, for example, a father with an obligation to pay child support leaves his current job and takes a lower-paying job that he likes better because it's more creative or less stressful. In this situation, a court may base the child support on the income from the original job (ability to earn) rather than on the new income level (ability to pay). The children's current needs take priority over the parent's career plans and desires. However, if income is reduced because a parent decides to go back to school for a degree that is likely to increase the parent's earning capacity, the court may be more flexible in setting support.

How Long Child Support Lasts

In general, state laws require that all parents support their child until:
- the child reaches the age of majority (this varies by state, but is usually 18) and sometimes longer if the child has special needs or is in college
- the child is on active military duty
- the biological parents' rights and responsibilities are terminated—for example, when a child is adopted by someone else, or
- the child has been declared emancipated by a court and has the legal rights of an adult (see Chapter 6 for details on emancipation).

In some divorce settlement agreements, the parents set a specific date to terminate child support—usually after the child finishes college or otherwise becomes self-supporting. If there's no such agreement, state law governs the date that support ends.

When a Parent Falls Behind on Child Support Payments

Each installment of court-ordered child support is due on a specific date set out in the divorce or parentage order from the court. Overdue payments are called arrearages or arrears—and federal and state governments take an aggressive approach to collecting them.

Can a Parent Ever Withhold Child Support?

A parent cannot withhold child support because of disputes over visitation, with one narrow exception. If the custodial parent disappears for a lengthy period so that no visitation is possible, a few courts have ruled that the noncustodial parent's duty to pay child support may be considered temporarily suspended.

As a rule, though, no matter what the circumstances, a parent must continue paying support even when the other parent is interfering with visitation rights. If you aren't seeing your kids as you are supposed to because the other parent isn't allowing it, go back to court to have your rights enforced or modified—for example, you could ask for a change in physical custody or time sharing, request supervised changeovers so that someone else witnesses your ex's failure to bring the kids on time or at all, or even ask the court to hold the other parent in contempt, which could result in fines or, in very extreme cases, even jail time. You will need to file a written request in order to make any of these changes and attend a court hearing.

Back Child Support: It Never Goes Away

Once child support is owed, it is owed until the parent pays it in full. Even filing for bankruptcy, which wipes out many debts, does not cancel child support debt. A parent who's fallen behind on payments can ask a judge to lower future payments (see "Modifying Child Support Payments," below), but that doesn't affect the past due amount, which must be paid in full. In fact, judges in most states are prohibited by law from retroactively modifying a child support obligation.

TIP

If you fall behind, immediately go to court and request a temporary modification of your payment amount. If you just let payments slide, you'll be on the hook for a debt you might not ever be able to pay off.

Collecting Delinquent Child Support Payments

All child support orders contain automatic wage assignment orders, meaning that a portion of the paying parent's paycheck can be taken and sent directly to the recipient parent if the receiving parent opts to use the wage assignment. (Some don't—if they're not worried about nonpayment, it is just as easy to have the paying parent send a check directly, and it keeps the employer out of the paying parent's personal life.) However, in order to get your money this way, you must provide the employer with the court order. And a wage assignment won't work for self-employed parents or those whose income is more sporadic.

Every state has a child support enforcement agency with the job of helping parents, whether married or unmarried, collect overdue child support. (They'll even help if the paying parent has moved out of state, as required by the Uniform Interstate Family Support Act.) These efforts might range from meeting with the ex-spouse and arranging a payment schedule to contacting an employer and getting money withheld (garnished) from every paycheck. All child support orders from a court include a wage garnishment order—cooperative parents usually don't enforce it, but if you're having trouble getting your support payments, you can use it. To garnish wages, you'll need to send the court order on child support (and some other paperwork) to your ex's employer, who will then deduct child support payments from every paycheck. The child support enforcement agency will help you do this, and most of these services are free or low cost. The website of the National Child Support Enforcement Association (www.ncsea.org) has contact information for every state child support enforcement agency.

State and federal governments and agencies may also withhold federal income tax refunds, deny a passport, and suspend or restrict a business, occupational, or driver's license when a parent is delinquent in paying child support. Once a state child support enforcement agency has listed a parent as delinquent, these actions will happen automatically the next time a license comes up for renewal or the parent applies for a passport. As a last resort, the court that issued the child support order can hold a delinquent parent in contempt of court and, in the absence of a reasonable explanation for the delinquency, impose a jail term. Jail terms aren't common, because courts would rather see the parent working and earning money to pay the support—but a parent who has repeatedly flouted court orders and failed to pay significant arrearages may see the inside of a jail cell.

Tracking Down Out-of-State Parents

If your children's other parent has moved out of state, you can use legal procedures, either on your own or with the help of your state's child support enforcement agency, to locate your ex and seek payment of current support as well as arrearages. You have several options, including:

- asking a court in your state to force the parent to pay (as long as your state has legal authority over the parent; if you got your divorce there, then the state has that authority, called jurisdiction)
- ask a court in your state to forward the current child support order, as well as any new orders made on arrearages, to a court in the state where your ex lives, and have that state's courts and agencies enforce the order
- file an enforcement request directly in the state where the other parent lives by contacting that state's child support enforcement agency or hiring a local attorney, or
- forward the support order to the other parent's employer and ask the employer to withhold the support amounts from paychecks. However, if there are significant arrearages, you may need to go back to court to get an order for a higher wage assignment to cover both current and past due support.

Finding a Delinquent Parent's Assets

The federal government tracks a delinquent parent's assets with resources such as the Federal Parent Locator Services, which is a government service designed to help parents collect past due child support and enforce child support payments. Federal law also requires employers to report all new hires to their state's child support enforcement agency (the Personal Responsibility and Work Opportunity Reconciliation Act of 1996, or PRWORA). The agency then forwards this data to the National Directory of New Hires, a centralized registry that searches lists of new employees for parents who owe child support and quickly sets up wage withholding orders for these delinquent parents. Under PRWORA, financial institutions—such as banks, savings and loans, credit unions, insurance companies, and money market funds—must also search the account records of parents who owe child support. When a match is identified, the information is sent to the state within 48 hours, so the accounts can be seized.

 RESOURCE
State child support enforcement agencies and information on programs and options for collecting (and paying) child support. See the website of the National Child Support Enforcement Association, www.ncsea.org or call 703-506-2880. You'll find information about the Federal Parent Locator Service at www.acf.hhs.gov/programs/cse/newhire.

Modifying Child Support Payments

You and your child's other parent may agree to increase or decrease child support amounts—and if there's a significant change in either parent's situation, it's a good idea to figure out something that will work for both of you, rather than spending time and money in court. However, even if you reach an agreement, make sure you write it down and have a judge approve it. If it's not approved by a judge, meaning that it becomes a court order, then the paying parent still owes the original support amount, and the recipient parent can try to collect the full amount even after agreeing to a lesser amount. If you had a lawyer for your divorce, you can ask the same lawyer to help you with a support modification—or you can try doing it yourself using your court's self-help materials.

If one parent wants a change and the other won't agree, the parent seeking the modification must ask the court to hold a hearing, at which each of you can argue your side. As a general rule, the court will not modify an existing order unless the parent proposing the modification can show changed circumstances—for example, a job layoff that resulted in lower income. This rule encourages stability and helps prevent the court from becoming overburdened with frequent modification requests. If the court does order a modification, depending on the circumstances, it may be temporary or permanent.

Temporary Modification

Changed circumstances that could support a temporary modification include:
- a child's medical emergency
- a temporary inability to pay—for instance, because of a medical emergency or job loss, or
- a temporary increase in need—commonly from some kind of economic or medical hardship—on the part of the parent receiving support.

Permanent Modification

A judge may permanently modify a child support order under one of the following circumstances:
- either parent receives additional income from remarriage
- changes in the child support laws
- job change of either parent
- cost of living increase
- disability of either parent, or
- changes in the needs of the child.

A permanently modified child support order will remain in effect until child support is no longer required or the order is modified again.

Child Support and Taxes

Child support doesn't have any tax consequences for either the paying parent or the receiving parent—it's neither taxable nor deductible. (This is different from spousal support, or alimony, which is tax deductible for the person who makes the payments and taxable to the recipient.)

Which Payments Are Child Support?

To qualify as child support, payments must be designated as child support in a divorce or separation agreement. If the agreement lumps the payments together as "family support" or "alimony" and doesn't designate a specific portion of each payment as child support, *none* of the payment will be considered child support for tax purposes. This can have adverse tax consequences for both the payer and the recipient of child support payments, because family support or alimony is taxable to the recipient, and the paying parent won't get the tax deduction either.

Who Gets to Claim a Child as a Dependent

When parents divorce or separate, only one of them can claim the dependent exemption each year for any given child. The IRS will come down hard if both try to claim it; the agency cross-references dependents' Social Security numbers to make sure taxpayers don't get away with this.

During a divorce, it can be unclear who is entitled to take the exemption when both parents are supporting the child and are sharing custody. The IRS rule is this: If parents lived apart during the entire last six months of the calendar year, or if they have a written divorce decree, maintenance agreement, or separation agreement, *and* more than half of the child's total support for the year came from one or both parents (the rest can come from relatives or public benefits), *and* the child was in the custody of one or both parents during the year, then the parent who had custody for the greater part of the year gets the exemption.

However, the parents may agree to give the exemption to the noncustodial parent if either of the following is true:

- In the divorce decree or separation agreement, the custodial parent gave up (waived) the right to claim the dependent exemption.
- The custodial parent signs a declaration (IRS Form 8332) relinquishing the right to claim the dependent exemption, and the noncustodial parent attaches this declaration to that year's tax return. Using this form, the custodial parent can relinquish the exemption for one year, a number of years, or forever.

If you relinquish the exemption, you also give up eligibility for the child tax credit (discussed in Chapter 6).

If the parents are not married, did not live apart during the last six months of the calendar year, or do not have a written agreement about support and custody, then the parent who provides more than 50% of a child's support during the tax year can claim the child as a dependent.

RESOURCE

Information on taxes and child support payments. See IRS Publication 504, *Divorced or Separated Individuals*, which you can download for free from www.irs.gov.

Adoption

Adoption, no less than birth, is a profound event. Like birth, it creates a new parent-child bond and changes the makeup of the family. Once an adoption is complete, the new parent-child relationship is recognized for all purposes, including child support obligations, inheritance rights, and custody.

All states have very specific and exacting rules governing the adoption process, and the Interstate Compact on the Placement of Children governs adoptions that involve a child crossing state lines. Every adoption must be approved by a court in the state where the adopting parents live. Birth parents must consent to the adoption, and adoptive parents must be fit to take on this most important responsibility. And most important, the court must rule that the adoption is in the best interests of the child.

 STATE RULES AND RESOURCES
The Adoption section of Appendix B contains resources for your state's rules on adoption issues, such as birth parents' consent, who can adopt, independent adoptions, and home studies, and where to find licensed adoption agencies, as well as courts that handle adoptions and family matters.

Who Can Adopt

Anyone who wishes to adopt must be a fit parent in the eyes of the court that's charged with approving or denying an adoption request. Before the court makes that determination, however, some states impose certain threshold requirements on adoptive parents:

- **Residence.** A few states or local counties require the adoptive parent to live in the state for a certain length of time before adopting. The residency period is usually a year or less.
- **Marital status.** Most states allow single people and unmarried couples to adopt, but a few do ban adoption by unmarried people petitioning together. Courts, adoption agencies, and birth parents, however, often favor heterosexual married couples. Unmarried singles or couples may have to wait longer to adopt or be flexible about the child they can adopt; it may be easier to adopt an older child or one with special needs.

- **Sexual orientation.** Only Utah and Mississippi prohibit openly gay people from adopting. An increasing number of states allow same-sex partners who are legally married or registered in a marriage-equivalent relationship to adopt a partner's child. Courts in 13 states and the District of Columbia have ruled that a gay couple may adopt a child together when neither is the child's biological or legal parent, and other states allow it although there are no laws explicitly permitting it. (See "Same-Sex Couples and Adoption," below.)
- **Race or ethnicity.** Adoptive parents do not need to be of the same race as the child, but some states give preference to prospective adoptive parents of the same race or ethnic background as the child; sometimes these preferences take the form of state laws, and sometimes they are policies of the state adoption agencies. Adoptions of Native American children are governed by special rules and procedures set out in a federal law, the Indian Child Welfare Act.
- **Age.** Most states require an adoptive parent to be ten or more years older than the child.

In addition to state rules, private adoption agencies may impose their own additional requirements or preferences, as long as the rules don't violate state antidiscrimination laws. (See "Agency Adoptions," below.)

Special Challenges of Single-Parent Adoptions

If you're a single person wishing to adopt, be prepared to make a good case for your fitness as a parent. When you apply to an agency to be matched with a birth parent, you can expect questions about why you haven't married, how you plan to support and care for a child on your own, what will happen if you do marry, and other questions that will put you in the position of defending your status as a single person. If you are accepted by the agency, you may face similar questions from prospective birth parents concerned about giving up their child to a single parent, and it may take longer to find a match.

The Birth Parents' Consent

For an adoption to be legal, in most instances, both birth parents must consent to it. Once a birth parent's consent is final, the birth parent gives up all parental rights, including the right to visit the child or make decisions regarding the child's life. Birth parents often have a great deal of control over who adopts their child: Commonly, with private agency and independent adoptions, birth parents choose the adoptive parents. The birth parents may also work out an arrangement with the adoptive parents so that they have continuing contact with the child—called an open adoption.

> **RESOURCE**
>
> **More on legal rights of birth parents.** The Child Welfare Information Gateway includes useful articles on the legal rights of birth parents intending to place a child for adoption. See www.childwelfare.gov/adoption/birth/for/pregnant_women or call 800-394-3366.

Who Must Consent

Both birth parents must consent to an adoption—a birth mother can't place a child for adoption without the consent of the child's presumed father. A presumed father is a man who was married to the child's mother at the time the baby was born, who put his name on a child's birth certificate, or who behaved like a father, including taking the child into his home and saying that he was the child's father. This legal presumption can be overruled if it's demonstrated by genetic testing that someone else is the child's biological father, but unless that happens, the presumed father has a right to be notified of any adoption proceeding and to either consent or object.

In some states, there's also a category called an alleged or putative father—someone who doesn't meet any of these requirements but who says he is the father or is identified by the birth mother as the biological dad. An alleged father is also entitled to notice of an adoption, but his rights aren't as strong as those of a presumed father—he doesn't have any greater claim to parentage than the adoptive parents do, and if he receives notice and doesn't file a paternity action within 30 days, his rights can immediately be terminated. A presumed father, on the other hand, has a presumptive right to custody of the child and can prevent the adoption if he does not consent, unless the birth mother can show he's not the biological father, in which case the adoption can proceed without his consent.

Of course, if either a presumed or an alleged father receives notice of the adoption and takes no action, the court can terminate the father's rights and allow the adoption to proceed.

Many states permit minor parents to place a child for adoption, although some require that an adult to be involved in the process in some way.

RESOURCE

State laws on minors' consent to adoption. For details on relevant laws in your state, see www.guttmacher.org (search "minors' rights as parents").

Most states require that a child 12 or older consent to adoption.

Other relatives—for example, the child's grandparents—don't need to consent, and in general aren't even entitled to receive notice of the adoption. A birth mother's parents don't have any legal right to stop her from placing the baby for adoption, and grandparents aren't necessarily favored as adoptive parents over nonrelatives. The only big exception to this rule is the adoption of Native American children, where a special federal law, the Indian Child Welfare Act applies and does favor adoption by Native American relatives.

If Birth Parents Change Their Minds

Although it's very common to make arrangements for a child to be placed with adoptive parents well before the due date, birth parents cannot give their legal consent to an adoption until after the child is born, and some states require them to wait three to four days after the birth before signing a consent form as part of the adoption process. The consent form is signed during the counseling procedure that birth parents must undergo, whether they're involved in a private agency adoption or an adoption being investigated by a county or state agency.

Until they give written consent, birth parents can legally change their minds about the adoption. Even after the birth parents have given their consent and the child is living in an adoptive home, the birth parents may have some time in which to change their minds and take the child back. In some states, birth parents have as long as three months to revoke their consent—a nerve-wracking time period for the adoptive parents caring for the child.

To help make sure birth parents understand the permanence of adoption and have considered their decision carefully and won't want to change their minds later, some states (and many adoption agencies) require birth parents to undergo counseling before giving consent. In general, the adopting parents pay for the counseling just as they pay most of the expenses of the adoption.

RESOURCE

State consent rules vary widely. See the adoption resources below for information on state consent rules.

Adoption Without Parental Consent

Under a few circumstances, it is possible to go forward with an adoption without a biological parent's consent. If a court terminates parental rights because of abuse, neglect, or abandonment, then the child is free for adoption. Most states' laws provide for termination of parental rights when a parent has willfully failed to support the child or has abandoned the child for a certain period, usually a year. Parental rights can also be terminated if a parent is considered permanently unfit because of drug addiction or child abuse or neglect. If a parent isn't capable of raising a child now but might be later—for example, after alcoholism treatment—the court would more likely order the child placed with a temporary guardian.

Parental rights can be terminated through proceedings in dependency or juvenile court, generally when the child has been removed from the home by an agency such as Child Protective Services. Often, these children are placed with prospective adoptive parents through a foster-adopt program under which the parents are licensed as foster parents with the intention of adopting the child if reunification efforts aren't successful. It's also not uncommon for parental rights to be terminated in the process of a private or agency adoption, in which case the adopting parents would ask the court directly to end the parental rights of an absent father, for example.

Ways to Adopt

Adoptive families come together in different ways. There are public agencies and private agencies, and most counties offer adoption programs as well as foster-adopt procedures. You can also make an arrangement to adopt without using an agency at all. Each option has its good and bad points, so if you're considering adoption make sure you evaluate what's best for you.

Open Adoption

An open adoption is one in which there is some degree of contact between the birth parents and adoptive parents both before and after the adoption. Often, this includes contact between the birth parents and the child as well, as the child grows up. An adoption can be open whether it's handled through an agency or independently.

There is no one standard for open adoptions; families work out the arrangement that they think will be best for them. Some adoptive parents meet the birth parents just once before the birth of the child and then don't have much contact afterwards, while others form ongoing relationships that may include written correspondence or visits. Although these visitation agreements are often part of the legal proceedings for the adoption, they are not enforceable by a court. If the adoptive parents don't allow contact after promising to do so, there's not much the birth parents can do.

If you are thinking about using an agency and want your adoption to be open, be sure to check the policies on open placements of any agency you're considering. Some agencies offer only closed or "semi-open" adoptions and will not provide identifying information even if both families want it shared. On the other hand, independent adoptions—where allowed—permit birth and adoptive families to determine what degree of contact is agreeable to all.

> **RESOURCE**
>
> **More on open adoptions.** The Independent Adoption Center (www.adoptionhelp.org, phone 800-877-OPEN (6736)) is a national nonprofit organization that specializes in open adoptions.

Agency Adoptions

A public agency or a private adoption agency licensed by the state can place a child with adoptive parents.

Public agencies generally place children who have become wards of the state because they were orphaned, abandoned, or abused. Many of these children have been in foster care before being freed for adoption. Most public agencies have many children ready to be adopted, many of whom are older or special needs children. Their adoption services are usually free or extremely low cost to the adopting parents, meaning the costs would be limited to incidental expenses.

Private agencies are sometimes run by charities or nonprofit social service organizations, but many are for profit as well. Private agencies specialize in matching would-be adoptive parents with expectant birth parents who want to choose the placement for their baby before the baby is born. The birth parents choose the adoptive parents from a collection of profiles prepared by the prospective parents with the help of the agency.

International adoptions are private agency adoptions, but differ from domestic adoptions in that the children being adopted are usually older, and the match is made by the agency rather than by the birth parents.

Pros and Cons of Private Agency Adoptions

Using a private agency for an adoption offers many advantages:

Experience and expertise. Agencies exist to find children, match them with parents, and satisfy the legal requirements of adoption. They do most of the legwork of an adoption and walk adoptive parents through the steps, such as going through the home study, obtaining the necessary consents, learning the state's legal requirements, and finalizing the papers (often with the help of an attorney).

Extensive counseling throughout the process. Agencies typically provide counseling for adoptive parents, birth parents, and the children (if they are old enough). Careful counseling can help everyone involved weather the emotional ups and downs of the adoption process. Preadoption counseling for a birth mother can help determine whether or not she is really committed to giving up a child for adoption, which reduces the likelihood that she might change her mind.

Specialization. Agencies tend to develop specialties in placing different kinds of children. That can be helpful if you want, for example, to adopt an infant, a child of a different race, a child from another country, or a child with special medical needs.

There are also drawbacks to working with a private agency:

Extreme selectivity choosing adoptive parents. Because private agencies often have a surplus of people who want to adopt, most have long waiting lists of prospective parents, especially for healthy white infants. Agencies sometimes discourage prospective parents from attempting to adopt if the agency believes they bring less than desirable criteria, such as marital status, income, health, religion, family size, and personal history. Many agencies prefer heterosexual married couples. However, for-profit agencies that advertise to the public must comply with state nondiscrimination laws, and can't refuse to do business with prospective parents for a discriminatory reason. The bottom line, of course, comes down to the birth parents, who will use their own criteria to select the adoptive parents with whom they'll place their child.

Lengthy adoption process. As is true in most types of adoption, with an agency adoption, the birth parents must consent to the adoption after the baby is born, and they have a period of time during which they can revoke their consent. In most cases, the agency will place the baby with the prospective adoptive parents anyway, on the assumption that the birth parents won't withdraw consent and that the adoption can be finalized in court after the consent becomes final. If the birth mother decides she wants the child back before the waiting period has expired, the adoptive parents must let the child go. For this reason, agencies sometimes wait to place a child in the adoptive home until all necessary consents have become final, which can be as long as three months in some states. As a result, a child may be placed in foster care for a few days or weeks, depending on the situation and the state's law. This delay concerns many birth and adoptive parents who want the child to have a secure, stable home as soon as possible.

Cost. Adoptive parents can expect to pay a fee of $15,000 or more to adopt a newborn through a private agency, less for placing older or special-needs children. Many agencies charge a flat fee; some use a sliding scale that varies with adoptive parents' income, usually with a minimum and maximum fee. Adoptive parents usually also pay for the birth mother's expenses (medical costs, living expenses during the pregnancy, and costs of counseling) as limited by state law. (See "Payments to Birth Mothers," below.)

> TIP
> **Adoptive parents may get a tax credit.** Many of the expenses that adoptive parents incur to legally adopt a child qualify for a federal adoption tax credit. The credit applies to both domestic and international adoptions. (See Chapter 6.)

How to Find and Screen an Adoption Agency

There are an estimated 3,000 adoption agencies, public and private, in the United States. You'll need to do some searching to find an agency that meets your needs and is able to work with you. Often, a personal referral from someone who has adopted a child is the best way to find a good agency. You can also contact a national adoption organization that offers referrals (some are listed at the end of this chapter).

Once you've got some names, get information from:
- **Your state's licensing department** (search "adoption licensing agency" on your state website). It can tell you whether a particular agency has been cited for licensing violations and whether the licensing office has received any complaints about it. You can also request a copy of the state's rules governing agencies so that you can see the standards the agency should be meeting.
- **The staff at your state's department of social services.** They may be able to give you information about the agency.
- **Your state or local department of consumer affairs.** It may handle complaints about adoption agencies or provide information about a particular agency.

- **Parents in similar circumstances who have successfully adopted through the agency.** They may provide valuable information about their experience. Ask the agency for names.

After you've done your homework, ask each agency about:

- its application process and eligibility requirements (parents' age, health, income, residence, and the like)
- the number of children available for placement by age and other characteristics, and how long a wait the parents might expect
- procedure and timeline for home study
- counseling services (before and after adoption, for birth parents and adoptive parents)
- fees
- accreditation, and
- policies on open adoptions, international adoptions, interstate adoptions, and anything else that's important to you.

Payments to Birth Mothers

It is, of course, illegal to buy or sell a baby. But all states allow adoptive parents to pay a birth mother to cover certain reasonable costs that are specifically related to the adoption process. Each state has its own rules on what kinds of expenses may be paid.

Most states allow adoptive parents to pay the birth mother's medical expenses, counseling costs, and attorneys' fees. Some states allow payments to cover the birth mother's living expenses, such as food, housing, and transportation, during pregnancy. Most states require all payments to be itemized and approved by a court before the adoption is finalized. Be sure you know and understand your state's laws, because providing or accepting prohibited financial support may jeopardize the adoption—and subject you to criminal charges.

Birth parents who revoke their consent within the time allowed are not legally required to return any of the money they received for expenses during the pregnancy.

A federal adoption tax credit is available for expenses incurred to legally adopt a child. See "Tax Breaks for Adoptive Parents" in Chapter 6 for details.

Independent Adoptions

In an independent or private adoption, a child is placed with adoptive parents without the assistance of an agency. Independent adoptions are arranged directly between the birth parents and the adoptive parents, without the intervention of an agency to make the match. Sometimes, birth parents and adoptive parents meet through personal contacts—for example, imagine two coworkers, one of whom has a niece who wants to place a baby for adoption and one of whom knows a couple who wants to adopt, and who discover the match and put the birth mother in contact with the adoptive parents. Other independent adoptions are established through an intermediary such as a lawyer, adoption facilitator, doctor, or member of the clergy. (In some states, adoption facilitators aren't allowed to match adoptive couples with birth parents; in others, it's legal to do so.) Some states allow prospective adoptive parents to advertise in order to meet birth parents, but this isn't legal everywhere. Regardless of how the match is made, adoptive parents in an independent adoption should have an attorney working with them throughout the process. Independent adoptions are quite heavily regulated, and the legal rules and paperwork are more than most adoptive parents will want to handle themselves—counseling before placement, a significant amount of paperwork required by the local county or state department that investigates the adoption petition, and legal paperwork to finalize the adoption in court.

Independent adoptions are attractive to many birth and adoptive parents for several reasons:

- **Control over the entire adoption process.** Rather than relying on an agency as a go-between, the birth parents and adoptive parents can meet, get to know each other, and decide for themselves whether the adoption should take place and what kind of ongoing communication they would like. (See "Open Adoption," above.)
- **Better information.** Adoptive parents can often get background information and medical history on the child and birth family.
- **Less red tape.** Independent adoptions avoid the long waiting lists and restrictive qualifying criteria that characterize many agency adoptions. Independent adoptions can happen much faster than agency

adoptions, often within a year of beginning the search for a child. (An agency adoption would take the same amount of time after placement, but the placement process can be lengthy and emotionally draining.)

There are also a few major drawbacks to independent adoptions:

Cost. Because each situation is unique, the expense of an independent adoption is unpredictable. If they advertise or use an adoption facilitator or attorney for the matching process, prospective adoptive parents must cover the cost of finding a birth mother. Even if they meet the birth mother without an intermediary, they'll still pay all costs related to the pregnancy and birth and significant legal fees. Expenses can be higher if the birth mother lives out of state. Some states also allow adoptive parents to pay the birth mother's living expenses during the pregnancy, although there are caps on all of these payments. (See "Payments to Birth Mothers," above.)

Risk. Independent adoptions carry the same risk as agency adoptions, that the birth parents will have a change of heart and withdraw consent during the period before the consent becomes final. In some states, that period is longer in an independent adoption. There's also the possibility that the birth parents won't get adequate preadoption counseling; if they don't fully work through the emotional aspects of giving up a child, it can make an adoption arrangement between birth and adoptive parents more vulnerable to unraveling.

Amount of work. Even with a lawyer's help, many adoptive parents spend enormous amounts of time and money finding a birth mother, not to mention following through and finalizing the adoption, especially if the birth parent lives in another state.

Interstate Adoptions

The Interstate Compact on the Placement of Children (ICPC) governs adoptions in which a child is transported across state lines for an adoption. This occurs fairly often with both agency and independent adoptions, and the ICPC is designed to make sure that the adoption is properly investigated by regulating which state is responsible for the home study and what information must change hands during the process. Each state must approve the adoption before it can be finalized.

Identified Adoptions

An identified, or designated, adoption is one in which the adopting parents locate a birth mother (or the other way around) and then ask a private agency to handle the adoption process. In this way, an identified adoption is a hybrid of an independent and an agency adoption. Prospective parents don't have to sit on an agency waiting list, but they reap the other benefits of working with an agency, such as experience with legal issues and counseling services. Identified adoptions provide an alternative to parents in states that don't allow independent adoptions.

Foster Care to Adoption (Fost-Adopt)

Children in foster care are wards of the state, often because they have suffered abuse or neglect or been abandoned by their birth parents. A foster parent is a temporary guardian of a child and is paid monthly support for the child's care. To become a foster parent, your home must be licensed by a state-approved agency. Being a foster parent is very different from becoming a child's guardian, which usually involves a child you already know and doesn't require the same level of screening. (See "Guardianship," below.)

Foster placements can last anywhere from days to years, during which time the parents are entitled to reunification services, which may include substance abuse treatment, anger management training, and education on parenting skills. During this period, the foster parents must cooperate with the reunification plan, even if their hope is to adopt the child. If reunification efforts are unsuccessful, the birth parents' legal rights will be terminated in court, and the child may be placed for adoption, either with the foster parents or another family.

RESOURCE

Resource for foster parents. The National Foster Parent Association (www.nfpainc.org, phone 800-557-5238) is a national support organization for foster parents that provides contact information for state and local associations and other foster care resources.

Stepparent Adoptions

The majority of adoptions in the United States are stepparent adoptions, in which the spouse of a parent adopts that parent's legal child. This type of adoption may occur when one biological parent has died or has left the family after a divorce, and the remaining parent remarries. Most stepparents do not formally adopt their stepchildren, but those who do obtain the same parental rights and responsibilities as biological parents, such as the right to custody and the obligation to pay child support after a divorce.

A stepparent adoption is usually much easier to complete than a nonrelative adoption. The general procedure is the same, but waiting periods are often dispensed with, the home study is fairly minimal, and the cost is significantly less than other types of adoption. After all, the child is already living in the prospective parent's home.

In all stepparent adoptions, however, if the child already has two legal parents, the other one will need to consent. Without consent, the adoption will not be allowed unless the legal parent's parental rights are terminated for some other reason, such as abandonment, unfitness, or failure to support the child. (See "Who Must Consent," above.)

Kinship Adoptions

When a child is related to the adoptive parent by blood or marriage, the adoption is a relative adoption, sometimes called a "kinship adoption." The most common example is a stepparent adoption, but it's also not unusual for grandparents to adopt grandchildren or for aunts and uncles to take responsibility for the children of their siblings if the parents die while the children are minors or if the parents are unable to take care of the children for other reasons. These adoptions are simpler than nonrelative adoptions. If the adopted child has siblings who are not adopted at the same time, kinship adoption procedures usually provide for contact among the siblings after the adoption.

Investigating Adoptive Parents: The Home Study

All states require adoptive parents to undergo an investigation, called a home study, to make sure that they are fit to raise the child they are seeking to adopt. With agency adoptions, parents often undergo a "preplacement" investigation that verifies they are appropriate adoptive parents. But in addition, all adoptive parents must go through a full investigation once a child is placed with them for adoption. (If there was a preplacement home study, then the second investigation is called "post-placement.")

Who conducts the home study depends on what type of adoption is involved. In an independent or stepparent adoption, a county or state agency is responsible for the investigation. When an agency does the placement, the same agency also does the home study. The home study process involves a licensed social worker employed by the county, state, or agency who interviews the adoptive parents, examines their home life, and collects other information from personal references and background checks. The investigating social worker gets information about issues such as the prospective adoptive parents':

- financial situation
- employment history
- marital and family history
- other children (current or planned)
- work and career obligations
- physical and mental health, and
- criminal history.

The social worker also gathers information from a number of personal references, verifies employment, and requires the prospective adoptive parents to be fingerprinted and checked against national criminal databases. Finally, the social worker must check into whether there's anyone else with a right to object to the adoption. If the child being adopted has a birth father who hasn't consented, for example, the social worker will explore the situation with the birth mother and encourage the adoptive parents to have his rights terminated before the final hearing. The social worker will include in the report whether there are any other involved parties and whether any additional consents are needed.

In recent years, the home study has become more than just a method of investigating prospective parents; it serves to educate and inform them as well. The social worker helps to prepare the adoptive parents by discussing issues such as how and when to talk with the child about being adopted, how to deal with the reactions of friends and family to the adoption, communicating with the birth parents in an open adoption, and other issues.

The home study typically takes several months. Once all of the information has been gathered, the social worker submits a report for the court with a recommendation about whether or not the particular adoption should be approved.

It doesn't happen very often, but if the social worker writes a negative report to the court, the prospective adoptive parents may contest the conclusion. Each state has different appeal procedures. Some states provide for a separate procedure, while other states make the appeal part of the adoption hearing.

Prospective adoptive parents may be charged a fee for a home study. It depends on the type of adoption and agency involved; there may be no fee with a public agency or a few thousand dollars fee with a private agency.

RESOURCE

More on home studies. See Appendix B for resources that provide details on home study requirements and appeals processes. See "International Adoptions," below, for information on home study requirements when the child is coming from another country.

Family Court Approval of Adoption

All adoptions, whether handled by an agency or done independently, must be approved by a local court—often the family court, but sometimes the probate department or the general civil court. (Appendix A includes information on state family courts.) The adoptive parents file an adoption petition when the child is first placed with them. In most cases, the home study is conducted after the petition is filed; once it's complete, the social worker files the report with the court and the judge holds a hearing.

Even the simplest stepparent adoption requires a hearing, in which the adoptive parents and the child appear before the judge and confirm their commitment to the adoption.

Giving Notice to Interested Parties

In general, all of the consents will be taken care of during the investigation process. If there is anyone whose consent is necessary and who has refused to consent, that person—usually a birth father—must be given notice of the adoption hearing and the right to appear and contest the adoption. If that person does show up at the hearing, the judge will have to decide whether to consider the arguments against the adoption at that time or postpone the hearing until everyone has had a chance to prepare for a contested trial. Most of the time, however, all of this will have been dealt with during the investigation process.

The Adoption Petition

An adoption petition generally includes:
- the names and address of the adoptive parents
- the name, age, and legal parentage of the child to be adopted
- the relationship between the adoptive parents and the child to be adopted, such as blood relative, stepparent, or nonrelative
- the legal reason that the birth parents' rights are being terminated (usually, because they consent)
- an assertion that the adoptive parents are the appropriate people to adopt the child, and
- an assertion that the adoption is in the child's best interest.

Sometimes, the written consent of the birth parents or a court order terminating their parental rights is filed along with the petition. Other times, the termination occurs later in the process. Adoptive parents also often include a request to have the child's name legally changed. If the child's name is not changed as part of the adoption, and the adopting parents later want to change it, they'll need to file a separate court proceeding.

Adoption Hearing and Order

When it's time for the adoption hearing, the judge will have a chance to review the home study report in advance. The adoptive parents and the child must appear in court and, in most cases, the judge will ask them some simple questions—usually just verifying that the facts in the petition are true, and that the parents are committed to the adoption. If the child is older, the judge may also ask the child some questions. Some judges make adoption hearings quite informal and hold them in chambers (the judge's office), and others do them in open court with a court reporter present. Either way, adoption hearings are private, and the public isn't allowed. However, most judges will allow you to bring other family members and friends to the hearing if you wish.

If the judge determines that the adoption is in the child's best interest, the judge will issue an order approving and finalizing the adoption. This order, often called a final decree of adoption, legalizes the new parent-child relationship, orders a name change if the new parents have asked for one, and is the final step in the adoption. Finalizing an adoption is one of the happiest things that ever happens in a courtroom.

Adult Adoptions

In most states, it's legal for one adult to adopt another as long as there's at least a ten-year age difference and the parties can show why the adoption is in the interests of both people and the public good. Often, adult adoptions are stepparent adoptions that the family didn't get around to when the younger person was a minor, but wants to complete now so the younger person will inherit from the older.

Sometimes, older adults who don't have children of their own meet younger persons who they wish to treat as their children for inheritance purposes. Although adult adoptions can generally be completed based on the two adults' agreement, without a home study or investigation, many states require investigations of adult adoptions where caregivers of the elderly are involved, in order to prevent older people from being manipulated or abused.

> **RESOURCE**
>
> **Helpful resources on adoptions:**
>
> - www.adoption.com. The National Adoption Information Clearinghouse provides information about adoption agencies, international adoption, and many other adoption issues, including links to a wide variety of state adoption laws, such as consent to adoption, regulation of adoption expenses, use of advertising in adoption, access to adoption records, and more. (See Appendix B or call 888-251-0075.)
> - www.childwelfare.gov/adoption. The Child Welfare Information Gateway, a program of the U.S. Department of Health and Human Services, provides information about adoption and referrals to state and local agencies and support groups. The site also includes the National Foster Care & Adoption Directory (see www.childwelfare.gov/nfcad) which lists public and licensed private adoption agencies in the United States as well as adoption support groups. See your state page for details, or call 800-394-3366.
> - *The Adoption Resource Book*, by Lois Gilman (HarperPerennial), is a comprehensive guide for anyone considering adoption.
> - http://topics.law.cornell.edu/wex/table_family. The Legal Information Institute at Cornell Law School provides links to many family laws, including laws governing adoption, child custody, and children's rights.

International Adoptions

Adopting a child from another country is complicated, not least because the rules always seem to be changing. In addition to satisfying the adoption requirements of both the child's country and the parents' home state in the United States, parents must get an immigrant visa for the child through U.S. Citizenship and Immigration Services (USCIS) and the State Department. USCIS has its own rules for international adoptions, such as the requirement that the child be under 16 years of age and that the adoptive parents of orphans be married and at least 21 years old or, if single, at least 25 years old. USCIS also requires adoptive parents to complete several forms and submit a favorable home study report from a licensed agency. The country from which you're adopting is likely to have its own requirements as well—many have both a minimum and a maximum age for adoptive parents, many require that adoptive parents be married, and no country permits same-sex couples or out LGBT people to adopt.

Most people go through an American agency that specializes in international adoptions. You can adopt directly, but it's less common, because the rules are so complicated. In general, the agency you choose will help you select a country to work with and help match you with a child. You can either wait to file your adoption petition until you've been matched with an identified child, or file a petition in advance to get things started.

If you've already identified the child you want to adopt, you must file a Petition to Classify Orphan as an Immediate Relative (USCIS Form I-600) with USCIS. The form states that the child's parents have died, disappeared, or abandoned the child, or that one remaining parent is not able to care for the child and consents to the child's adoption and immigration to the United States. (If there are two known parents, then the child cannot be classified as an orphan, and you'll need to meet a whole different set of requirements, including that the child has lived in your legal custody for two years before you begin the immigration process.)

Along with the I-600 form, you will need to submit a significant number of documents, including a favorable home study report, financial and employment information, and references. If USCIS approves the petition, and there are no disqualifying factors, such as a communicable disease, the child can be issued an immigrant visa.

If you haven't yet identified a specific child to adopt, you can, and should, still get started on the paperwork. You'll use USCIS Form I-600A, Application for Advance Processing of Orphan Petition. It's a good idea to get your application started as soon as possible, because USCIS often takes a long time to process the paperwork. If it's not finished by the time you are matched with a child, it could hold up the child's arrival in the United States, even after all international requirements have been met.

Finally, be sure to check your own state laws for any preadoption requirements. Some states, for instance, require you to submit the written consent of the birth mother before they approve the entry of the child into the state.

Parents who adopt overseas may very often readopt the child in their own state in order to make sure that the adoption fully conforms to state law.

Sometimes, readoption is a legal necessity—required either by the state in which you live or by the country in which you adopted. Doing so also has the advantage of allowing you to obtain a birth certificate in English, which you often will not have when you leave the host country.

RESOURCE

More on international adoptions.

- The U.S. State Department, http://travel.state.gov/family/adoption/ adoption_485.html, and United States Citizenship and Immigration Services, www.uscis.gov (click on "Resources" then "Adoption-Based Resources" or call 800-375-5283) provide information and forms related to international adoption.

- *U.S. Immigration Made Easy*, by Ilona Bray (Nolo), discusses the rules and application procedures for international adoptions and citizenship for adopted children. See www.nolo.com for a sample chapter and full table of contents.

Same-Sex Couples and Adoption

Given the confusing and quickly changing status of same-sex marriage and marriage-like relationships (domestic partnerships and civil unions), it's not surprising that the laws surrounding the children born or adopted into same-sex relationships are also in flux.

Second-Parent Adoption

When one person in a same-sex couple has a child—by adopting, giving birth, or, in the case of a gay man using a surrogate to carry a child conceived with his sperm and a donor egg—the other partner generally has no biological relationship to the child. In most states, that person has no legal relationship to the child, either, and to become the child's legal parent, the partner must adopt the child through a second parent or coparent adoption. (The exception is in states with marriage or marriage-equivalent laws, discussed in Chapter 1, where a married person is a legal parent of a child born into the legal partnership. However, adoptions are still recommended in those cases, to protect the second parent's rights in other states and where federal law is involved.)

There are more than 20 states where laws are in place allowing second-parent adoption. In other states, there's no specific law, but many courts will allow the adoptions. However, some states—including Kentucky, Nebraska, and Ohio—have expressly disapproved of this type of adoption.

Adopting Together

Many same-sex couples have happily adopted children together. But there's no denying that same-sex couples who seek to adopt may face obstacles at several steps along the way. Some adoption agencies don't accept same-sex couples, or at least actively discourage them from seeking to adopt. Some birth parents won't choose them. Some judges might refuse to approve them as adoptive parents. However, at least 13 states have expressly ruled that a gay couple may adopt a child together when neither is the child's legal parent, and such adoptions have been granted in a number of other states as well.

RESOURCE

Resources on same-sex couples and adoption.

- The Human Rights Campaign website (www.hrc.org) includes information on state adoption laws affecting LGBT individuals and same-sex couples (see www.hrc.org/issues/parenting/adoptions/adoption_laws.asp). You can also phone the HRC at 800-777-4723.
- The National Center for Lesbian Rights (www.nclrights.org, phone 800-528-6257), Lambda Legal Defense and Education Fund (www.lambdalegal.org, phone 866-542-8336), and Gay and Lesbian Advocates and Defenders (www.glad.org, phone 617-426-1350) all offer information and resources.
- *Legal Guide for Lesbian & Gay Couples*, by Denis Clifford, Frederick Hertz, and Emily Doskow (Nolo), has more about same-sex parenting, including adoption. See www.nolo.com for a sample chapter and full table of contents.

Working With a Lawyer

Although there is no legal requirement that a lawyer be involved in an adoption, the process can be complex, and many adopting families seek out someone with experience and expertise. This is especially true when parents pursue an independent adoption and don't go through an agency. Even adoptive parents who work with an agency, however, often hire a lawyer to prepare the adoption petition and represent them at the hearing. Many stepparents, however, represent themselves, as the process is quite simple in most places.

See Chapter 9 for advice on finding and working with an attorney.

Adopted Children's Right to Their Birth Records

After an adoption is completed, the state where the child was born will issue a new birth certificate showing the adoptive parents as the child's parents. The original birth certificate, showing the birth parents, is sealed so that no one can see it without court permission. Only a few states offer adult adopted children open access to their original birth certificates. Generally, a court will unseal a record only for an urgent reason, such as a need for medical or genetic information.

But as attitudes toward adoption have become more open, states have come up with ways for adopted children to find their birth parents, some of which do not require the unsealing of records.

One system is called "search and consent." Someone who was adopted as a child contacts the birth parent through an intermediary agency; if the birth parent agrees, the agency gives the contact information to the child. This only works when the birth parent's information is available, and the most common system is a mutual consent registry, used in about 25 states, in which birth parents and adopted children provide identifying information about themselves to the registry. If a birth parent and that parent's adopted child both appear within a registry, the agency in charge shares the information with each of them, allowing them to get in touch.

TIP

Let an agency help you. If you're searching for a birth parent, contact a local adoption agency that is familiar with states' laws and procedures for contacting birth parents. The National Adoption Information Clearinghouse (www.adoption. com) and other resources listed above often provide referrals to local agencies.

Guardianship

A guardianship is a legal arrangement in which an adult has the court-ordered authority and responsibility to care for a child. A guardianship may be necessary if a child's parents die or if the child has been abandoned, neglected, or abused. Guardianships usually involve people who know each other or are related, in contrast to foster care situations, where a family is licensed to provide foster care in its home and then takes in whatever child is in need of care. A guardian does not have to be licensed in advance by the state, but before a formal legal guardianship will be granted, the county does investigate the request.

Typically, a guardian takes care of a child's personal needs, including shelter, education, and medical care. A guardian may also provide financial management for a child, though sometimes a second person (often called a "guardian of the estate") is appointed to manage the child's assets.

A guardianship does not sever the legal relationship (regarding custody, support, and inheritance) between the biological parents and the child the way an adoption does. For example, if a biological parent dies without a will, the child who is under a guardianship may inherit under state law. A child who has been adopted generally does not inherit from a biological parent who dies without a will.

As a general rule, guardianships are not granted unless:

- the parents consent
- the parents have abandoned the child, or
- a judge finds that it would be detrimental to the child for the parents to have custody.

If the court decides parents are unfit, a guardian will be appointed even if they object. The person who wants to be the guardian begins the process (generally, but not always, with a lawyer's help) by filing papers in court. A court investigator will interview the prospective guardian, the child, and the child's parents and make a recommendation to the judge. A judge will review the case, including any objections from family members to the proposed guardian, and decide who, if anyone, should be appointed guardian.

RELATED TOPIC

Naming a guardian in a will. To name a guardian for your own children in case you aren't around to take care of them, use your will to name the person you want to take care of them. (For details, see Chapter 8.)

A guardianship ordinarily lasts until:

- the child becomes a legal adult (age 18 in most cases)
- the child dies
- the child's assets are used up—if the guardianship was set up solely for the purpose of handling the child's finances, or
- a judge determines that a guardianship is no longer necessary.

A guardian may step down from the role only with permission from the court. In that case, a judge will appoint a replacement guardian.

RESOURCE

The Guardianship Book for California, by David Brown and Emily Doskow (Nolo), contains all of the forms and instructions necessary to become a California child's guardian. See www.nolo.com for a sample chapter and full table of contents.

Alternatives to Legal Guardianship

Some adults raise children—often grandchildren or other relatives—without legal court authorization. There are simple forms that parents can use to authorize other adults to care for their children in many circumstances, and those work fine for a short-term care situation. (For example, California has a form called a Caregiver's Authorization Affidavit, which gives a nonparent permission to enroll a child in school and make medical decisions on the child's behalf without going to court; other states have similar forms.) However, if the caretaking role is going to last longer than a couple of months, it's best to get a legal guardianship—otherwise you could run into problems with institutions that won't accept your authority to make decisions for the child.

Research the laws for your state or talk to a knowledgeable family law attorney to find out whether there are ways for you to take legal responsibility for a child—short of becoming a legal guardian.

Are You Prepared to Be a Guardian?

If you're considering becoming a child's guardian, honestly answering these questions may help you determine whether you're ready for the job:

- Do you want the ongoing responsibilities of a legal guardianship, including potential liability for the child's actions?
- If you're managing the child's finances, are you willing to keep careful records, give a court periodic accountings, and go to court for permission to handle certain financial matters?
- What kind of personal relationship do you have with the child?
- Will the guardianship adversely affect you or your family because of your own children, health situation, job, age, or other factors?
- Do you have the time and energy to raise a child?
- What is the financial situation? If the child will receive income from Social Security, public assistance programs, welfare, a parent, or the estate of a deceased parent, will it provide a decent level of support? If not, are you able and willing to spend your own money to raise the child?
- Do you anticipate problems with the child's parents or other relatives?

Children

Many local, state, and federal laws are designed to protect children, whether it's prohibiting them from drinking alcohol or working long hours, or requiring them to go to school. There are special juvenile courts to handle kids who get in trouble, with an emphasis on rehabilitation rather than punishment. Kids even help their parents qualify for tax breaks—but may also cost them if the kids cause damage, because parents are held responsible for many of their children's actions.

STATE RULES AND RESOURCES

The Children section of Appendix B contains resources for your state rules on issues that affect children, including bullying, access to health care without parental consent, special education, child labor, juvenile crime, and other topics covered in this chapter, plus courts that handle family matters.

Baby's First Legal Documents

A birth certificate and Social Security card are the first two legal documents a child needs.

Birth Certificate

A birth certificate serves as proof of your baby's name, date of birth, citizenship, and parentage. You will need a copy of the birth certificate when enrolling your child in school, applying for a passport for your child, and at other important points in your child's life.

The birth certificate process begins with a birth registration form, which new parents are given before a newborn baby is discharged from the hospital. The form asks for the parents' names and Social Security numbers, the child's date of birth, and the child's name. If parents complete the form in the hospital, the staff will submit it to the state department in charge of issuing birth certificates, often called the department of vital statistics.

If the baby isn't born in a medical facility, the mother or the physician or midwife assisting in the delivery must notify health officials of the birth. If you're planning a home birth, you can contact your state's department of health or bureau of vital statistics for more information. Your doctor or midwife should be familiar with the procedures as well.

When parents are not married, the father must sign a voluntary acknowledgment of paternity to be named as the child's father on the birth certificate. The "Unmarried Parents" section of Chapter 4 covers paternity.

Most issuing agencies—either the state or the local county registrar—will automatically send new parents a copy of the birth certificate once it's issued; in other states, parents have to make a formal request to the appropriate department and pay a small fee. You can always get additional copies of your child's birth certificate from your county registrar or from the state vital statistics department.

Naming Your Baby

In most states, you may give your child any first, middle, and last name you like. Whether you are married or not, you don't have to give your baby the last name of either parent if you don't want to, and the child does not have to have the father's last name to be considered his legal child.

Social Security Number

Your child will need a Social Security number. You will need the number to add your new baby to your health insurance plan, set up a college savings plan or bank account for your child, or apply for government benefits that could help your child and family. It's also required if you want to claim child-related tax breaks (discussed below) on your income taxes.

The easiest way to apply for a Social Security number for your child is through the same birth registration form that you used to get your child's birth certificate. The birth registration form has a box you can check to request a Social Security number for your child. To complete the form, you will need to provide both parents' Social Security numbers.

If you didn't get a birth registration form in the hospital, you can visit your local Social Security Administration (SSA) office and request a number in person. This process requires you to do three things:

- Complete Form SS-5 (*Application for Social Security Number*) and provide both parents' Social Security numbers on the form. To save time, download Form SS-5 from the SSA website (www.socialsecurity. gov/online/ss-5.pdf) and complete it before you go.
- Provide at least two documents proving your baby's age, identity, and citizenship status. One document should be your child's birth certificate. The other document can be your child's hospital birth record or other medical record.
- Provide proof of your own identity. Your driver's license and passport are both acceptable.

Social Security Numbers for Adopted Children

If you adopt a child who is a U.S. citizen, your child probably has a Social Security number already. If not, you can obtain an Adoption Taxpayer Identification Number (ATIN) to claim child-related tax breaks while the adoption is pending. To apply for one, complete IRS Form W-7A, *Application for Taxpayer Identification Number for Pending U.S. Adoptions*, available at www. irs.gov. The ATIN will be valid for two years, at which point you can extend it if your child's adoption is still not final. Once the adoption is final, you must stop using the ATIN and get a Social Security number for your child following the process described above.

If you are adopting a child from another country, you will have to wait until the adoption is final and your child has entered the United States before you can obtain a Social Security number for your child. Once that happens, you can use the process described above.

Find the SSA office nearest you by logging on to the SSA's Office Locator at www.ssa.gov/locator. If you'd prefer, you can mail in a completed Form SS-5 along with your identification documents to your local SSA office To find yours, call the SSA at 800-772-1213. Most people apply in person, however, because you'll need to give the SSA originals or certified copies of all identification documents, and going in person means you don't let those important documents out of your hands (or spend money getting additional certified copies).

Once you've submitted your application, you should receive your child's Social Security card in six to 12 weeks. It may take substantially longer to process your application if your child is one year of age or older, because the SSA will contact your state's department of vital statistics to confirm that the birth certificate you have provided is valid.

Is Your Baby a U.S. Citizen?

Every baby born in the United States is an American citizen, regardless of the parents' citizenship. In other words, a new baby is a citizen even if the parents are resident aliens or undocumented immigrants. All that is required is that your baby be born on U.S. soil. (There is one exception to this rule for certain children of diplomatic personnel, but it does not apply to the vast majority of people who live in the United States.)

There is no special paperwork to complete to establish your child's citizenship status—your child's birth certificate will serve as proof of citizenship. If you are not a legal U.S. resident, then your child may someday be able to petition for you to receive lawful permanent residency—but only after the child turns 21. And you have no right to live in the United States while waiting, unless you are able to maintain a separate, valid visa (which is unlikely). If you somehow managed to stay in the United States without documentation all that time, current immigration laws would punish you by mandating a ten-year stay outside the United States before returning as a permanent resident. See a lawyer for a personal analysis.

Citizenship rules are much more complex for children born outside of the United States to U.S. citizen parents. If both parents are citizens and married at the time the child is born, the child will be a U.S. citizen provided that at least one parent actually lived in the United States at some point before the child was born. Different (and more complicated) requirements apply if the parents are not married. To find out whether your foreign-born child meets the standards for citizenship, contact your local U.S. consular office. If your foreign-born child qualifies for citizenship, you will need to register the birth with your local U.S. consular office and obtain a Consular Report of Birth Abroad of a Citizen of the United States of America (FS-240). You can find contact information for your local consular office at www.usembassy.gov. To

learn more about citizenship rules for children born abroad, log on to http://
travel.state.gov/family/family_issues/birth/birth_593.html.

If you adopt a child who is not a U.S. citizen, either from overseas or
from within the United States, that child will, in most cases, become a
citizen automatically. The timing, however, as well as the way you'd obtain a
certificate proving citizenship, depend on various factors. Ask the adoption
agency or lawyer assisting you to analyze the details in your case. For more
information on adoption, see Chapter 5.

Tax Breaks for Parents

The federal government offers parents several money-saving tax breaks to
ease the financial burden of caring for children.

Dependent Exemption

The dependent exemption allows qualified parents to deduct a certain
amount—$3,650 per child in 2010—from their taxable income. With some
exceptions, parents can claim this exemption for any child who:
- is your biological, step-, adopted, or foster child
- lived with you for more than half the year
- is younger than 19 at the end of the tax year, is a full-time student
  younger than 24, or is permanently and totally disabled
- didn't provide more than half of his or her own support for the year,
  and
- is a U.S. citizen or a resident of the United States, Canada, or Mexico.

For 2009, the dependent exemption is subject to phaseout if your income
exceeds certain threshold amounts. However, you only lose up to two-
thirds of the exemption amount under these rules. You can calculate your
exemption amount under the phaseout rules using the worksheet in IRS
Publication 501, *Exemptions, Standard Deduction, and Filing Information*,
available on the IRS website at www.irs.gov. There are no phaseout limits for
tax year 2010.

When parents are divorced, a child is the dependent of the parent who
has physical custody, because the child lives with that parent for more than

half the year. (Parents who share physical custody equally often designate one of them as having 51% custody in order to allow that person to take the exemption.) Divorced parents can also agree that the noncustodial parent take the dependent exemption for the child; the custodial parent must sign a form transferring the exemption to the other parent. See Chapter 4 for more on the subject of dependent exemption and child support.

RESOURCE

More about the dependent exemption. See IRS Publication 501, *Exemptions, Standard Deduction, and Filing Information*, available at www.irs.gov. Also, *Nolo's Essential Guide to Divorce*, by Emily Doskow, includes a detailed discussion of taxes and children, including when a noncustodial parent may take the dependent exemption. See www.nolo.com for a sample chapter and full table of contents.

Child Tax Credit

The child tax credit allows qualified parents to subtract $1,000 per child (through 2010) from their federal tax bill. The eligibility requirements are essentially the same as those for the dependent exemption, with two notable exceptions: The child must be younger than 17 (rather than 19, as is the case with the dependent exemption), and there's a lower income limit for the child tax credit. For the 2010 tax year, married couples filing jointly cannot claim any part of the child tax credit if their adjusted gross income exceeds $110,000.

If you and your child's other parent are divorced, the custodial parent will take the child tax credit, unless the noncustodial parent is taking the dependent exemption by agreement with the custodial parent. In that case, the noncustodial parent can take the child tax credit as well as the dependent exemption.

RESOURCE

More about the child tax credit. See IRS Publication 972, *Child Tax Credit*, available at www.irs.gov.

Tax Breaks for Adoptive Parents

Through the adoption tax credit, the federal government in essence reimburses adoptive parents for the expenses they incur to legally adopt a child. The credit allows you to subtract your adoption expenses from your tax liability for the year. For tax year 2010, the maximum credit available for qualifying expenses is $13,170 per adoption.

To claim the credit, the following rules apply:

- Your child must be younger than 18 (or, if older than 18, must be incapable of caring for himself or herself because of a disability)
- You must have out-of-pocket costs related to the adoption, such as adoption fees, court costs, attorneys' fees, and travel expenses.
- Your income must be within certain limits. For the 2010 tax year, the credit phases out at $222,520.

Expenses of stepparent adoptions or surrogate parenting arrangements do not qualify for the adoption tax credit.

> **RESOURCE**
>
> **More about the adoption tax credit.** Find out more about income limits, rules for children with special needs, and rules for domestic and international adoptions in IRS Form 8839, *Qualified Adoption Expenses*, available at www.irs.gov.

Child Care Tax Breaks

The federal government offers two tax breaks to help offset the cost of child care: the child care credit and dependent care accounts.

Child Care Credit

The child care credit provides a tax credit of 20% to 35% of the first $3,000 in child care costs you incur per child per year (with a maximum of $6,000 for two or more children). The exact percentage is determined by your income level. For example, in 2009, families with an adjusted gross income (AGI) of $15,000 or below were entitled to a 35% credit; those with an AGI above $43,000 were entitled to a 20% credit.

You must meet all of the following requirements (with some exceptions) to be eligible for the child care credit (the same rules apply to dependent care accounts, discussed below):

- Your child must be your biological, adopted, step-, or foster child.
- Your child must live with you for more than half the year.
- Your child must be younger than 13 or permanently and totally disabled.
- You must pay more than half the cost of keeping up a home in which you and your child live during the year.
- You (and your spouse, if you are married) must work, look for work, or be a full-time student.

In addition to the above, your child care expenses must meet all of the following criteria:

- Your child care provider must be someone whom you can't claim as a dependent—this may include a licensed day care provider, preschool, or on-the-books nanny, but can't include anyone you pay under the table.
- You must have used the child care to enable you to work, look for work, or attend school full time (for example, you cannot claim a credit for babysitter costs incurred to run errands or go out on Saturday night).
- Payments to a child care provider must have been for child care only, not for items such as food, lodging, clothing, education, and entertainment for the child care worker. (Expenses for household services, such as housekeeping, qualify if they are at least partly for the well-being and protection of your child.)

Claiming the child care credit is easy. Keep your child care expense receipts for the year and then input the appropriate information onto your tax return.

RESOURCE

More about the child care credit. See IRS Publication 503, *Child and Dependent Care Expenses,* available at www.irs.gov.

Dependent Care Accounts

A dependent care account (sometimes called a dependent care flexible spending account or a cafeteria plan) is like the 401(k) plan of the child care world. Through your employer, you set aside pretax dollars that you can access to pay your nanny, day care, or preschool bills during the year. All of the money you contribute to the account is exempt from federal taxes. Not all employers offer dependent care accounts, and you can't set up an individual account—they're only available through work. Also, if you sign up for a dependent care account, you can't also claim a child care tax credit for the same child care expenses.

Federal law sets limits on the amount you can contribute to your dependent care account. Regardless of how many children you have, married couples filing jointly can contribute a maximum of $5,000. Single people or married couples filing separately can contribute up to $2,500. Your employer can set an amount lower than the federal maximum.

The eligibility rules for a dependent care account are the same as for the child care credit discussed above.

The amount you can use from your dependent care account is limited by your earned income. You cannot claim more than your earned income or your spouse's earned income, whichever is less.

If your employer sponsors a dependent care account, you'll be able to enroll during your general benefits enrollment period. At that point, you decide how much money to contribute for the year (you can't change this amount during the year—and if you don't spend it by the end of the year, you will usually lose it).

To access money from your dependent care account, you must have already incurred the expense—you can't take money out in advance. You'll submit a form and the receipt to your employer, who will reimburse you for the expense directly or through a third-party administrator. Consult your employee benefits manual or check with your human resources administrator for more information on your company's reimbursement policy.

You will also have to include this information on your tax return.

RESOURCE
More about dependent care accounts. See IRS Publication 503, *Child and Dependent Care Expenses* (and IRS Form 2441), available at www.irs.gov.

Child Care by the Books

To take advantage of child care tax breaks, you must comply with appropriate laws. For example, if you hire a nanny, you are subject to several federal and state employment laws. These include:

- verifying your caregiver's immigration status
- delivering regular paychecks
- withholding and paying Social Security, Medicare, and other applicable taxes
- getting an employer identification number, and
- paying for workers' compensation insurance.

For detailed legal and practical advice on hiring in-home child care, see *Nannies & Au Pairs*, by Ilona Bray (Nolo). See www.nolo.com for a sample chapter and full table of contents.

Keeping Children Safe

Many local, state, and federal laws treat children differently from adults.

Alcohol, Drugs, and Tobacco

Many states have special rules designed to protect children from drinking and drugs.

Alcohol. In every state, the legal drinking age is 21. There are related rules and penalties regarding possession of alcohol, driving under the influence, and carrying or using a fake ID. Parents may be found liable if they serve alcohol to minors and damage ensues—including injuries or damage from a car accident caused by an underage child who was allowed to drink in their home. See "Parental Responsibility for a Child's Misbehavior," below.

Tobacco. State laws prohibit a minor from buying cigarettes or other tobacco products, and require stores to check ID before selling them.

Drugs. Punishments for the possession, use, or sale (or intent to sell) of illicit drugs, such as marijuana, heroin, cocaine, and amphetamines, depend on the substance (marijuana penalties are less severe) and the age of the person. Where the violation occurred also matters; selling or possessing marijuana on school grounds carries more severe penalties.

RESOURCE

More about state alcohol, tobacco, and drug laws. See Appendix B for relevant government agencies and resources for federal and state rules.

Bikes, Scooters, and Skateboards

Local governments often set rules limiting the places where kids can bike, skateboard, or ride a scooter. Many states require all kids under 18 to wear helmets while bicycling.

Kids in Cars

All states require special child car seats, though the exact rules about their use vary. For instance, some states require car seats for children until they're eight years old, but others end the requirement when kids reach six years old or weigh 60 pounds. In California, kids must ride in the back seat, even when they no longer are required to use a car seat. State laws also prohibit leaving young children alone in a car.

RESOURCE

Vehicle-related rules. Contact your state motor vehicle agency for information on laws that affect minors (see the Children section of Appendix B for advice on finding yours).

Tattoos and Piercing

Many states prohibit children under age 18 from getting their ears, lips, or other parts of their body pierced without parental consent. Some prohibit tattooing of children under age 18 whether or not the parents consent.

> **RESOURCE**
>
> **Tattoo and piercing rules.** See your state rules at the National Conference of State Legislatures' website, www.ncsl.org/Default.aspx?TabId=14393. Also, check your state department of health.

Online Dangers

The Internet offers children as well as adults many great activities, both educational and fun. But the online world also presents dangers to children, from inappropriate use of kids' personal information to exposure to pornography and sexual predators. Federal and state laws regulate Internet use involving children by controlling things such as what can be sent to a child. The Children's Online Privacy Protection Act (COPPA) limits information that websites can collect from kids under age 13, including information kids post about themselves or personal information such as their addresses or phone numbers. COPPA requires websites to post their privacy policies. Many states are also setting rules against "cyberbullying" (See "Bullying and Harassment," below.)

Ultimately, it is parents who need to supervise their children's computer use and set rules on smart and safe use of the Internet and websites like YouTube and Facebook. See the resources that follow to learn more.

> **RESOURCE**
>
> **How to protect your kids online.** For detailed advice on Internet safety for children, see www.protectkids.com, a sister site of the national nonprofit Enough Is Enough (www.enough.org). The protectkids.com site includes tips for both parents and children on safe use of the Internet, including use of monitoring and filtering software. The federal government's website www.onguardonline.gov provides lots of

articles on Internet safety. For information on federal privacy rules under the Children's Online Privacy Act, see www.ftc.gov/bcp/edu/pubs/consumer/tech/tec08.shtm. To report unsolicited obscene material sent to a child, contact the National Center for Missing and Exploited Children at www.cybertipline.com or call 800-843-5678.

> **TIP**
>
> **How to remove personal information from the Internet (including information your kids have posted online).** Make sure your kids know not to post any personal information (such as name, address, and phone number) online. The Privacy Rights Clearinghouse (www.privacyrights.org) has useful advice on the subject of controlling personal information online in the "Online Privacy and Technology" section (www.privacyrights.org/fs/fs1-surv.htm).

Bullying and Harassment

Bullying, both physical (hitting and punching) and verbal, is an increasing concern of children and families, and many states and local school districts have responded by passing strict antibullying rules and instituting educational programs. Many rules prohibit specific bullying behavior, including harassment based on sexual orientation. Increasingly, schools are required to notify parents when their child is involved in bullying (as either victim or instigator). Depending on the situation, penalties for bullying may include suspension or expulsion from school to charges of felony assault.

"Cyberbullying" is a relatively new form of torment. It occurs when a kid (or group of kids) bullies someone online, via cell phone, or by some other form of technology. Cyberbullying can include sending cruel or threatening emails and posting negative comments, photos, or videos online, whether via instant messaging or on a Facebook page or another social networking site. Although cyberbullying involves the Internet service provider (ISP) as the place where the messages are posted, it's difficult to get an ISP to block such activities. Under the Communications Decency Act, ISPs are immune from liability for such activity and, as a result, have little incentive to cooperate in removing it.

> **RESOURCE**
> **More about bullying and how to stop it.** An excellent website that provides advice for families, children, and schools on how to identify and prevent bullying is www.stopbullyingnow.hrsa.gov, a special program of the U.S. Health and Human Services Administration. The site also lists states with antibullying laws. For information on the "Stop Bullying Now" program, call 888-ASK-HRSA. Other useful sites with advice for parents and teachers on how to stop bullying are the Gay, Lesbian and Straight Education Network (www.glsen.org/bullying, phone 212-727-0135) and the Anti-Defamation League (www.adl.org/combatbullying).

Teen Driving

Many states have age-specific rules about driving—for example, when a teen can get a learner's (or instructor's) permit to drive, requirements for a set number of hours of professional driver education training, and mandatory supervised training with an adult. Once a minor gets a license, states may restrict the age and number of passengers who can be in a car with the new driver and the hours a novice driver can be on the road. In California, for example, in a minor's first year driving, the new driver may not drive with anyone under the age of 20 in the car and may not drive between 11 p.m. and 5 a.m. unless accompanied by a driver who is 25 years of age or older. Penalties for drunk driving also vary for young drivers. Rules vary from state to state, so check your state department of motor vehicles for details.

Unfit Parents

Parents who abuse, neglect, or abandon children can be considered unfit. Where the children have another fit parent, the offending parent may lose custody or visitation rights; in other cases the parent can lose parental rights, either permanently or temporarily.

When a parent completely abandons a child—providing no care or financial support—and there's no other adult to care for the child, the state's foster care system will take charge. (If there is a relative available, guardianship is usually a better option.) When a parent is abusive or neglectful or is abusing substances or otherwise failing to care for children appropriately, a relative can step in and care for the child under an informal or formal guardianship, or the child can be placed in foster care while the state attempts to help the parent deal with the issues and reunite with the child. If these efforts aren't successful, the child will usually be freed for adoption. In especially severe cases, parents may be charged with a crime. (For more on foster care and guardianship, see Chapter 5.)

Parents who physically abandon a very young child may be criminally prosecuted. But there are "safe haven" or "legal abandonment" laws in almost every state that designate certain places or people as drop-off locations where a parent can leave an infant without fear of prosecution. These are usually hospitals, fire stations, or with an emergency responder. These laws only apply to very young babies—in some states, the child must be less than 72 hours old, while other states extend the time period all the way to 90 days.

Leaving a Child Home Alone

When does a child have enough maturity and physical, mental, and emotional ability to stay at home alone safely? Many states advise against leaving children younger than 12, but age isn't the only factor. The time of day, length of time the child will be left alone, and the safety of the neighborhood are also major considerations. Depending on your state laws and child protective policies, leaving a young child unsupervised may be considered neglect. For more information, see the *Leaving Your Child Home Alone* factsheet of the Child Welfare Information Gateway at www.childwelfare.gov/pubs/factsheets/homealone.cfm.

Crimes Against Children

All states make child abuse (physical, sexual, or emotional) a crime and require physicians, teachers, and other professionals with knowledge of child development to report suspected abuse to the police or a child protective services agency. Penalties are severe for someone who abuses a child (or allows abuse by another) and can include lengthy prison terms.

Arguably less serious than child abuse, child endangerment is also a crime. Examples include leaving a child unattended in a car, inflicting physical punishment that results in bodily injury, manufacturing drugs in the presence of a child, or leaving a young child unsupervised in an unsafe area.

RESOURCE

Find your child protective services agency. For immediate help, contact your local police. You can also find the websites and phone numbers of your state's agencies designated to investigate suspected child abuse and neglect at the Child Welfare Information Gateway, www.childwelfare.gov, a service of Children's Bureau, Administration for Children and Families, U.S. Department of Health and Human Services (phone 800-394-3366). You can also contact the Childhelp National Child Abuse Hotline at 800-4-A-CHILD (or see their website at www.childhelp.org). This hotline offers crisis intervention and referrals to emergency, social service, and support resources. All calls are anonymous and confidential.

Many federal laws protect children from sexual crimes, particularly as concerns child pornography and sexual exploitation. See www.fbi.gov for details.

Age of Consent to Have Sex

Men having sex with girls younger than a specified age has for centuries been known as "statutory rape." The age of consent when the first statutory rape laws were written in 1275 was 12, and that remained largely unchanged until the late nineteenth century, when feminists sought to raise the age of consent in order to end the widespread abuse of working class girls. Then, in the 1970s, a second wave of feminists argued successfully for gender-neutral laws that would also punish older females who had sex with younger males, and the laws now apply in both directions. (However, the need to protect young women from sexual coercion and exploitation was never repudiated.)

Today, there is no nationwide age at which girls are deemed capable of giving consent. Instead, most states vary the age of consent depending on the age differences between the partners, the age of the "victim," or the age of the defendant. For example, one state might make 16 the age of consent, but require an age differential of four years or more before the activity is illegal. Sexual relations between a 17-year-old and a 15-year-old would be legal in such a state, but not relations between the same 15-year-old and someone who's 21. In other states, the age of consent itself may change depending on the age of the perpetrator: In such a state, the normal age of consent (16) will drop to 13 if the perpetrator is no more than four years older and younger than 19. Yet other states specify a minimum age of the perpetrator, making it illegal to have relations with someone below the age of consent only if the perpetrator is over 18 years old.

Most statutory rape laws do not allow perpetrators to argue that they reasonably thought that the victim was over the age of consent.

Medical Care

Until a child is legally an adult, parents have the right to make decisions about their child's medical care and treatment. There are a few important exceptions to this rule, however, designed to protect teenagers who can't rely on parental support. For example, depending upon the state and the age of the child, a minor may be able to make decisions without parental consent when it comes to seeking prenatal care (in the case of a pregnant teen, for example), treatment related to a sexually transmitted infection, drug problem, or rape, or access to birth control. A few states allow minors to consent to abortion services without parental consent, although many states require some kind of parental involvement in a minor's decision to have an abortion, such as the prior notification to or consent of at least one parent. Many states allow minors to place children for adoption.

RESOURCE

State minors' consent laws. An excellent resource for state laws on minors' access to contraceptive services and other health care without parental consent is the Guttmacher Institute (www.guttmacher.org, phone 800-355-0244). This respected national nonprofit organization publishes a series of state fact sheets on issues and laws affecting sexual and reproductive rights, including abortion laws. It also provides monthly updates on state legislation.

Health Insurance

Health insurance is key to any family's financial security. Without it, a family can be bankrupted by medical bills as a result of a serious accident or illness. Many employers offer their employees some type of group insurance plan, and the federal health care reform law of 2010 (the Affordable Care Act) began phasing in some coverage in 2010.

A good place to learn more about health insurance (private and public) is www.healthcare.gov, a website of the U.S. Department of Health & Human Services. Your state department of health or insurance may also have details on health insurance options.

School

Children between the ages of about six to 16 (depending on the state) must attend school. Parents can pick the school, though: Public school, private school, and home schooling can all satisfy the legal requirement of school attendance.

States generally make rules on curriculum, special education, testing requirements, and discrimination and harassment. There are fewer federal laws about education, but some important ones, such as the No Child Left Behind Act, significantly affect how much federal money a school district receives. There are also important federal laws governing special education. (See "Educating Children With Special Needs," below.)

In most states, local school boards are responsible for day-to-day management of, as well as compliance with federal and state rules for, public schools. They supervise schools within their districts, make annual operating budgets, and hire and fire staff.

School Authority to Regulate and Discipline

Public school boards often set local rules on topics such as district transfers, dress codes, drug and alcohol testing at school dances, locker searches, and grounds for student suspension or expulsion. Schools are increasingly coming down hard on kids who bully or harass other students (see "Bullying and Harassment," above).

Over time, students and parents have challenged many rules and procedures employed by state schools. Whether a particular policy or rule is legal varies from state to state and depends heavily on the facts of each situation. For example, the U.S. Supreme Court held in 1985 that schools are subject to the Fourth Amendment and that students have a legitimate expectation of privacy. But the school has an equally legitimate need to maintain an environment in which learning can take place. For this reason, school officials need not obtain a warrant before conducting a search (of a locker, for example), nor need they have "probable cause" before searching. Instead, the search must be reasonable, under all of the circumstances.

Not all states follow the federal rule, however. Individual states may give students heightened privacy rights in this and other areas. For example, federal law permits random drug testing for student athletes, but in the state of Washington, such a policy is against the state's guarantee of protection from unreasonable searches and seizures.

Whether a particular rule or policy will pass federal and state constitutional muster is often a very tricky question. Parents and students who are concerned about the intrusiveness of a particular procedure will almost always need the help of an experienced First Amendment or criminal defense attorney.

RESOURCE

Information on school choices and rules. To find rules for your child's school, contact your local school board. You'll find a wealth of information at your state department of education website, such as requirements regarding compulsory attendance and home schooling. If you want to check out federal laws affecting schools, such as the No Child Left Behind Act, which sets testing requirements and accountability standards, see the U.S. Department of Education website at www. ed.gov. This federal government site is also a good place to find state profiles and statistics on schools in your state. Finally, the National School Boards Association (www.nsba.org) has extensive information in its "School Law" section on the latest topics, such as school safety and student rights.

Educating Children With Special Needs

Children with disabilities and their parents have important legal rights when it comes to education. The federal Individuals with Disabilities Education Act (IDEA) gives families of special education children the right to:

- have their child assessed or tested to determine special education eligibility and needs for specific programs and services
- inspect and review school records relating to their child
- attend an annual "individualized education program" (IEP) meeting and develop a written IEP plan for the child with representatives of the local school district, and
- resolve disputes with the school district through an impartial administrative and legal process.

IDEA defines children with disabilities as individuals between the ages of three and 22 with one or more of the following conditions:

- mental retardation
- deafness or another hearing impairment
- speech or language impairment
- blindness or another visual impairment
- serious emotional disturbance
- orthopedic impairment
- autism
- traumatic brain injury
- specific learning disability, or
- another health impairment.

For a child to qualify for special education under IDEA, it is not enough to have one of these disabilities. There must also be evidence that the disability adversely affects the child's educational performance.

Once a child is found eligible for special education, subsequent evaluations take place at least every three years. If parents are not satisfied with the initial evaluation or feel the child's disability or special education needs have changed, they are entitled to more frequent assessments, and even outside or independent assessments.

RESOURCE

More information on IEPs and special education law. The Special Education & IEPs section of www.nolo.com contains useful articles. Nolo also publishes two books on the subject, both by Lawrence Siegel: *The Complete IEP Guide: How to Advocate for Your Special Ed Child*, and *Nolo's IEP Guide: Learning Disabilities*. See www.nolo.com for each book's table of contents and sample chapter. Both books include state-by-state resources on special education. For detailed information on state and federal special education law and programs, see www.wrightslaw.com. For resources focused on learning disabilities and ADHD, see LD Online at www.ldonline.com.

Children at Work

Federal and state laws seek to protect younger workers by restricting the type of work they can do and the number of hours they can work in a day. The Fair Labor Standards Act, which governs child labor, affects nearly all employers and businesses (with a few exceptions, including small farms). Some state laws are even stricter.

Types of Work

Under federal law, anyone 18 or older may work at any job, hazardous or not. Younger folks, however, face special restrictions:

- **Teenagers who are at least 17 years old** may get jobs that involve driving on public roads, if they have valid driver's licenses and no moving violations.
- **16- and 17-year-old teens** may perform any nonhazardous job. Jobs that are considered hazardous involve mining, wrecking and demolition, logging, and roofing.
- **14- and 15-year-old teens** may work in various nonmanufacturing, non-mining, and nonhazardous jobs, with some restrictions. They may not do construction or work as ride operators at amusement parks or in certain cooking or baking jobs. Fourteen-year olds may not lifeguard at a lake or beach, but a 15-year old may if properly certified as a lifeguard at a traditional swimming pool or water amusement park.

Days and Hours of Work

Younger teens, ages 14 and 15, cannot work more than three hours on a school day, 18 hours in a school week, eight hours on a nonschool day, or 40 hours in a nonschool week. Also, the work cannot begin before 7 a.m. or end after 7 p.m., except from June 1 through Labor Day, when evening hours are extended to 9 p.m.

Exceptions

Some industries have special exemptions from child labor restrictions. For example, youths of any age may deliver newspapers or perform in movies or plays.

Also, people who own or operate a farm or another type of agricultural business may hire their own children, of any age, to do any kind of work on the farm.

Other farm owners or agricultural businesses may hire a worker who is:
- 16 years or older for any work, whether hazardous or not
- 14 or 15 years old for any nonhazardous work outside of school hours
- 12 or 13 years old for any nonhazardous work outside of school hours if the child's parents work on the same farm or if the parents have given their written consent, and
- 10 or 11 years old if the farm has been granted a waiver by the U.S. Department of Labor to employ the youngster as a hand harvest laborer for no more than eight weeks in any calendar year.

Work Permits for Teens

Most states require teens (the age varies by state) to get a work permit. Applications for work permits, also known as employment certificates, are typically available from a school guidance counselor.

RESOURCE

Federal and state child labor rules. The U.S. Department of Labor website, www.dol.gov (see the "Youth and Labor" section) provides information on federal labor laws affecting minors (or you can call 866-4-USA-DOL). State laws may be more protective. To find yours, contact your state department of labor.

Teens and Taxes

Many teen workers will have some taxes withheld from their paychecks, even if the employment lasts for only a few months. Teens, like other employees, must complete all relevant IRS forms, including a W-4 form (*Employee's Withholding Allowance Certificate*) for every job held. Tax forms are available on the Internal Revenue Service website, www.irs.gov.

Encourage your teen to file a tax return; that way you'll ensure that they don't pay taxes unnecessarily. Most teen workers will get some, if not all, their withheld taxes refunded by filing a return.

Many teen jobs—waiting tables, for example—involve tips. Tips are taxable and need to be reported as income, so encourage your teen to keep a log of all tips received, including any share of tips that are split with other workers. Keeping a record will ensure that your teen doesn't get taxed on the basis of the employer's estimate of tips, which will usually be higher than what your child actually received.

To learn more about filing taxes, see articles in the Taxes section of www.nolo.com. For tax forms and instructions see www.irs.gov.

Juvenile Crime

When a juvenile is suspected of committing a crime, the procedure that's followed is very different from that used for adults. All states have special juvenile court systems for minors who get into trouble with the law. And although some minors are ultimately judged to be delinquent by these juvenile courts, the players in a typical juvenile case—including police officers, prosecutors, and judges—have broad discretion to fashion other outcomes.

Although the procedure for juvenile delinquency cases varies from state to state, here is a rundown of a typical juvenile case.

Laws Aimed at Kids

Many local ordinances, even if they are not age specific, have a special impact on children. Examples include restrictions on using cell phones or texting while driving, setting off fireworks, painting graffiti on someone else's property or committing other acts of vandalism, blasting loud music while driving, and acting rowdy at a sporting event. Many communities set curfews for minors, limiting when they may be out late at night without a valid reason. Penalties for violating local ordinances may range from fines to community service, or even jail time in some cases. To check local rules and ordinances, search the name of your county, city, or town, or check out www.statelocalgov.net which links to the websites of many cities and counties. Or you can call your city manager's or mayor's office for this information.

Eligibility for Juvenile Court

Most cases involving young people up to 18 years of age (usually called minors or juveniles in this context) are adjudicated in juvenile court. In certain serious cases, such as murder, juveniles can be tried in adult criminal court, especially if they have a lengthy juvenile court record.

Crimes Committed by Young Children and Preteens

Our legal system is based on the idea that people should be punished only when they have acted with an intent or purpose that makes them morally blameworthy. Based on this principle (known as "mens rea" or guilty state of mind), most states consider children under the age of seven to be legally incapable of forming the guilty state of mind necessary to be morally blameworthy and, therefore, subject to criminal punishment. As a result, children under age seven are almost never charged with crimes. But if a very young child does cause injury or damage, the parents are on the hook to compensate the victim. In some cases, a court might even conclude that the parents' neglect led to the child's bad behavior and place the child with relatives or foster parents.

Children between the ages of seven and 14 occupy a middle ground. They are often presumed to be incapable of forming the guilty mind necessary to be morally to blame and therefore subject to criminal punishment. But if a prosecutor is able to show otherwise, the child can be criminally punished.

Once minors reach age 14, most states regard them as fully capable of forming a guilty mind, and they are usually held accountable for the crimes they commit, either in juvenile or adult court.

How Police Deal With Juveniles

Police arrest some minors for theft, simple assault, disorderly conduct, drug possession, or other common crimes. Other kids are referred to the police by parents or school officials. Regardless of how the police get wind of a potential juvenile case, they have several options for handling the situation.

Issue a warning. A police officer can detain a minor, issue a warning against further violations, and then let the minor go (perhaps meeting with parents later). This is often referred to as the "counseled and released" alternative.

Hold the minor until a parent comes. Sometimes a police officer detains a minor, issues a warning, and then releases the minor to the custody of a parent or guardian.

Refer to juvenile court. In instances of serious or repeat offenses or misbehavior, an officer may place the juvenile in custody and refer the case to juvenile court.

Hiring a Lawyer for Your Child

If your child is arrested, you may have little or no time to research the law. See Chapter 9 for advice on finding legal help for your child. Minors who can't afford a lawyer are entitled to have one provided by the state.

Types of Cases Heard in Juvenile Court

Two types of cases are heard in juvenile court:
- cases involving "status offenses" or violations that apply only to minors. Examples include truancy (skipping school), violating a city curfew, running away from home, and underage drinking.
- juvenile delinquency cases involving minors who are alleged to have committed crimes and would, if they were 18 or older, be in regular criminal court.

Juvenile courts also hear cases involving children who are abused or neglected. See "Unfit Parents," above, for more on the subject.

When Cases Go to Juvenile Court

States have a juvenile court system because they recognize that many kids who run afoul of the law can be helped by being gently steered in the right direction, rather than punished. Minors who commit crimes often receive counseling and get to stay at home instead of going to jail.

Once a police officer refers a case to juvenile court, a prosecutor or juvenile court intake officer (often a probation officer) takes over. That person may decide to dismiss the case, handle the matter informally, or file formal charges.

In deciding how to proceed, the prosecutor or intake officer typically considers:

- the severity of the offense (serious offenses, such as robbery, rape or murder, may be transferred to adult criminal court)
- the strength of the evidence in the case
- the juvenile's age and any prior contact with the juvenile court system
- the juvenile's history of problems of home and at school, and
- the ability of the juvenile's parents to control his or her behavior.

Parental Responsibility for a Child's Misbehavior

Parental liability is the term used to refer to parents' obligation to pay for damage done by negligent, intentional, or criminal acts of their children. Most states hold parents responsible for all malicious or willful property damage done by their children (such as graffiti) and may set dollar caps on their liability. Many state laws also make parents responsible for all malicious or willful personal injuries inflicted by their children.

Parental liability usually ends when the child reaches the age of majority (usually 18).

Informal Proceedings

If the prosecutor or probation officer decides to proceed informally, usually the minor must appear before a probation officer or judge. No formal charge is entered against the juvenile, but the judge or court officer will usually require that the juvenile:

- listen to a stern lecture
- attend counseling
- attend after-school classes
- compensate the victim for losses
- pay a fine
- perform community service work, or

- enter probation, a program of supervision that allows minors to remain free if they fulfill specified conditions, such as regular counseling or community service. (A minor who violates a condition of probation may be incarcerated.)

A judge who suspects a juvenile is being abused or neglected may initiate an investigation, which may lead to proceedings to remove the minor from the home.

Formal Proceedings

A prosecutor or probation officer who decides to proceed formally will file a petition in juvenile court. The minor is then formally charged (arraigned) in front of a juvenile court judge or referee. In some serious cases, the court may decide to send the juvenile to adult criminal court.

The court will also determine whether the minor should be detained or released until the initial hearing. In most juvenile court cases, the judge allows the minor to go home while awaiting the hearing.

If the case remains in juvenile court, one of three things may happen:

The minor enters into a plea agreement. Often, a plea agreement hinges on the juvenile's compliance with certain conditions. For example, as part of a plea deal, a juvenile may need to attend counseling, obey curfews, or reimburse the victim for losses.

The minor is sent for counseling or community service. When a judge directs a minor to complete a program (such as counseling) or perform some act (such as community service or payment of restitution), the judge keeps authority over the case. If the juvenile doesn't fulfill the obligations, the court may reinstate formal charges. (These are often called diversion programs.)

The judge holds a hearing. A juvenile trial (called an "adjudicatory hearing") is much like the criminal trial of an adult. Both sides present evidence, and attorneys argue the case. In most states, the hearing is held before a judge, not a jury. At the conclusion of the hearing, the judge will determine whether or not the juvenile is delinquent.

If the court makes a delinquency ruling, a probation officer will evaluate the juvenile, order psychological examination or diagnostic tests if necessary, and then make recommendations at the disposition hearing, which is similar to a sentencing hearing in adult criminal court. The judge then decides what is in the best interest of the juvenile and may order any number of things, including:

- counseling
- placement with someone other than the parents, such as a relative or foster care
- confinement in a juvenile detention facility
- reimbursement of the victim, and/or
- probation.

The judge may also order the juvenile to appear in court periodically (called postdisposition hearings) so that the judge can monitor the juvenile's behavior and progress.

Sealing Juvenile Court Records

Most states let people seal (expunge) records of certain juvenile offenses. Essentially, this wipes them off the books, and it is as if the juvenile court proceedings never took place.

Some states automatically seal certain types of juvenile records after the offender reaches a certain age. But in most places, records are not sealed unless the offender pays a fee and files an official request (petition) with the juvenile court clerk in the county where the offense occurred.

Which juvenile records may be sealed? It varies from state to state. Usually, whether or not a record can be sealed depends on several factors.

Age. The person seeking the sealing must be an adult. In most states, this means the person making the request must be at least 18 years old.

When the offense was committed. Often, a juvenile record cannot be sealed until five years have passed from the date of the offense or from the end of the juvenile court proceedings.

Type of offense. Some states limit the types of offenses that can be expunged from a juvenile record. Many states don't allow people to expunge serious juvenile offenses—such as a violation that would be a felony in adult criminal court.

Subsequent arrests or convictions. In many states, if the person asking for expungement of a juvenile record has later criminal arrests or convictions as an adult, the request to seal the juvenile record will be denied.

If the court approves the petition and seals the juvenile records, the court then treats the juvenile court proceedings as if they never occurred. In most states, this means that if someone is asked whether they have a juvenile offense history, they can legally say "No." Likewise, if an employer, educational institution, government agency, or another entity does a background check, the juvenile court history will not come up. So having a juvenile record sealed can have tremendous advantages to someone applying for a job or professional license or in any other situation that might involve inquiries about criminal history.

Sealing is not absolute, however. In certain circumstances, an expunged juvenile record may be accessible. For example, if someone applies for a job with a law enforcement agency, chances are the juvenile record will be visible to that agency when it runs a background check. If a juvenile record contains a vehicle-related violation, an insurance company may be able to access a record of that offense when someone applies for car insurance. Finally, juvenile offenses that are expunged from a record may still be used to increase the severity of a sentence that's handed down after a later juvenile offense or criminal court conviction. And it must be said, in this age of computers and online databases, that often even a properly sealed record remains accessible to anyone with enough ingenuity to look long and hard through the ether.

RESOURCE

More information about juvenile court.

See Appendix B for resources for your state's juvenile justice system, including the Office of Juvenile Justice and Delinquency Prevention in the U.S. Department of Justice (www.ojjdp.gov) and the National Center for Juvenile Justice (www.ncjj.org).

See *The Criminal Law Handbook*, by Paul Bergman and Sara Berman (Nolo), for more about the rights of minors in juvenile proceedings and how to help if your child gets in trouble with the law. See www.nolo.com for a sample chapter and full table of contents.

When Does a Child Become an Adult?

All the special rules that restrict and protect children cease to apply when a child reaches adulthood, or what's called the age of majority. In certain circumstances, a child may be legally emancipated before reaching the age of majority.

The Age of Majority

In most states, the age of majority is 18. At 18, you can vote, make a will, enter into binding contracts (such as to buy a house), enlist in the armed forces, and make your own decisions (without parental consent) regarding finances, medical care, and employment. A few adult rights and responsibilities, however, come later than the age of majority—notably drinking alcohol, which no state allows for anyone under age 21.

Emancipation of Minors

A minor who is "emancipated" assumes most adult responsibilities, free from parental control or support, before reaching the age of majority. Eligibility depends on state law, but usually minors can be emancipated by:

- getting married (as long as they comply with state marriage requirements, covered in Chapter 1)
- joining the military (because military policies require enlistees to have a high school diploma or GED, most young people are at least 17 or 18 before they become emancipated through enlistment), or
- getting a court order (see "Emancipation by Court Permission," below).

A few states and territories (for example, Louisiana and Puerto Rico) allow a fourth form of limited emancipation that requires only parental consent, not the court's permission.

Parents may not unilaterally declare their child emancipated, and a child cannot decide, alone, to become emancipated—for example, by running away from home. Instead, parents must support their children until the children reach adulthood—and longer if a child is disabled.

Emancipated minors are not under the care and control of parents and may function as adults in society. An emancipated minor can keep earnings from a job, sign contracts like leases, sue or be sued in court, decide where to live or attend school, make his or her own medical decisions, and more.

Most states place some limits on what an emancipated minor can do. For example, many states don't allow emancipated minors to:

- get married without parental consent
- quit school before age 16 (or whatever age the state allows)
- buy or drink alcohol, or
- vote or get a driver's license before the legal age at which other minors are allowed to.

Emancipation by Court Permission

Some (but not all) states allow a minor to be emancipated by court order. Usually, the minor must be at least 16 years old—although in California, minors as young as 14 may petition the court for emancipation. The court will grant emancipation if it believes that it's in the young person's best interest. That determination is typically based on factors such as whether the minor is:

- financially self-sufficient (usually through employment, as opposed to government aid or welfare)
- currently living apart from parents or guardians or has made alternative living arrangements
- sufficiently mature to make decisions and to function as an adult, and
- going to school or has received a high school diploma.

Minors who are seeking emancipation through a court order must follow the procedures that are set out by their state's law. Though the process varies from state to state, here's what the court procedure typically looks like:

- **Petition.** The emancipation petition must be filed by the minor (or by an attorney on the minor's behalf). Usually, the petition includes an explanation of why the minor is seeking emancipation, information about the minor's current living situation, and evidence that the minor is or soon will be financially self-sufficient.

- **Notification of parents.** In most states, minors must notify their parents or legal guardians that a petition for emancipation has been filed—or explain to the court why they do not want to do so.
- **Hearing.** In most cases, the court schedules a hearing, at which the judge asks questions and hears evidence to decide whether emancipation is in the minor's best interest.
- **Declaration of emancipation.** If the court decides that emancipation should be ordered, it will issue a Declaration of Emancipation, which the newly emancipated minor must give to schools, doctors, landlords, and provide in any other situation that would normally require parental consent.

Alternatives to Emancipation

There are many reasons why a young person might seek emancipation. A minor who is very wealthy (a child actor, for example) might seek emancipation for financial and tax reasons. Some young people who are physically or emotionally abused want to get away from a bad home environment. Others just cannot get along with their parents or guardians. Emancipation is just one option in these situations. Other avenues to explore include:

- getting help from government or private agencies, such as child protective services
- getting family counseling or arranging mediation for everyone involved
- living with another responsible adult, or
- living away from home with the informal consent of parents.

Elder Care

Americans are living longer and healthier lives than at any time in history. Many older people just need help with daily activities in their own homes, but some require ongoing, long-term care. Whether you are thinking about your own future or seeking care for a relative who needs help (now or down the road), you have many options to consider.

The time may also come when you or loved ones will need to make financial and health care decisions for an older relative. It's a good idea to have documents giving you the legal authority you need to do so: an advance health care directive or power of attorney for finances. If your relative is no longer capable of making decisions or executing a power of attorney, you may need to go to court to request a conservatorship, which allows another person to make legal decisions under the supervision of the a local court that appoints the conservator.

STATE RULES AND RESOURCES
The Elder Care section of Appendix B provides contact information for government and nonprofit programs that serve the elderly in areas such as health insurance and long-term care for each state.

Getting the Right Documents in Place

Everyone who qualifies for a senior citizen discount at the local restaurant needs to get a few key legal documents signed. It's not a difficult process, and it will bring peace of mind to everyone in the family. The big ones are:

- a will (discussed in Chapter 8)
- an advance medical directive
- a durable power of attorney for health care, and
- a durable power of attorney for finances.

Wills let you leave your property as you wish and choose someone, called an executor, to wrap things up when the time comes. But powers of attorney, though often overlooked, can actually be much more important. If necessary, they can take effect during your lifetime, giving authority over your medical and financial matters to a trusted person. Having such powers in place, just in case illness or accident means you are unable to make your own decisions, can save your family anguish and money and help stave off destructive family disputes.

Health Care Power of Attorney and Advance Directive

To make sure your wishes for your medical treatment will be honored, even if you're unable to communicate them, you need two documents:

- a **durable power of attorney for health care**, which names a trusted person to make health care decisions for you if you can't or don't wish to, and
- an **advance medical directive**, also known as a living will or declaration, which lets you spell out your wishes for end-of-life care.

In some states, these documents are combined in a single form, commonly called an advance health care directive. But even when they're separate, they work together. In your medical directive, you state (in as much or as little detail as you wish) what kind of medical care you want to receive. The power of attorney grants someone legal authority to carry out those wishes.

Depending on the state, the person to whom you give this authority may be called an agent, attorney-in-fact, health care proxy, health care surrogate, or something similar. The power of attorney is called "durable" because, unlike a standard power of attorney, it isn't invalidated if you become incapacitated. You can also make your durable power of attorney take effect only if you are incapacitated. (This is called a "springing" durable power of attorney.)

The health care agent confers with doctors and other health care providers to make sure you get the kind of care you wish to receive (or not receive, such as life support). When arranging care, the agent is legally bound to follow the document maker's treatment preferences to the extent that they're expressed in the document or have been expressed to the agent previously.

RESOURCE

Health care directives for your state. Contact a local hospital or your state's medical association for a form that's valid in your state. The U.S. Living Will Registry website, www.uslivingwillregistry.com, has free health care directive forms for every state. You can also create a health care directive that's valid in your state (for all states except Louisiana) with *Quicken WillMaker Plus* software from Nolo.

Financial Powers of Attorney

A durable power of attorney for finances lets you give someone else authority to handle your financial matters. The person you appoint is usually called your agent or attorney-in-fact (but most definitely doesn't have to be an attorney).

The agent can handle mundane tasks such as sorting through mail and depositing checks, as well as more complex jobs like watching over retirement accounts and other investments and even filing tax returns. The agent doesn't have to be a financial expert, just someone who is trustworthy and has a good dose of common sense. If necessary, the agent can hire professionals to help with complicated tasks.

A financial power of attorney can be drafted so that it goes into effect as soon as it's signed. For example, many spouses have active financial powers of attorney for each other in case something happens to one of them—or in case one of them is out of town when something must be done or a paper signed. Or the document can state that it takes effect only if you become incapacitated. Usually, incapacity is certified by a doctor's written statement.

A durable power of attorney is usually a fill-in-the-blanks form that's a few pages long. It should specify that the power of attorney is "durable." If it's not, the power of attorney will automatically end if you ever become incapacitated—which is exactly when you would need the document.

Where do you get the right form? Some states have their own forms, but it's not mandatory that you use them. Some banks and brokerage companies have their own durable power of attorney forms. It's fine to create different powers of attorney to cover different assets, so go ahead and use the bank's form if you want your agent to have access to your accounts there. An agent who presents a familiar form will have an easier time dealing with the staff.

You must sign the durable power of attorney in front of a notary public. In some states, witnesses must also watch you sign. If the agent will have authority to deal with real estate, record (file) a copy of the document at the local land records office, usually called the county recorder or register of deeds.

An agent's authority automatically ends at the death of the person who made the power of attorney. That means that you can't give an agent authority to handle matters after death, such as paying debts, making funeral or burial arrangements, or transferring property to the people who inherit it. Those jobs fall to the executor named in your will. So if you want your agent to have authority to wind up your affairs after death, use your will.

Helping Older Relatives With Their Finances

Many people worry about the ability of aging parents to handle money and financial affairs because of a mental, visual, or physical impairment. Or perhaps the spouse who handled all the finances has passed away, leaving the survivor feeling overwhelmed by financial record keeping and decision making.

An elderly relative may not need you to take over all financial matters, but might appreciate some help with money management—making sure bills get paid on time, keeping an eye on spending for things like contests and purchases from television shopping networks, and warning of telemarketing scams or investment frauds. The "Elder Care & Seniors" section at www.nolo.com includes useful articles on helping elders with finances, including applying for benefits such as Medicaid and avoiding elder financial abuse.

RESOURCE

Financial power of attorney forms and more information. You can use *Quicken WillMaker Plus* (software published by Nolo) to create a durable financial power of attorney, along with a will and other important documents. To see everything Nolo has to offer when it comes to creating a financial power of attorney and planning your estate, visit the Wills, Trusts & Estates section of at www.nolo.com.

Conservatorships and Guardianships

If a family member is already incapacitated and didn't sign durable powers of attorney for finances and health care in advance, you may need to ask a court for authority over your loved one's finances and personal affairs.

Generally, conservatorships are established for people who are in comas, suffer from severe dementia, or have other serious illnesses or injuries.

A conservatorship is what a durable power of attorney for finances is designed to avoid. Court proceedings to establish conservatorships are expensive, time-consuming, and public—not what a family wants when dealing with a crisis involving a family member.

The person appointed by a court, called a conservator or guardian, has a legal duty to act in the incapacitated person's best interests. A court usually names a spouse or another close family member to this position, taking into account evidence of what the incapacitated person would have wanted and other information about what's in the person's best interest.

Conservators are subject to court supervision, which is designed to safeguard the incapacitated adult's property and welfare. To prevent conservators from mismanaging property or otherwise taking advantage of the people they are supposed to be helping (sometimes called the conservatee), most courts require conservators to provide periodic reports detailing their actions. Many courts also require the conservator to seek permission before making major decisions, such as selling real estate or terminating life support (if the conservator is in charge of health care decisions).

Conservators aren't required to use their own money to support an incapacitated person. Instead, it's their job to manage the incapacitated person's own assets and make personal decisions as needed. A conservator does, however, have the responsibility to seek all financial benefits that might be available. These benefits may include Social Security, health insurance, Veterans Administration benefits, pension and retirement benefits, disability benefits, health insurance coverage, public assistance, and Supplemental Security Income.

A conservator must act until the court issues an order ending the conservatorship. This ordinarily happens when:

- the incapacitated person dies
- the incapacitated person no longer needs this level of assistance, or
- the conservator resigns or can no longer handle the responsibilities. In this situation, someone else takes over the conservator's duties.

Medicare and Medicaid

Medicare and Medicaid have similar names, and both can help with medical expenses, but they are two very different programs:

- **Medicaid** is for low-income, financially needy people.
- **Medicare** is not tied to individual need; instead, eligibility is based primarily on age and work history.

Although you may qualify for and receive coverage from both Medicare and Medicaid, there are separate eligibility requirements for each program. Being eligible for one program does not mean you are eligible for the other.

RESOURCE

More on Medicare and Medicaid.

- **Nolo's Medicare & Medicaid section**, www.nolo.com/legal-encyclopedia/ medicare, provides easy-to-understand information about choosing a Medicare managed care plan, using Medigap to fill in gaps in your Medicare coverage, how Medicare Parts A and B work, and whether and when to enroll in Medicare Part D, Prescription Drug Coverage.
- *Social Security, Medicare & Government Pensions: Get the Most Out of Your Retirement & Medical Benefits,* by Joseph L. Matthews and Dorothy Matthews Berman (Nolo), provides extensive advice on Medicaid, medigap insurance, Medicare, and Medicare managed care plans. See www.nolo.com for a sample chapter and full table of contents.
- **The official U.S. government Medicare site**, www.medicare.gov, provides forms to apply for Medicare and help choosing a policy to supplement Medicare coverage, finding doctors, and much more.
- **The Social Security Administration's website**, www.ssa.gov/pgm/links_ medicare.htm, contains a wealth of information about Medicare benefits, applying for benefits, and information about Medicare prescription drug plan costs.
- **The Centers for Medicare & Medicaid Services' website**, www.cms.gov, has lots of research and data about how these programs are administered and who receives benefits.

Medicare

This federal program was created to deal with the high medical costs that older people face—especially troublesome given the reduced earning power of retired people. But your actual need is irrelevant when it comes to eligibility. You are entitled to Medicare not because you can't pay for medical services but because you or your spouse paid for it through your taxes.

Generally, if you are 65 or older and paid Medicare taxes for at least ten years, you will qualify for Medicare Part A, which helps cover the costs of care in a hospital or skilled nursing facility. If you didn't pay Medicare taxes for that long, you can buy Part A coverage. You may apply for coverage by calling the Social Security Administration or going to your local office.

Medicare doesn't pay for everything, and so the majority of Medicare recipients aged 65 or over buy what's called "medigap" insurance. That's insurance that's designed to pay health care bills not covered by Medicare, such as deductibles.

CAUTION

Read the fine print. Before buying a medigap insurance policy, consider not only the services covered (long-term custodial care is not), but the amount of benefits, the monthly cost of the policy, how much premiums may rise, and renewal policies. The Medicare website (www.medicare.gov) has useful articles on choosing medigap insurance.

Medicaid

Medicaid is set up by the federal government and administered differently in each state. This program goes by different names in some states; for example, it's called MassHealth in Massachusetts and Medi-Cal in California.

If you qualify for both Medicare and Medicaid, Medicaid will pay for most Medicare Part A and B premiums, deductibles, and copayments.

Comparing Medicare and Medicaid		
	Medicare	**Medicaid**
Who is eligible	Medicare covers almost everyone 65 or older, certain people on Social Security disability, and some people with permanent kidney failure.	Medicaid covers low-income and financially needy people, including those over 65 who are also on Medicare.
Who administers the program	Medicare is a federal program whose rules are the same all over the country. Medicare information is available at your Social Security office.	Medicaid is administered by each state; rules differ in each state. Get information at your county social services, welfare, or department of human services office.
What it covers	Medicare hospital insurance (Part A) provides basic coverage for hospital stays and posthospital nursing facility and home health care. Medicare medical insurance (Part B) pays most basic doctor and laboratory costs and some outpatient medical services, including medical equipment and supplies, home health care, and physical therapy. Medicare prescription drug coverage (Part D) pays some of the costs of prescription medications.	Medicaid provides comprehensive inpatient and outpatient health care coverage, including many services and costs. Medicaid does not cover prescription drugs, diagnostic care, or eyeglasses. The amount of coverage, however, varies from state to state. Medicaid can pay Medicare deductibles and the 20% portion of charges not paid by Medicare. Medicaid can also pay the Medicare premium.
How much you pay	You pay a yearly deductible for both Medicare Part A and Part B, and make hefty copayments for extended hospital stays. Under Part B, you pay the 20% of doctors' bills Medicare does not pay, and sometimes up to 15% more. Part B also charges a monthly premium. Under Part D, you pay a monthly premium, a deductible, copayments, and all of your prescription drug costs over a certain yearly amount and up to a ceiling amount, unless you qualify for a low-income subsidy.	In some states, Medicaid charges consumers small amounts for certain services.

Long-Term Care Insurance

Long-term care (LTC) insurance, also known as nursing home insurance, is widely advertised as protection against the costs of long-term care, particularly residential nursing facilities. However, this kind of insurance is expensive, and it often provides only limited benefits—with many restrictions and conditions—that may end up covering only a small percentage, or nothing at all, of total long-term care costs.

Insurance companies market long-term care (LTC) insurance by suggesting that consumers are likely to wind up spending years in a nursing facility—a prospect that would wipe out their savings and perhaps leave them without a roof over their heads. However, the actual odds of a long nursing facility stay are considerably lower than the insurance industry would like you to imagine, and with the protection afforded by Medicaid laws, there is little risk of being thrown out of a nursing facility and into the street.

When you consider the true odds of a long nursing facility stay along with the high cost of LTC insurance and the other things you could do with that premium money, you may find that for you—as for the 95% of the population over age 65 who have not invested in it—LTC insurance is not a good bet.

If you are considering LTC insurance, be a very careful consumer. Comparison shop among several policies, checking each for exclusions and limitations. Don't base your decision solely on advice from an insurance agent or broker who is trying to sell you a policy. Check out state-certified (called "state-partnership") long-term care insurance policies which offer some of the best terms available.

RESOURCE

More on long-term care insurance. Check *Consumer Reports* magazine at www.consumerreports.org, for their latest analysis of LTC insurance policies, and the National Clearinghouse for Long-Term Care Information's website, www.longtermcare.gov, for useful advice, including average costs of LTC insurance in your area.

Finding At-Home or Long-Term Residential Care

Arranging long-term care for yourself or a senior relative can be extremely difficult. Here's an overview of some of your options.

RESOURCE

More on choosing at-home and long-term care.

- **Nolo's Long-Term Care & Assisted Living section,** www.nolo.com/legal-encyclopedia/long-term-care, explains how to find the right long-term care (in home, assisted living, or nursing home) at the right price, and includes articles on topics such as long-term care insurance.

- *Long-Term Care: How to Plan & Pay for It,* by Joseph Matthews (Nolo) explains the full range of options from in-home care to nursing homes with detailed advice on how to find the best care you can afford. See www.nolo.com for a sample chapter and full table of contents.

- **American Association of Homes for the Aging,** www.aahsa.org, provides information about member residential facilities.

- **Medicare,** www.medicare.gov/longtermcare/static/home.asp, offers a user-friendly checklist on choosing long-term care, as well as summaries of the types of long-term care that are available, comparisons of financing options, and advice on finding and evaluating the quality of nursing homes. The Resources page provides links to counseling and assistance resources for more long-term care information.

- **Administration on Aging,** www.aoa.gov (phone 202-619-0724), is a federal government clearinghouse for a broad array of information of interest to elders and their families. The Clearinghouse for Long-Term Care Information provides information and resources to help consumers plan for long-term care needs.

- **www.longtermcareliving.com** provides information on nursing homes, assisted living facilities, residential care, and other types of long-term care, plus helpful tips on coping with the transition of a family member into an assisted living residence, caring for someone with Alzheimer's, and writing an advance directive.

- **The National Consumer Voice for Quality Long-Term Care,** www.theconsumervoice.org, provides state and local resources for residents or family members advocating for quality long-term care, and consumer fact sheets with information on federally guaranteed residents' rights, selecting a nursing home, forming family councils, and more.

- **Family Caregiving 101,** www.familycaregiving101.org, is a resource for people caring for an ill or disabled family member. Whether you are anticipating caring for a loved one, currently providing care, or transitioning a family member to a nursing home, this site provides useful information and links to resources.
- **AARP,** www.aarp.org, has a "Caregiving" section in the Health area of its site that provides useful consumer information on long-term care options.
- **Family Caregiver Alliance,** www.caregiver.org, provides advice and support for caregivers and referrals to local government, nonprofit, and private programs of interest to caregivers and the recipients of long-term care.
- **www.caring.com** provides information and support for people who care for aging parents, spouses, and other loved ones. The site covers a wide range of topics, including geriatric medicine, law, finance, housing, and other key areas of health care and eldercare.

At-Home Care

Lots of older people don't need medical or nursing care, but could use help with day-to-day activities. Fortunately, more and more options are available for people who want to "age in place," as staying in one's home is sometimes called.

 RESOURCE

More on aging in place. The AARP website, www.aarp.org, has several useful articles on the subject. AARP also publishes a book, *The AARP Guide to Revitalizing Your Home: Beautiful Living for the Second Half of Life*, by Rosemary Bakker, on the topic.

The term "home care" encompasses a multitude of medical and personal services provided at home to an elder. These services often make it possible for an older person to remain at home or with a relative. Depending on what is available in your community, home care and related supplemental services can include:

- **health care:** nursing, physical and other rehabilitative therapy, medicating, monitoring a chronic health condition, and medical equipment
- **personal care:** assistance with personal hygiene, dressing, getting in and out of a bed or chair, bathing, and exercise
- **nutrition:** meal planning, cooking, meal delivery, or driving to meals away from home
- **housekeeping:** cleaning, shopping, home repair, and household paperwork
- **social needs:** escort and transportation services and companions, and
- **safety:** especially for people with dementia or other cognitive impairment, includes making sure that the person does not become lost, disoriented, or injured.

Home care needs may be filled by community agencies or organizations, adult daycare or senior centers, individuals hired through informal networks or a certified home care agency, and family and friends. Geriatric care managers can be especially helpful if you want to arrange care for an elderly relative who doesn't live nearby. A geriatric care manager will assess long-term care needs of an elderly person and organize appropriate services, including in-home care and supporting services from various providers.

RESOURCE

More on geriatric care managers. The National Association of Professional Geriatric Care Managers, www.caremanager.org, offers referrals and information about caregivers and how a geriatric care manager can help.

Finding Good Home Care

Many people hire one or more individuals to take care of an older relative. The best way to find a good home care worker is by referral. Ask your family physician about getting in-home help, or see whether your local hospital has a registry of visiting nurses. Your local area office on aging (find yours at www.aoa.org) can also provide referrals for reputable home-care services, as can the Elder Care Locator (see www.eldercare.gov or call 800-677-1116).

And don't forget to ask family, friends, and neighbors for referrals. Most of all, you want someone you can trust.

Anyone providing medical care must be licensed or certified by your state's home care licensing agency. So when you need medical or nursing care—not just assistance with daily activities—you should seek help from certified agencies rather than independent caregivers.

If you need nonmedical care, you can hire an independent caregiver or an agency—the caregiver does not need to be licensed or certified. But it is very important to check references carefully and to find out what credentials a potential caregiver has. For example, ask whether the caregiver has had CPR and first aid training or any other health care training. Also, be sure to define the tasks that you need the caregiver to perform, such as shopping and meal preparation, bathing and personal care, and light housekeeping, and make sure that the person is willing and able to do them.

If you hire someone directly, not through an agency, you'll need to comply with federal and state employment laws, such as verifying the legal status of the caregiver and withholding taxes from paychecks (see your state department of labor for your rules). You'll also need a plan for who will step in when the caregiver gets sick or takes time off.

Cost of In-Home Care

The cost of nonmedical home care averages $15 to $30 per hour or more, depending upon the amount of time a caregiver works each day, whether or not they live in, their skills, and other factors. A nurse practitioner or registered nurse will be much more expensive than someone who is providing nonmedical home care. If a doctor prescribes medically necessary home health care for a homebound senior, Medicare will cover some of the costs if you use a Medicare-approved home health agency. Medicare will not, however, pay for a caregiver who provides nonmedical assistance.

Assisted Living

Assisted living is the fastest growing type of senior residence. It meets the needs of millions of seniors who don't need nursing care but do want help with housekeeping and other chores and who enjoy the meals, activities, and socializing that a well-run assisted living residence provides.

Assisted living offers extensive personal assistance and services, which are not offered by independent living residences and would be extremely expensive if arranged through home care. Residents maintain the privacy and independence that are lost in more institutional, and more expensive, nursing facilities.

Typically, people in assisted living rent their own room or small apartment. It may be equipped with an emergency call system, so help can always be summoned quickly. Residents can choose from a range of services, typically including:

- domestic services, including meals and housekeeping
- assistance with personal care and the activities of daily living, but not nursing care, and
- close monitoring to help ensure their health and safety, such as keeping track of and helping a resident take the correct dose of medications or helping a resident with self-administered health aids, such as prostheses and oxygen.

Assisted living facilities range widely in cost, from $1,500 to $5,000 per month or more, depending on the size of the living space and the services provided. The cost is generally one-third to one-half the cost of a nursing facility of the same quality in the same area. Assisted living is not covered by insurance.

Long-Term Residential Care

Some seniors are too ill or frail to live at home or in an assisted living residence. They need the 24-hour monitoring, extensive personal help, and nursing care that can be found only in a residential care facility.

Several types of care are available in long-term residential facilities. Skilled nursing facilities provide short-term, intensive medical care and monitoring for people recovering from acute illness or injury. Other facilities—called nursing homes, board and care homes, sheltered care homes, or something similar— provide custodial care, long-term room and board, and 24-hour assistance with personal care and other health care monitoring, but not intensive medical treatment or daily nursing. Some facilities provide only one level of care (skilled or custodial), while others offer several levels at the same location.

For someone with severe physical or mental limitations, it is crucial to find a facility that provides the kind of attention and care that meets the individual's specific needs. For people who need little actual nursing care, the task is to find a facility that provides physical, mental, and social stimulation, not just bed and board.

Special Considerations for People With Memory Loss and Dementia

Elders with Alzheimer's and other conditions that involve memory loss or dementia face unique risks and often need special types of care. When you're looking for an appropriate facility, consider these factors:

- **Space.** Look for a facility that allows active residents to move about freely while keeping them safe.
- **Other residents.** Facilities that are devoted to those with dementia often have educational programs, family counseling, and support groups that might not be available elsewhere. And the staff can organize meals, activities, and care with just the needs of these residents in mind.
- **Staff.** Try visiting at different times of day, including meal times, to see how well the staff interacts with the residents. Is the staff calm and soothing, treating the residents with respect and acknowledging their comments and requests? Do the residents seem comfortable with the staff?
- **Special programs.** People with dementia can benefit from programs to help them stay mentally alert, such as arts and crafts work, music, reading, word games, and outings. Find out what special programs are offered.
- **Medication and medical care.** Find out whether the facility is licensed to administer drugs by injection and deliver other types of medical care that a patient cannot self-administer.

Finding a Good Residential Care Facility

The best way to find a good, affordable facility is usually to ask for referrals. Here are some good places to start:

- relatives, friends, and neighbors who have experience with a long-term care facility or know someone who does
- doctors (including your older relative's) who have personal experience with facilities in your area
- the hospital discharge planner, if your loved one is going straight from a hospital to a long-term care facility
- organizations focusing on your older relative's specific illness or disability, such as the American Heart Association, the American Cancer Society, the American Diabetes Association, or the Alzheimer's Disease Foundation
- national long-term care organizations, such as the American Association of Homes for the Aging (www.aahsa.org), that specialize in long-term care and give referrals to local facilities
- government agencies, such as your state Area Agency on Aging (find yours at www.aoa.org) or your local county social services that often provide targeted referrals, and
- church, ethnic, or fraternal organizations that may be affiliated with a particular facility or whose members may have recommendations.

See the list of resources above for organizations that provide referrals to and advice on choosing a nursing home or long-term care facility.

Paying for Residential Facility Care

Residential care is expensive. There is, however, a significant range in nursing home and other residential facility costs, depending on location, size, and facilities.

Skilled nursing facilities run between $300 and $500 per day, but, fortunately, stays there are usually relatively short, and Medicare or private health insurance will usually pick up much of the tab. To be covered by Medicare, you must receive the services from a Medicare-certified skilled nursing home after a qualifying hospital stay. (Generally, a stay of at least three days is required.)

Long-term custodial care—the kind that may last for years—costs several hundred dollars per day. Neither Medicare nor medigap private insurance supplements pay any of the cost. Medicaid will pay the full cost of custodial nursing facility care for people with very low income and few assets.

Eligibility varies by state; check your state's requirements to find out whether you are eligible. Medicaid will pay only for nursing home care provided in a facility certified by the government to provide service to Medicaid recipients. Long-term care insurance will pay for this type of care if you're one of the small percentage of people who have that type of insurance.

RESOURCE

Free financial counseling and assistance. The State Health Insurance Assistance Program (SHIP) in your state, sometimes called the Health Insurance Counseling and Advocacy Program (HICAP), provides counselors who can review your existing coverage and find any government programs that may help with your health insurance and long-term care expenses. See www.shiptalk.org.

RESOURCE

More elder care resources.

- **Nolo's Elder Care & Seniors section**, www.nolo.com/legal-encyclopedia/elder-care-seniors, provides easy-to-understand information on topics such as hospice care, senior home sharing, long-distance caregiving for seniors, helping a widowed parent, elder abuse, using reverse mortgages to finance home care, safety issues involving elderly drivers, late-life divorce, taking family leave to care for an older relative, and more. Other sections of Nolo.com include useful articles for seniors planning for retirement and applying for Social Security.

- *The Sharing Solution: How to Save Money, Simplify Your Life & Build Community,* by Janelle Orsi and Emily Doskow (Nolo), includes a section on sharing related to elder care, including sharing an in-home care provider with another adult. See www.nolo.com for a sample chapter and full table of contents.

- **National Center on Elder Abuse (NCEA),** www.ncea.aoa.gov, phone 302-831-3525, is the government-affiliated agency charged with investigating reports of elder financial abuse and offering assistance to victims and provides links to state Adult Protective Service's offices (see "State Resources").

Wills & Estate Planning

Y ou don't take care of making a will and other estate planning tasks for yourself—you won't be around to benefit from it. Instead, you do it for your family. Good estate planning will save your family members money, spare them confusion, and take away the burden of making wrenching decisions during emotionally difficult times. The only thing you'll get from your estate planning efforts is peace of mind—which, on second thought, might be pretty valuable in itself.

Estate planning lets you:

- determine who gets what after your death
- name someone to care for your minor children if someday you and the other parent can't
- appoint someone you trust to handle your financial affairs if you're not able to
- express your wishes regarding end-of-life medical treatment
- give someone authority to carry out your health care wishes in case you're ever unable to communicate them
- arrange it so that probate court proceedings won't be necessary after your death, saving your family money and hassle, and
- minimize estate tax, if you're wealthy enough to need to worry about it.

Writing a will should be at the top of your estate planning list, especially if you have children. Creating a valid will is surprisingly easy to do, and most people don't even need a lawyer's help. And once it's done, you can rest a little easier, knowing that your wishes will be known and followed when the time comes.

Preparing a Basic Will

Just about everyone should have a basic will. (If you're married, each spouse makes a separate will.) With a will, you can do the following:

Leave your property. You can divvy up things however you want: for example, everything to your spouse, or a few heirlooms to friends and relatives and the rest to your two grown children, or half to a charity and half to your niece. Except where state laws give your spouse the right to claim some of your property, it's up to you. See "A Spouse's Right to Inherit," below, for more on this subject.

Name an executor. This is the person who has a legal responsibility to carry out the terms of the will. The executor gathers and safeguards your assets, pays bills and taxes, and transfers your property to those named in the will to inherit it.

Choose a personal guardian for children. For parents of young children (under 18), this is probably the most important part of a will. You choose a person who you want to raise your children in the unlikely event that you and the other parent can't.

Arrange for someone to manage money children inherit. It's unusual for minors to inherit large sums, but in case your children might, you can set up a trust or another method that will put a trusted adult in charge.

Do You Need a Lawyer to Prepare Your Will?

Most people do not need a lawyer's help to make a basic will that leaves a home, investments, and personal items to their loved ones and names a guardian for young children. Making a will rarely involves complicated legal rules, and most people can draft their own wills with the aid of a good software program, online tool, or do-it-yourself book. Some useful resources are listed at the end of this section.

Consult a lawyer if you have questions that aren't answered by the resource you're using, or if:

- You expect to leave a very large amount of assets—over $3.5 million— that could be subject to estate tax.
- You own a business and have questions about the rights of surviving owners or your ownership share.
- You want to provide for both your current spouse and your children from a previous marriage, and you fear conflict between them.
- You are concerned that someone might contest your will, claiming that you were not mentally competent when writing it, or that the will was procured by undue influence or fraud.
- You wish to leave nothing or very little to your spouse.

See Chapter 9 for advice on finding and working with an attorney.

Who Will Inherit Your Property

For most people, it isn't hard to decide who gets what—generally the largest part of the estate goes to a spouse, long-term partner, or children. Most married couples leave everything to each other and name their children (if any) as alternates, to inherit only if both parents die.

After you make your first choices, don't forget to choose alternate (contingent) beneficiaries, too, in case your first choices don't survive you.

What Passes Through Your Will

You may be surprised to learn that lots of property—including, possibly, some of your most valuable assets—won't pass through your will. In fact, the terms of your will won't have any effect on this property whatsoever.

Basically, wills control property that:

- you own entirely yourself—that means no co-owners, and
- you have not already named a beneficiary for.

Here are some common kinds of assets that do NOT pass through a will:

- a house owned in joint tenancy
- a joint checking account
- life insurance proceeds
- retirement accounts for which you've named a beneficiary (which people commonly do when they open a retirement account)
- a jointly owned car.

Jointly owned assets generally pass to the surviving owner unless you co-own the property as "tenants in common," which is unusual for spouses. Life insurance and retirement account money go to the beneficiary you named in a separate document that the insurance company or account administrator provided to you when you opened the account.

None of this may matter much if you're married and, like a lot of people, simply want to leave everything to your spouse. Put a provision to that effect in your will, and your spouse will inherit everything that passes under the will.

If you're married and don't want to leave everything to your spouse, keep in mind that your will can pass only items you own yourself. For example, the rocking chair you inherited from your grandma or a savings bond she gave you are yours alone, but things you own with your spouse aren't, so you can't leave them to someone else in your will. (See Chapter 1 for more on state systems for dealing with marital property.)

Your spouse may also have the right, under state law, to claim some of your property. The details vary widely from state to state. In some places, a surviving spouse can claim one-third of the deceased spouse's property even if the will says otherwise; in others, the amount depends on the length of the marriage. If this is an issue for you, see a lawyer.

Your Executor

Every will must name someone to serve as executor—the person whose job it is to carry out the terms of the will and handle one's property after death. The executor, called a personal representative in many states, must be prepared to carry out a long list of tasks prudently and promptly. This includes paying bills, taxes, and ongoing expenses, such as mortgage payments; accounting for property; making sure items are passed to the people and organizations named in the will; and notifying banks and government agencies (such as Social Security) of the death.

An executor may want some help from an attorney or another professional, especially if probate court proceedings (discussed below) are required or there are disputes among inheritors. Fees for these experts can be paid from the estate funds.

The person you choose as executor should be trustworthy, conscientious, and good at keeping track of details. If possible, name someone who lives nearby and who is at least somewhat familiar with your financial matters; that will make it easier to do chores like collecting mail and locating important records and papers. Most people name a spouse, close friend, or relative as executor. You should also name an alternate executor, who would take over if your first choice can't serve.

There are some restrictions on who can act as executor in probate court. You can't name a minor or a convicted felon (not that you'd want to). Most states let you name someone who lives in another state, but a few require that an out-of-state executor be a relative or a primary beneficiary under your will. Some probate courts also require that nonresident executors obtain a bond (an insurance policy that protects your beneficiaries if the executor steals or misuses estate property) or name an in-state resident to act as the executor's representative. These rules underscore the benefits of naming someone who lives nearby. If you feel strongly about naming an executor who lives out of state, be sure to familiarize yourself with your state's rules.

RESOURCE

State rules on executors. *The Executor's Guide,* by Mary Randolph (Nolo) provides details on legal and practical issues involving executors. See www.nolo.com for a sample chapter and full table of contents.

A Guardian for Your Children

If you have children under 18, you will need to decide who you want to raise them in the unlikely event that both you and the other parent can't. For many parents, choosing a guardian is the most difficult part of writing a will. There's never a perfect choice, but it is important to choose someone, so do your best and remember that you can always change your mind later.

A guardian's legal authority comes from a court. So if a guardian were ever needed for your children, a probate judge would look at your will and appoint your nominee unless the judge concluded (based on a review of your prospective guardian's background and home) that it was not in the best interests of your children. If you don't name a guardian in your will, it would be up to the court to select and appoint someone without your input—not necessarily someone you would want.

In your will, name the person you've chosen and an alternate, in case your first choice can't serve. To avert conflicts, you and the other parent (you make separate wills, remember) should each name the same guardian for a child. If you have more than one child, however, you do not need to name the same guardian for all of them.

If you are a single parent sharing custody of a child, keep in mind that the other parent would raise the child if you couldn't, unless there was a problem serious enough (drug addiction, for example) for a court to take the child away from that parent. If you have primary custody and you don't think the other parent should raise the child full time, you can name another guardian in your will. Be sure to state, either in your will or in a separate document, the reasons that you are nominating someone who isn't the other parent. The judge is unlikely to follow your wishes—the parent-child relationship is too important—but you can try it. And the nomination will be useful if, for some reason, it turns out the other parent isn't available to parent.

If you are raising a child with your same-sex partner, but you are the only parent with legal (custodial) rights, you will name your partner as the personal guardian. If you have family members who might argue against your partner becoming the guardian, consider writing a letter to explain why it would be crucial for your partner to be named guardian and continue raising the child—and why your family members might not be appropriate choices. If it were ever necessary, the letter could be given to the judge who was deciding who should be guardian.

You should have complete confidence in the person you nominate, and you should be certain that the person is willing to accept this big responsibility should the need arise. See "Are You Prepared to Be a Guardian?" in Chapter 5 for more on this. It's wise to pick just one person, rather than a couple. Couples can split up, opening up the possibility of disputes over the guardianship.

RESOURCE

More on guardians. *The Mom's Guide to Wills & Estate Planning*, by Liza Hanks (Nolo), provides extensive common sense advice on choosing a guardian. See www.nolo.com for a sample chapter and full table of contents.

You may or may not choose the same person to be both a personal guardian and a property guardian. It may be that the person who would be the best surrogate parent would not be the best person to handle the money. Ideally, if you choose different people for the different jobs, they would be people you expect to get along and work together well for your children's welfare.

Someone to Manage Children's Property

If a child might inherit from you, you should pick someone to manage the inheritance until the child is old enough to manage it. You can name this person, called a property guardian, in your will. If you don't, the court will appoint someone to manage any significant property your children inherit. The court would then supervise the guardian until the kids turned 18, when the children would receive anything left outright.

Choose someone who is a good money manager, responsible, trustworthy, and diligent. Ideally, this will be the same person you name as your child's personal guardian, but it doesn't need to be—and it shouldn't be, if the personal guardian is not good with money.

There are many ways to use your will to give the person you've chosen control over a child's money. Here are the most useful.

Name a custodian under the Uniform Transfers to Minors Act (UTMA). In every state except South Carolina and Vermont, you can use a law called UTMA to choose someone, called a custodian, to manage property you leave to a child. If the child inherits property, the custodian will step in to manage it until the child turns the age specified by your state's law—21 in most states. At that time, the child receives what's left of the trust property outright. If you want property management to last longer, you may want to set up a trust, which allows you more control over the property. See below for more about trusts.

Set up a trust for each child. You can use your will to name a trustee (usually a trusted relative or friend) who will handle any property the child inherits. The trustee must act in the child's best interests and follow your written instructions. Generally, the trustee can spend trust money for the young person's health, education, and living expenses. When the child reaches the age you specify in the trust—which can be older than 21 if you wish—the trustee turns over whatever trust property is left to the child.

Set up a pot trust for your children. If you have more than one child, you may want to set up just one trust for all of them. This arrangement is usually called a pot, sprinkling, or family trust. In your will, you appoint a trustee. The trustee doesn't have to spend the same amount on each child; instead, the trustee decides what each child needs, and spends money accordingly.

When the children reach the ages you set, the trust ends. At that time, any property left in the trust will be distributed as you direct in your will—often it's given outright to the children in equal shares at that point.

Signing and Storing Your Will

After making your will, you'll need to sign and date it in the presence of two witnesses, who also sign the document. (They don't have to read it or know what's in it—they just need to know it's your will.) Your witnesses should be people who won't inherit anything under the will.

You don't have to have your will notarized. In many states, though, if you and your witnesses sign an affidavit (a notarized statement), it will be easier to prove the validity of the will in court after you die.

Keep your will in an envelope on which you have written your name and the word "Will." Place the envelope in a fireproof metal box, file cabinet, or home safe. It's usually better not to place the original in a safe deposit box— your executor might not have access to the box after your death. Wherever you keep your will, make sure your executor (and at least one other person you trust) knows where it is and has access to it. A will does not need to be recorded or filed with any government agency.

Handwritten Wills

Handwritten wills that are not signed in front of witnesses are called "holographic" wills. They are legal in about 25 states. To be valid, a holographic will must be handwritten, dated, and signed in the handwriting of the person making the will. Some states allow people to use a fill-in-the-blanks form if the rest of the will is handwritten and the will is properly dated and signed.

If it's valid in your state, a holographic will is better than nothing. But a will signed by witnesses is always better, because its legal validity should be clear after your death, when the document is filed with the probate court.

> **RESOURCE**
>
> **Will-making resources from Nolo:**

- *Quicken WillMaker Plus* software lets you create a valid will, customized to the laws in your state, and many other important estate planning documents, such as health care directives, a durable power of attorney for finances, and a final arrangements document.

- *Nolo's Online Will*, at www.nolo.com, lets you make a basic will online, customized for your situation and the laws in your state.

- *Quick & Legal Will Book*, by Denis Clifford, contains forms and instructions for creating a basic will.

- *The Mom's Guide to Wills & Estate Planning*, by Liza Hanks, leads you through ten simple steps to take to plan your estate, including lots of information on choosing guardians for children.

For details on these products and more information about wills and estate planning, see the Wills, Trusts, & Estates section of www.nolo.com.

If You Die Without a Will

If you don't make a will or use some other legal method to transfer your property when you die, you lose your chance to have a say over what will happen to your property—and who will raise your children.

State law will determine what happens to your property, under a process called "intestate succession." The exact rules vary from state to state, but in general:

- If you're married, your property will be distributed to your spouse and children, if you have them.

- If you don't have a spouse or children, your property will go to your closest relatives.

- If no relatives can be found, your property will go into your state's treasury.

- If you are a registered domestic partner or have entered a civil union, your partner will have the same inheritance rights as a surviving opposite-sex spouse (the same is true for same-sex married couples). In states that don't have or recognize registered domestic partnerships or civil unions, your surviving partner will not inherit anything.

If you have minor children, a court will determine who will care for them and their property if the other parent is unavailable or unfit.

Estate Planning and Blended Families

Second marriages present special challenges in estate planning. You and your spouse have probably brought both children and assets to the relationship, and you've now got to think about both. If you're like most people, it's important to you to provide for your current spouse and also for all your children, whether they're from your current relationship or a previous one. Relying on your spouse and children to work it out later is *not* a plan.

You'll probably want to work with an estate planning attorney who has experience crafting plans for blended families. There are several kinds of trusts that can work well in second marriages, reassuring everyone concerned and heading off disputes.

You'll also want to:

- Review any beneficiary designations you have made on insurance policies or retirement accounts, and make sure they are up to date. (People often forget to remove former spouses.)
- Make a list of special family items your children have their hearts set on inheriting, and make sure you specifically take care of these items in your will or trust.

RESOURCE

Help for people in second marriages. *Estate Planning for Blended Families: Providing for Your Spouse & Children in a Second Marriage*, by Richard Barnes (Nolo), explains what to consider when you're making an estate plan that takes into account a current spouse and children from previous relationships. See www.nolo.com for a sample chapter and full table of contents.

Planning for Loved Ones With Special Needs

If you want to leave money or property to a loved one with a disability, you must plan carefully. Otherwise, you could jeopardize your loved one's ability to receive Supplemental Security Income (SSI) and Medicaid benefits—and Medicaid can be crucial to someone who may never be able to get private health insurance through employment. By setting up a special needs trust now or in your will, you can avoid some of these problems.

How a Special Needs Trust Can Help

Owning a house, a modest car, furnishings, and normal personal items does not affect eligibility for SSI or Medicaid. But other assets, including cash in the bank, will disqualify your loved one from benefits. For example, a loved one to whom you left $10,000 in your will would be disqualified from receiving SSI or Medicaid.

A way around this is to create what's called a special needs trust and transfer assets to it, either now or at your death. You choose a trustee who will have complete control over the trust property and will be in charge of spending money on your loved one's behalf. Funds are commonly used to pay for personal care attendants, vacations, home furnishings, out-of-pocket medical and dental expenses, education, recreation, vehicles, and physical rehabilitation. Because your loved one has no control over the trust money, SSI and Medicaid administrators ignore it for eligibility purposes.

Pooled Trusts

If you don't know someone who will make a good trustee or don't want to set up a separate special needs trust, consider a pooled trust. These trusts (also called community trusts) are special needs trusts run by nonprofit organizations that pool and invest funds from many families. Each trust beneficiary has a separate account, and the trustee chosen by the nonprofit spends money on behalf of each beneficiary. Pooled trusts are available in many areas of the country.

RESOURCE

More on trusts for beneficiaries with disabilities. *Special Needs Trusts: Protect Your Child's Financial Future,* by Stephen Elias (Nolo), explains how special needs trusts work and gives you the tools to make one yourself. See www.nolo.com for a sample chapter and full table of contents.

Spouses' and Children's Right to Inherit

The law doesn't want surviving spouses left out in the cold, so it protects them from being disinherited. Children, however, rarely have the right to claim anything from a parent's estate. And nothing requires you to leave a thing to your brother, your cousin, or any other relatives.

A Spouse's Right to Inherit

If you're married and live in a community property state (Arizona, California, Idaho, Louisiana, Nevada, New Mexico, Texas, Washington, or Wisconsin), you and your spouse each automatically own half of all the property and earnings (with a few exceptions) either of you acquires during your marriage. So each of you can leave your half of the community property, and all of your separate property (generally, all property you owned before marriage or received through gift or inheritance during marriage), to anyone you choose; the surviving spouse, in turn, gets to keep his or her half of the property. (See Chapter 1 for more on community property rules.) Your spouse has no right to inherit your half if you don't leave it to him or her.

In all other states, there is no rule that property acquired during marriage is owned by both spouses. To protect spouses from being disinherited, these states give a surviving spouse a legal right to claim a portion of the deceased spouse's estate, even if the will says something different. In some states, the amount a surviving spouse can claim depends on how long the couple was married. These provisions protecting a spouse from disinheritance kick in only if your spouse challenges your will. If your spouse doesn't object to a will that leaves less than the statutory share, the court will honor the will as written.

These rules also apply to registered domestic partners and couples in civil unions in states that grant the rights and responsibilities of marriage to domestic partnerships (see Chapter 1 for a list).

The upshot of all this is that if you don't plan to leave at least half of your property to your spouse or registered domestic partner or civil union partner, you should consult a lawyer—unless your spouse or partner willingly consents, in writing, to your plan.

> **TIP**
>
> **Inheritance rules do not apply to ex-spouses.** In most states, getting divorced automatically revokes gifts made to a former spouse in your will. But to be on the safe side, if you get divorced, make a new will that revokes the old one. Then you can simply leave your former spouse out of your will if you want.

Children's Rights to Inherit

Generally, it's legal to disinherit a child. Some states, however, protect minor children against the loss of a family residence. For example, the Florida constitution prohibits the head of a family from leaving a residence to anyone other than a spouse if there's a minor child. Louisiana has special and complicated laws that give minor children and disabled offspring of any age the right to inherit.

The goal in most states, however, is simply to protect children from being *accidentally* disinherited. Most of these state laws assume that if you make a will, later have a child, and the child is neither named in your will nor specifically disinherited, you just forgot to update your will and include that child. The overlooked child (sometimes call a pretermitted or omitted heir) has a right to the same share of your estate as if you'd left no will. The share usually depends on whether a spouse survives you and on how many other children you have, but it is likely to be a significant percentage of your property. In some states, these laws apply not only to your children but also to any of your grandchildren born to a child who has died.

To avoid legal battles after your death, if you decide to disinherit a child or the child of a deceased child, expressly state your wishes in your will. And if you have a child after you make your will, remember to make a new will.

Providing for Your Pet

If you own pets, you undoubtedly want to make sure that they will be cared for after you die. Many people make informal arrangements with a friend, neighbor, or relative to care for their pets, but you may want to make more formal provisions. You can't just leave money in your will to your pet, though. Instead, take one or more of these steps:

- **Choose a new owner for your pet.** Make your decision legally binding by leaving your pet to someone in your will.
- **Leave money in your will to provide for your pet.** This can include leaving money for the new owner who will care for your pet and arranging in advance for the costs of your pet's veterinary care.
- **Set up a pet trust.** In most states, you can set up a pet trust, in which you leave property for the benefit of your pet. You put someone else, called a trustee, in charge of managing and spending the money, and you provide that trustee with a set of written instructions. One advantage of a trust is that it can take effect if you become ill and are unable to care for your pet. A will takes effect only upon your death.

For more on providing for pets, including pet trusts and sample will provisions, see *Every Dog's Legal Guide: A Must-Have Book for Your Owner*, by Mary Randolph (Nolo). See www.nolo.com for a sample chapter and full table of contents.

Probate and How to Avoid It

Probate is a legal process that takes place after someone dies. It commonly includes these steps, all of which are the responsibility of the executor named in the will:

- proving in court that a deceased person's will is valid (usually a routine matter)
- identifying and inventorying the deceased person's property
- having the property appraised
- paying debts and taxes, and
- distributing the remaining property as the will (or state law, if there's no will) directs.

Will Probate Be a Hassle?

Probate generally takes several months to a year and necessitates hiring a lawyer, meaning that it involves considerable delay and expense to the family. But it isn't always a big or expensive hassle. Here are some important factors that can affect how onerous probate is, or whether it will be necessary at all:

Where you live. About 20 states have probate court processes that are straightforward and involve almost no court supervision. In other words, it's mostly paperwork. Most of these states have adopted a set of laws called the Uniform Probate Code.

How much property was left. Almost every state offers simplified probate procedures for small estates. What qualifies as a small estate is different in every state, but even fairly large estates—those of several hundred thousand dollars—commonly qualify because many assets are not counted toward the limit.

What kind of property was left. Generally, only solely owned property goes through probate. So if a couple owns their house together, and one spouse dies, ownership will probably pass to the surviving spouse without probate. The same thing goes for joint bank accounts.

> RESOURCE
>
> **Help for executors.** *The Executor's Guide*, by Mary Randolph (Nolo), explains what executors can expect and how to deal with legal and practical issues, such as insurance, benefits, wills, trusts, probate, debts, and taxes. See www.nolo.com for a sample chapter and full table of contents.

Avoiding Probate

Because probate can be time-consuming and expensive and usually doesn't yield any benefit to the surviving family, many people plan in advance to avoid it. But avoiding probate takes time and money, too. Whether or not it makes sense for you and your family depends on a number of factors, especially your age, health, and wealth.

If you're young and in good health, there's little point in adopting a complex probate-avoidance plan—you'll just have to redo it as your life situation changes. And if you have very little property, you won't want to spend your time planning to avoid probate; your estate will probably qualify for simple probate (or none at all) under state law. But if you're older, in ill health, or own a significant amount of property, you'll probably want to do some planning to avoid probate.

If you decide you want to pursue probate avoidance, you have lots of options, including:

Joint ownership. If you and your spouse or partner own assets together—for example, real estate or bank accounts—they'll probably pass to the survivor when the first person dies. (Check to be sure you're holding title in the correct form under your state's laws.) If, however, you own valuable property by yourself, think twice before adding someone (an adult child, for example) as a co-owner just to avoid probate. If you do make someone a co-owner, you're making an irrevocable gift. And that half of the property could be lost to creditors or in a divorce, if the new co-owner runs into financial trouble down the road.

Beneficiary designations. You can avoid probate for bank accounts and certificates of deposit by adding a "payable-on-death" (POD) designation to the account registration. It's free and simple (just get a form from the bank and fill it in). At your death, the funds in the account will go directly to the person you named as POD beneficiary, no probate required. You can get the same result for securities and mutual funds by adding a transfer-on-death (TOD) beneficiary designation to brokerage accounts. In some states, you can even add a TOD beneficiary to a deed, so that real estate will pass without probate.

A revocable living trust. A basic living trust is a popular probate-avoidance device. It isn't much more complicated than a will, and you probably won't need to hire a lawyer to create a trust document, if you get a good do-it-yourself software program or book (see the resources below). Once the trust is created, you can hold property in trust, without giving up any control over it. At your death, the trust property can be distributed directly to the beneficiaries you named in the trust document, without the blessing of the probate court. It's all handled by the person you name in the trust to be successor trustee, whose role is similar to that of the executor of a will. When all of the property has been transferred to the beneficiaries, the living trust ceases to exist. A simple trust has no effect on your taxes.

> **RESOURCE**
>
> **Help with avoiding probate is available from Nolo:**
>
> - The Wills, Trusts & Estates section of www.nolo.com contains lots of articles about probate avoidance and living trusts.
> - *Living TrustMaker* software lets you make a basic probate-avoidance trust.
> - *Nolo's Online Living Trust*, at www.nolo.com, lets you make a basic probate-avoidance trust online, customized for your situation and the laws in your state.
> - *8 Ways to Avoid Probate*, by Mary Randolph, explains simple and inexpensive methods of sparing your family the hassle and expense of probate after your death.
> - *Plan Your Estate*, by Denis Clifford, offers an in-depth discussion of almost all aspects of estate planning, including living trusts and other means of probate avoidance as well as ways to reduce estate tax.
> - *Make Your Own Living Trust*, by Denis Clifford, contains forms and instructions for preparing two kinds of living trusts: a basic probate-avoidance trust and a tax-saving AB trust.
> - *The Trustee's Legal Companion*, by Liza Hanks and Carol Elias Zolla, explains the ins and outs of being the trustee of a living trust.
>
> For details on these products and more information about probate and estate planning, see the Wills, Trusts, & Estates section of www.nolo.com.

Estate and Inheritance Taxes

Most people don't need to worry about estate tax. The federal estate tax and most state taxes are imposed on the wealthiest families. For deaths in 2011 and 2012, the federal estate tax applies only to taxable estates of more than $5 million—fewer than 1% of all estates.

How the Taxes Work

The federal gift and estate tax are really just one tax; the same lifetime exemption and the same tax rate apply to property that you either give away during life or leave at your death. In other words, you can transfer, either while you're living or at your death, up to $5 million of property tax-free. More than that, and your estate pays a 35% tax on the excess.

Federal gift tax. Individuals can give away up to $5 million in taxable gifts tax-free. (Under the prior law, the limit was $1 million.) Most gifts are tax-free, which means they don't count against the $5 million limit. Only gifts of more than $13,000 per year to any one person or noncharitable institution are taxable. Making gifts of $13,000 or less, however, can yield substantial estate tax savings if you keep at it for several years. Some gifts are exempt from the gift/estate tax no matter what their amount. For example, if your spouse is a U.S. citizen, you can give your spouse an unlimited amount of property (a noncitizen spouse can receive up to $134,000 per year free of gift tax). Any property given to a tax-exempt charity avoids federal gift taxes, and money spent directly for someone's medical bills or school tuition is exempt as well.

Federal estate tax. Individuals can leave up to $5 million without owing any estate tax. Married couples can leave up to $10 million free of estate tax, split between their estates in any way they want. (Under the prior law, they had to create a complicated trust to make sure each spouse used up his or her separate exempt amount.) Property left to a spouse (as long as the surviving spouse is a U.S. citizen) or to a tax-exempt charity passes free of estate tax.

State estate tax. Many states also impose their own estate tax, which may affect estates that are much small than those subject to federal estate tax. Rates are typically less than 20%.

Inheritance tax. A few states impose a separate tax, called an inheritance tax, on those who inherit property. The tax rate depends on the inheritor's relationship to you; spouses pay nothing, close relatives pay the lowest rates, and unrelated recipients pay the highest rates. Tax rates vary from state to state but are much lower than federal estate tax rates.

Reducing Estate Taxes

Consult a tax attorney if you're concerned about estate tax. Lawyers can help you reduce the eventual tax bill with trusts and gift-giving strategies.

You can achieve substantial estate tax savings by making large gifts to reduce the amount of property you leave at your death. To avoid running into federal gift tax liability, you'll want to pay attention to the size of individual gifts. Currently, you can give away $13,000 per year per recipient tax free (the amount is indexed to inflation). That means a couple can give $26,000 a year to a child free of gift tax. If you have a few children or other people you want to make gifts to (such as sons- or daughters-in-law), you can significantly reduce the size of your taxable estate over a few years. Any property given to a tax-exempt charity also avoids federal gift tax, as does money spent directly for someone's medical bills or school tuition.

Funeral Planning and Other Final Arrangements

Wills are typically not read—or even found—until days or weeks after a death. That's too late to be of help to the people who must make immediate decisions about the disposition of your body and funeral or memorial services. So, instead of including funeral and other instructions in your will, make a separate document spelling out your wishes and tell your executor where to find it when the time comes.

There are many good reasons to spend some time considering what kind of arrangements you want after death, including any ceremonies and observances. Most important, letting your survivors know your wishes saves them from making these decisions at a painful time. Many family members and friends find that discussing these matters ahead of time is a great relief, especially if a person is elderly or in poor health and death is expected soon. Clear instructions also minimize disputes—for example, about a choice between burial and cremation. Planning some of these details in advance also helps ensure that costs will be controlled.

If you die without leaving written instructions about your preferences, state law will determine who will have the right to decide how your remains will be handled. In most states, the right—and the responsibility to pay for the reasonable costs of disposing of remains—rests with the following people, in order:

- spouse or registered domestic partner
- child or children
- parent or parents
- the next of kin, or
- a public administrator, who is appointed by a court.

What to Include in a Final Arrangements Document

What you choose to include is a personal matter, likely to be dictated by custom, religious preference, or simply your own whims. A typical final arrangements document might include:

- the name of the mortuary or another institution that will handle burial or cremation
- whether or not you wish to be embalmed
- the type of casket or container in which your remains will be buried or cremated, including whether you want it present at any after-death ceremony
- who your pallbearers will be, if any
- how your remains will be transported to the cemetery and gravesite
- where your remains will be buried, stored, or scattered
- the details of any marker you want to show where your remains are buried or interred, and
- the details of any ceremonies you want before, at the time of, or following burial, interment, or scattering.

 RESOURCE

Funeral or memorial societies. Nonprofit funeral or memorial societies offer useful, localized information to help you make plans. The Funeral Consumers Alliance, www.funerals.org, can help you find a society near you.

Body and Organ Donations

In addition to making arrangements for your funeral and burial or cremation, you may want to arrange to donate some or all of your organs. The principal method for donating organs is by indicating your intent to do so on a donor card (available from the department of motor vehicles in most states) or in a health care directive (discussed in the Chapter 7 section "Health Care Power of Attorney and Advance Directive"). Some states also have online registries where you can state your wish to become an organ donor.

Arrangements for whole body donations must usually be made while you are alive, although some medical schools will make arrangements after death. Start by contacting the nearest medical school or the National Anatomical Service at 800-727-0700.

Even if you have not signed a card or another document indicating your intent to donate your organs, your next of kin can approve a donation after you die. If you do put your intent in writing, make sure you tell family members you have done so. Even if you have indicated in writing that you want to donate your organs, an objection by your next of kin will often defeat your wishes; medical personnel usually do not proceed in the face of an objection from relatives. The best safeguard is to discuss your wishes with close friends and relatives, emphasizing your strong feelings about donating your organs.

Keeping Your Estate Plan Up to Date

Your estate plan should be tailored to your current family and financial situation, not your circumstances of five years ago or maybe even just last year. Take a fresh look at your will, living trust, and beneficiary designations whenever any of these important life events happens:

- **You get married.** You and your new spouse should create new wills. In most states, your spouse is legally entitled to claim a percentage of your property after you die, unless you have a written agreement to the contrary.

- **You are unmarried but have a new partner to whom you wish to leave property.** Write a new will. Without a will or alternate arrangements, your partner will inherit nothing unless your state has a method—registered domestic partnership or civil union—of granting same-sex couples the same inheritance rights that married couples get.

- **You get divorced.** In most states, a final judgment of divorce (or an annulment) revokes any gift made by your will to your former spouse. But in some states, it doesn't. So no matter where you live, you should make a new will after a divorce. Also look at old paperwork where you named your former spouse to inherit retirement plans or insurance proceeds—you may want to make a change. See Chapter 2 for more on estate planning after divorce.

- **You bring a new baby into the family.** Make a new will to name a personal guardian for your new child.

- **You have new stepchildren.** Unless you legally adopt stepchildren, they probably won't have any right to inherit from you. If you want to leave them a share of your property, you should adjust your will.

- **You acquire or dispose of substantial assets, such as a home.** If you leave all of your property to one or more people or organizations, there is no need to change your will when your assets change. But if you've left specific gifts of property that you no longer own, you'll want to avoid leaving the intended beneficiaries out in the cold. Likewise, if you obtain new property (for example, through an inheritance) and you want to leave it to a specific person, you'll need to change your will to make your wishes clear.

- **You're married and move from a community property state to a common law property state, or vice versa.** Community property and common law property states view the ownership of property by married couples differently (see Chapter 1 for details). This means that what both you and your spouse own may change if you move from one type of state to the other.

- **You change your mind about who you want to inherit a significant portion of your property.** If your main beneficiary dies before you do, or if you just change your mind, you'll need to create a new will.

- **You want to name a new guardian.** If the guardian named in your will is no longer close to you or your children or has moved away, you will probably want to name a new guardian. You may also want to name a new guardian if your children are older and have different needs.
- **You want to name a new executor.** This might occur if the person you named moved out of state or is no longer available or appropriate to serve as executor.

RESOURCE

Organizing now pays benefits later. *Get It Together,* by Melanie Cullen and Shae Irving (Nolo), helps you organize and store all of your important records, including your will, living trust, insurance policies, financial accounts, and final arrangements. See www.nolo.com for a sample chapter and full table of contents.

Updating a Will or Trust

The best way to modify a will is just to make a new one. In it, you revoke your old will by including a simple statement like this: "I revoke all wills and codicils that I have previously made." (A codicil is an addition to a will, signed in front of witnesses just like a will.) It's also a good idea to gather all copies of your old will and destroy them. To update a trust, it's more common to add an amendment to the original trust document.

Lawyers

I f you have a question about the law and how it applies to you, you can try to find the answer yourself or you can hire a lawyer to find it for you. Which strategy is best depends on your own very personal circumstances—the complexity of the question, its importance, and your own comfort with diving in and doing research on your own or even representing yourself.

Many people conclude that a hybrid approach is best: educating themselves in the basics and then consulting a lawyer for the thornier stuff. Throughout this book, we've highlighted books, websites, and other resources that can help you get up to speed on a family law matter.

If you're going through a big life change—getting a divorce or adopting a child, for example—and need legal advice that's tailored to your particular family situation, a knowledgeable lawyer is absolutely essential. Especially when you're dealing with matters involving your family, it's important to find not just an experienced lawyer or a smart lawyer, but the right lawyer— someone you're comfortable with and whose counsel you trust. It may take you some time to find someone who's a good fit, but your efforts will pay off in the long run.

STATE RULES AND RESOURCES
Appendix A lists your state court that handles family matters.

Will You Need a Lawyer?

Some family law matters consist of fairly straightforward paperwork. You may not need a lawyer's special skills at all if you have good instructions from the court, a book, software, or relevant website. For example, many people don't use a lawyer to:

- arrange an amicable divorce where there is little money or property involved, no one is asking for spousal support, and there are no children
- handle a stepparent adoption where there is no opposition from the child's other biological parent, or

- prepare a simple will, financial power of attorney, or health care directive.

There are, of course, many situations when it makes sense to hire a lawyer. As a general rule, if you're in an adversarial proceeding and the other side has a lawyer, you'll be better off getting one yourself. Here are a few other examples of instances when you'll want to get a lawyer to represent you:

- You and your fiancé are considering a prenuptial agreement (in most states, the law requires that both people see a lawyer when preparing a prenup).
- You are going through a contested divorce, especially if there is a dispute about child custody or spousal support.
- You want to terminate a same-sex marriage, especially if you live in a state that doesn't recognize the marriage.
- You want to annul your marriage and your spouse doesn't.
- You are adopting a child from another country or arranging an independent adoption.
- Your teenager is charged with a criminal offense.
- You or your spouse is applying for a green card.
- You are fighting your school over an issue such as special education services or ongoing bullying of your child.
- You want to do some estate planning and there is a lot of money and property involved, or you are in a second marriage and want to provide for your children and your current spouse.
- You want a temporary restraining order in a domestic violence case, there are children involved, and the abuser has a lawyer.
- You want strategic advice on how to handle a particular legal problem or task, such as how to shelter a house when applying for Medicaid or how to adopt a newborn as a single person.
- You want help preparing a specialized legal document, such as a conservatorship or a complex trust.
- You want a lawyer to review a document you've prepared, such as a simple will or a straightforward marital settlement agreement.

Looking Up the Law Yourself

You can now find most statutes (laws) and court decisions online, at no cost. If you want to read a particular law or court case, check out websites listed on your state sheet, including court websites, www.nolo.com, the Legal Information Institute at Cornell Law School (www.law.cornell.edu), and www. justia.com. These sites have information and links on state, local, and federal laws as well as court cases.

   If you need help finding something, go to the reference desk at your public library; many have good law collections. If your county maintains a law library that's open to the public, you can get help there, too.

RESOURCE

Legal research help. *Legal Research: How to Find & Understand the Law,* by Stephen Elias and the Editors of Nolo, explains how to find answers to your legal questions. See www.nolo.com for a sample chapter and full table of contents.

Free or Low-Cost Legal Help

Most likely, you will need to pay a lawyer for help in a divorce or family law matter. Here are some exceptions.

   If you face criminal charges. Anyone charged with a crime who cannot afford to hire a lawyer has a constitutional right to an attorney at govern-ment expense. The court will appoint an attorney, often from a public defender's office, to represent you.

   If you qualify for legal aid. If you can't afford an attorney, you may qualify for free legal assistance. Legal aid lawyers are government-funded lawyers who represent people with low incomes in a variety of legal situations, including eviction defense, denial of unemployment compensation, and consumer credit problems. If you think you might qualify, call the nearest legal aid office—if you can't find the number, ask a local attorney, bar association lawyer referral service, or your elected representative.

Bar association volunteer legal services programs. Some local county bar associations operate volunteer legal services programs. People who qualify receive legal services at a very low fee or even at no charge. Some of these programs also have "modest means" programs for people who make too much to qualify for free services but can't afford expensive lawyer fees.

Law school legal clinic. As part of law students' education, some law schools operate legal clinics through which students give legal advice and even, in some circumstances, represent clients in court. This isn't all that common, but it's worth checking with your local law school to find out whether there are any available services.

Self-help centers at courts. Many counties have staffed self-help programs at courthouses where you can make an appointment for advice on a particular legal issue.

Working With Lawyers

If you do decide to hire a lawyer, you don't necessarily have to turn over the entire case and have the lawyer do everything—though that is still the typical model for many divorce cases. Even in that situation, you're in charge of making decisions—but the lawyer is responsible for moving the case forward. If you want to be more involved and hands-on, there are quite a few other ways you can work with a lawyer.

If you just need a little help but you're intending to represent yourself, you may be able to find a lawyer who will serve as a legal coach. A coach will guide you through the process, explaining the law and your rights, provide strategic advice, and review legal documents you've prepared. For example, you may receive a request from your ex-spouse for certain information, and you're not sure whether you have to turn it over. Instead of researching the law yourself, you can ask your legal coach and get a quick answer. The legal coach might also counsel you on whether a particular settlement offer is to your advantage or not, or advise you on negotiating tactics.

You can also have a lawyer do a particular task for you, like preparing paperwork for a request to change child support or appearing in court for you just once. Offering services in this piecemeal way is sometimes called "unbundling legal services." It's becoming a more popular way for lawyers to provide affordable and appropriate legal services. Be sure you and the lawyer have a clear understanding of exactly what the lawyer is going to do for you, and make sure it's in writing.

Finally, you can have a lawyer review a document that you've prepared yourself, like a will or a trust. For example, some attorneys in Nolo's lawyer directory (described below) have agreed that they will review documents prepared using *Quicken WillMaker Plus* software or Nolo's online will. Check the profiles on Nolo's lawyer directory to find one who will review documents or conduct your own search for a lawyer willing to do so.

Before You Start Looking for a Lawyer

Write down:

- your goal—for example, adopting a newborn, gaining sole custody of your children, keeping your child out of juvenile hall, or mediating a divorce settlement versus fighting it out in court
- the kind of help you're seeking—full representation, legal coaching, or assistance with a particular task, and
- how much time and money you can devote to achieving your goal.

How to Find a Good Lawyer

You might need to speak with several lawyers before finding one who is right for the job. Don't hire the first lawyer you pick out of the phone book—treat this like the important (and potentially expensive) decision it is.

What Kind of Lawyer Do You Need?

Like doctors, most lawyers specialize. Some handle divorces, some give tax advice, some work on corporate mergers, some do criminal defense. And a few general practitioners still do a little of this and a little of that. But unless a lawyer has experience in your particular legal area of concern, keep looking.

If your legal issue involves a divorce, child custody, child or spousal support, or adoption, hire a lawyer who specializes in the specific area of family law you're looking for. After all, a lawyer with deep experience in mediating child custody disputes may not have done many contested divorces. It pays to work with a lawyer who knows the field.

Similarly, if you need help with estate planning, elder care, special education, or criminal law, find someone with legal expertise in that area. A family law expert is probably not the right person.

Certified Specialists in Family Law

Many states certify attorneys in specific areas of specialization. Requirements vary, but most states require lawyers to have several years of experience in the field—often with detailed requirements like how many trials the lawyer must have completed—and pass an exam demonstrating their expertise. Several states certify specialists in family law or domestic relations (check with your state bar association).

Whether a lawyer is a certified specialist shouldn't be the main criterion when you are searching for an attorney. Many very experienced, skilled lawyers aren't certified specialists. You should pay more attention to the specifics of the lawyer's experience, how good a fit that experience is with your needs, and how comfortable you feel with the lawyer and the office staff. Also ask what organizations the lawyer belongs to; groups like the American Academy of Matrimonial Lawyers (AAML) or the American Academy of Adoption Attorneys (AAAA) also have strict criteria for joining, so you can be confident that an attorney who is a member of such a group has significant experience and skills.

Getting Recommendations

The best way to start looking for a lawyer is to get recommendations from sources you trust.

Lawyers and other legal professionals. If you know a lawyer who doesn't do the kind of work you need, you should still ask for recommendations—that lawyer is very likely to know someone who specializes in family law or whatever specific area you're looking for. Your divorce lawyer may know an expert on special needs trusts; your business attorney may recommend a lawyer who can help your teenager whose case is in juvenile court.

Friends, family, and social and professional networks. It can be very useful to canvass friends and acquaintances to get the names of lawyers they found helpful for a similar legal task or problem, such as parents who have adopted or friends who have gone through a divorce. However, don't make a decision solely on the basis of someone else's recommendation. A lawyer who does well for one client, or has the time and energy to devote to one case, won't necessarily do as well on another case. Your friend's divorce may have been quite different from yours; her lawyer might have been great about working out all the financial details, while your main concern may be child custody. Your cousin's adoption lawyer may have successfully arranged an international adoption of a toddler, while you hope to adopt a newborn from this country. You might be on a tight budget, while your friend wasn't. And different people have different responses to a lawyer's style and personality—so the bottom line is, you should meet with any attorney to make sure it's a good fit.

Other professionals. A family therapist may have good recommendations for a divorce or adoption attorney. Your accountant may refer you to an estate planning attorney. Your pastor or rabbi may know a good elder care attorney.

Nonprofit, government, and other organizations. Nonprofit organizations that work in the area that concerns you are sure to know lawyers. A few examples:

- A women's center may have a list of well-regarded family and divorce lawyers.
- A social services organization may recommend an adoption agency.
- A women's shelter may be able to give you names of attorneys who can help in a domestic violence case.
- An LGBT legal rights group will know lawyers who can help a same-sex couple terminate their marriage.

- A local government agency on aging may have referrals to elder care attorneys.

Lawyer directories. Many online lawyer directories, including Nolo's (www.nolo.com) can help you find an attorney. Other reputable directories include Justia's (www.justia.com) and the Martindale-Hubbell Legal Directory (www.martindale.com). Some websites that address specific topics, like divorce or adoption, may also have lawyer listings, but it's difficult to gauge the quality of these listings.

Nolo's Lawyer Directory

To help consumers choose the right attorney, Nolo's lawyer directory provides a detailed profile for each attorney listed. The profile contains information about the lawyer's experience, education, fees and, perhaps most important, the lawyer's general philosophy of practicing law (information not typically available from other lawyer directories). Nolo has confirmed that attorneys have valid licenses and are in good standing with their bar associations. All attorneys have taken a pledge to communicate regularly with clients, provide an estimate of the time and cost involved, and provide a clear, fair written agreement that spells out how they will handle the legal matters and how clients will be charged. For more information, see www.nolo.com/lawyers.

Bar association referral services. Many county and city bar associations will refer you to a local lawyer who practices in the subject area you're interested in. You can contact these services by calling your local bar association and asking for a lawyer referral or checking online (see www.abanet.org). However, most bar associations do not screen lawyers for competency or experience—though they do make sure the lawyers have malpractice insurance—so a referral is not the same as a recommendation.

Narrowing Down Your Choices

Once you have the names of some attorneys whose experience matches your needs and who look like they might possibly be a fit for you, it's time to do some checking before you whittle your list to the top two or three candidates.

Here are some ways to get started:

- Check the attorney's website and any other online resources to find out as much as you can about the lawyer's background, experience, attitude, and fees. Does this person sound like someone you want to work with? For example, if a divorce lawyer advertises "aggressive" representation when you think you could work things out fairly amicably with your spouse, stay away.
- Check with your state bar association (see www.abanet.org to find yours) to see whether the lawyer has been the subject of any disciplinary action.

Once you're ready to meet likely candidates, call to make an appointment. A member of the lawyer's staff will usually ask you questions about your issue. They may also ask who referred you and the names of other people involved in your case, in order to avoid conflicts of interest—if they've represented your spouse or another family member in the past, they won't be able to represent you now. If the lawyer is available and handles your type of legal matter, you can arrange a meeting at the lawyer's office. The lawyer may send you an intake form to complete before you come and might ask you to bring certain documents with you, such as financial statements or information about property you own, depending on your particular legal issue.

Some lawyers don't charge for an initial meeting to discuss the possibility of representing a client, and some charge a relatively low flat fee, like $50 or $75, for a half hour or hour's consultation. However, most will charge their regular hourly rate for the first meeting to discuss the facts and law relating to your legal problem and the possibility of working together. Generally, this fee should cover any time the lawyer spends before the meeting reviewing documents or researching the law and the time spent in meeting with you.

How to Make Your First Meeting Successful

Your first meeting with each of the lawyers on your short list should give you enough information to decide about who you want to hire. To get the most from these meetings, be sure you do some homework first.

Preparing

Before you call a lawyer, bring yourself up to speed on your legal issue, so you can converse knowledgeably. You can get background information from:

- an organization dedicated to your issue—for example, a website for the families of children with disabilities that can direct you to resources about special needs trusts
- your local court's website that may have step-by-step information on getting a restraining order or getting a child support order enforced
- other government websites—for example, on Medicaid eligibility
- your court's self-help center, if it has one, where staff (and sometimes volunteers) help nonlawyers navigate the family law system, and
- the websites, books, and other resources listed throughout this book.

Then gather documents that the lawyer requested or that you think might be relevant to take with you to the meeting; for example, if you're hiring a special education lawyer, bring your child's school records and copies of any correspondence between you and the school.

Finally, write down all your questions so you'll be prepared when you meet the attorney. Otherwise it's just too easy to forget even important things you want to ask.

At the Meeting

You and the lawyer will have a lot to talk about at your first meeting. The lawyer may have a questionnaire for you to fill out, and you'll have your own list of questions. But keep in mind that you're not going to solve all your problems at this meeting. You're here primarily to decide whether or not you want to hire this lawyer. The lawyer will also use the meeting to decide whether to take your case, considering the type of work, your schedule, how lucrative the arrangement might be, how much work it will require, and how the two of you are likely to get along.

First, clearly explain what type of legal help you're seeking. Do you want a few consultations, full representation, or something in between? Especially if you just want the lawyer to serve as a coach, make sure the lawyer is willing to provide this limited type of representation.

Other things to ask about:

- The lawyer's experience that's relevant to your situation, typical clients , and outcomes—for example, if you are interviewing adoption attorneys, ask about the specific type and number of adoptions the attorney has arranged and how long they took. (You can ask for references from clients, but attorney-client confidentiality will prevent the lawyer from giving you the names of other clients without their permission, so you may have a hard time getting any.)
- Fee arrangements (more on this below) and a ballpark cost estimate. The lawyer will be reluctant to predict the cost, but should be willing to give you at least a very broad range, especially if you make clear that you know it's impossible to guarantee how much the case will cost.
- The general process and timeline of the legal work.
- Legal strategy and any challenges in your case.
- Whether other professionals (such as paralegals in the law office or an outside psychologist in a custody dispute or juvenile court case) will be involved.
- Who will do most of the work, and who you'll have most contact with—the lawyer you're talking to, a different lawyer in the firm, or a legal assistant?
- How you will be able to contact the lawyer, and how quickly they will return your communications. Don't skip this step even if the lawyer is friendly and easy to talk to. You want a lawyer who will work hard on your behalf, communicates well, and will follow through promptly on all assignments—not someone who is slow to return your phone calls or emails.

You should feel free to ask any other questions you have. And pay attention to the personal chemistry between you and your lawyer. No matter how experienced and well recommended a lawyer is, if you feel uncomfortable during your first meeting or two, you may never achieve a good lawyer-client relationship. Trust your instincts and seek a lawyer whose personality is compatible with your own.

Legal Fees

When choosing a lawyer, an important consideration is the amount of the lawyer's fee and how it will be calculated. Discuss fee arrangements at the outset, before you decide whether or not to hire a lawyer.

How Lawyers Charge

In family law matters, you're most likely to be charged an hourly rate. But there are variations.

Consultation fee. If you are consulting an attorney on a one-time or an occasional basis, you will usually pay an hourly rate, as described below.

Hourly fee. Most lawyers bill by the hour. The rate depends on the attorney's location, experience, reputation, and type of legal work. For example, the rate for trial work is usually higher than for other work. If your lawyer works for a law firm (rather than on his or her own), other members of the firm will also charge hourly, often at different rates. For example, your lawyer might charge $250 per hour and bill a paralegal's time at $100 per hour and an associate's time at $200.

Fixed or flat fee. Lawyers sometimes charge a flat fee for work that's fairly predictable, like preparing a will or trust or representing a parent in a simple stepparent adoption.

Contingency fees. You're not likely to run into this kind of fee arrangement in a family law matter; in fact, many states prohibit lawyers from using contingency fees in divorce cases. Contingency fees are most often used in personal injury lawsuits. Instead of billing by the hour, the lawyer waits until the case is over and then takes a certain percentage of the amount won (one-third is fairly standard, but it can vary by geographic location, type of case, and how far along in the court process the case goes). If you win nothing, the lawyer gets no fee. In this way, the lawyer shares your risk of losing or of winning less than expected—and is rewarded for winning more.

> ### Attorneys' Fees in Divorce Cases
>
> In a divorce case, it's not uncommon for one spouse to have control over the money or to earn a lot more than the other spouse. In some cases, the court will order the higher-earning spouse or the spouse who controls the money to pay the attorneys' fees of the other spouse. This isn't automatic, however, and most lawyers will require that you pay their fee up front, rather than relying on getting it back from the other spouse.

How to Create a Fee Agreement With Your Lawyer

You should always sign a fee agreement with a lawyer. Many states require that lawyers enter into written agreements, often called retainer agreements or representation agreements, with clients to set out fees and other terms of the lawyer-client relationship. Whether or not your state requires one, get your fee agreement in writing.

Your written agreement should explain:

- the lawyer's fee, how it will be calculated, and whether there's any cap on the fee
- hourly fees of anyone else who might work on the case, such as legal assistants, psychologists, or investigators, and what that work might be
- how the lawyer's fees will be paid (for example, within 15 or 30 days of billing)
- who will pay for costs, such as court fees (in most cases, that will be you, the client; in contingency cases, it will occasionally be the lawyer)
- how often you will be billed
- how much detail the bill will include (an itemized monthly statement is standard), and
- whether you will need to pay a deposit in advance (often called a "retainer"), how much this will be, and how it will be used.

A written agreement will help prevent disputes about legal fees and clarify the relationship you expect to have with the attorney and the services the lawyer will provide. Some agreements state how each of you can end the agreement and explain how you expect to work together, such as any decisions the lawyer can make alone and which require your approval.

How to Help Your Lawyer Do the Best Job

There are many things a good lawyer should do to keep your relationship on the right track, such as informing you of important developments in the case, including you in the decision-making process, and preparing you for important legal events, like answering questions in a deposition.

There are also some things you can do to help your lawyer advocate more effectively on your behalf. Following these tips will save you time and money—and may lead to a more successful result in your case.

Carefully prepare all materials a lawyer requests, such as important facts about your family in an adoption case or contact information for people who can support your efforts for custody. Your lawyer may ask you for a particular document or certain financial information, such as an inventory of assets and liabilities, bank and retirement account records, insurance policies, and the like. Try to answer these requests promptly.

Keep your lawyer informed. As soon as you hire a lawyer, tell the lawyer everything that might pertain to your case. Hand over any documents or other items that might be relevant. If you aren't sure whether a particular fact is important, err on the side of full disclosure. Lawyers are trained to sift through information and determine what is useful and what is not.

Be honest. Under a rule called the attorney-client privilege, a lawyer is under the strictest duty never to reveal anything a client tells the lawyer. A court can never order a lawyer to violate the attorney-client privilege by disclosing anything you say. The protection provided by this privilege extends to your statements to any member of the lawyer's staff and to anyone hired by the lawyer to work on the case. Because the attorney-client privilege is so broad, you don't need to worry about telling your lawyer information that might reflect badly on you or even damage your case—something like the fact that you had an extramarital affair, for example. A lawyer who knows about potential problems can come up with ways to counter or explain them—that is part of a lawyer's job. It is the things you don't tell your lawyer that often cause the most trouble. If the lawyer is caught by surprise by a piece of information that undermines your side, it might be too late for damage control.

RESOURCE

More information about finding and working with a lawyer:

- *The Lawsuit Survival Guide: A Client's Companion to Litigation,* by Joseph Matthews (Nolo), is a step-by-step guide for people who are involved in a lawsuit. It can help you find a good lawyer, work together successfully, and avoid problems right from the start. Available as a downloadable eBook at www. nolo.com.
- www.nolo.com. Nolo's website offers helpful articles on working with lawyers and handling any problems that come up over fees or other matters.

State Rules & Resources: Marriage, Divorce, Child Custody & Support

This appendix summarizes key state laws and provides useful websites on specific topics covered in the first four chapters of this book: Marriage, Divorce, Child Custody, and Child Support. It also includes links for state, federal, and local statutes as well as court information and family law forms. See Appendix B for resources and links to websites that provide state-by-state information on adoption, children, and elder care, such as where to find state rules on consent to adoption or local agencies to help with elder care services.

TIP

Keep up to date. Be aware that contact information may change, and that the law itself is not static. Always make sure you have the most up-to-date information by checking for legal updates at www.nolo.com.

Alabama

Statewide Legal Resources

State website:
- www.alabama.gov. Links and information for many state agencies and departments.
- www.dhr.alabama.gov/list.asp?pagetype=Service&cat=Family. Especially relevant for state family law issues.

State and federal statutes:
- Nolo, www.nolo.com/legal-research/state-law.html.
- The Legal Information Institute at Cornell University, http://topics.law.cornell.edu/wex/table_family.
- Justia, www.justia.com/family.
- www.usa.gov: Federal government site.

State court information and family law forms:
- www.alacourt.gov: Do-it-yourself court forms and instructions, links to local court websites. Search by topic, such as divorce, adoption, or custody.
- National Center for State Courts, www.ncsc.org: Links to state courts (browse by state under "Information and Resources").

Local laws:
- www.statelocalgov.net: Links to websites of many cities and counties, where you can check local rules and ordinances, such as graffiti rules.
- www.municode.com: Municipal codes.

Marriage

Requirements: No blood test required. You must be of the age of consent, not be too closely related to your intended spouse, not be married to anyone else, and have sufficient mental capacity, meaning you understand what you are doing when you marry. You can marry immediately after your marriage license is issued, and your license is good for 30 days. For more details, check your county clerk's office.

Common law marriage: Yes. A couple must intend to be married, live together for a significant period of time, and hold themselves out as a married couple.

Community property: No.

Same-sex marriage: No.

Marriage-equivalent relationship: No. Alabama does not recognize domestic partnerships, civil unions, or reciprocal beneficiaries.

Divorce

Grounds for divorce: Fault or no-fault grounds are allowed, or you can base your divorce on the fact that you've been separated from your spouse for at least two years.

Residency requirement: At least one spouse must be a resident of Alabama for six months or 180 days before filing for divorce.

How property is divided: Equitable division.

State laws, forms, and resources:
- Alabama state court website, www.alacourt.gov.
- Women's Law Initiative, www.womenslaw.org: State-by-state information on divorce, custody, and related topics.
- www.divorcenet.com, www.divorcesupport.com, www.divorceinfo.com, www.divorcecentral.com: Helpful divorce websites.

Divorce attorneys and mediators in your area:
- Nolo's Lawyer Directory, www.nolo.com: Divorce attorneys in your area.
- National Center for Lesbian Rights, www.nclrights.org, 800-528-6257: Attorneys experienced in same-sex divorces.
- www.mediate.com, 541-345-1629: Mediators in your area.

Child Custody

Child custody guidelines: Alabama courts begin with a presumption that it's best for a child to have frequent and continuing contact with both parents after a divorce. If possible, judges want to support joint custody arrangements.

Alabama

State laws, forms, and resources: See list in "Divorce," above.

International custody disputes: International Parental Child Abduction Division in the Office of Children's Issues of the U.S. State Department, http://travel.state.gov/childabduction, 888-407-4747.

State surrogacy laws:
- Human Rights Campaign, www.hrc.org (search "surrogacy laws").
- National Infertility Association, www.resolve.org (click "Family Building Options," then "Surrogacy").

Child Support

Child support guidelines: Alabama requires all parents to support their children. The amount of child support depends primarily on each parent's income and other resources and how much time each parent spends with the children.

State laws, forms, and resources: See list in "Divorce," above.
- www.supportguidelines.com: Links to state and federal laws and agencies.

State child support enforcement agency:
- Child Support Enforcement Division, www.dhr.state.al.us/page.asp?pageid=288.
- National Child Support Enforcement Association, www.ncsea.org: Information about federal programs and links to state agencies.

Federal child support enforcement programs and laws: Federal Parent Locator Service, www.acf.hhs.gov/programs/cse/newhire: Links to child support enforcement programs like the passport denial program.

Child support calculators to determine state guidelines: www.alllaw.com/calculators/childsupport: Search your state.

Alaska

Statewide Legal Resources

State website:
- www.alaska.gov. Links and information for many state agencies and departments.
- www.hss.state.ak.us. Especially relevant for state family law issues.

State and federal statutes:
- Nolo, www.nolo.com/legal-research/state-law.html.
- The Legal Information Institute at Cornell University, http://topics.law. cornell.edu/wex/table_family.
- Justia, www.justia.com/family.
- www.usa.gov: Federal government site.

State court information and family law forms:
- www.courts.alaska.gov: Do-it-yourself court forms and instructions, links to local court websites. Search by topic, such as divorce, adoption, or custody.
- National Center for State Courts, www.ncsc.org: Links to state courts (browse by state under "Information and Resources").

Local laws:
- www.statelocalgov.net: Links to websites of many cities and counties, where you can check local rules and ordinances, such as graffiti rules.
- www.municode.com: Municipal codes.

Marriage

Requirements: No blood test required. You must be of the age of consent, not be too closely related to your intended spouse, not be married to anyone else, and have sufficient mental capacity, meaning you understand what you are doing when you marry. You can marry immediately after your marriage license is issued, and your license is good for three months. For more details, check your county clerk's office.

Common law marriage: No.

Community property: Yes (for specific assets, if spouses sign an agreement).

Same-sex marriage: No.

Marriage-equivalent relationship: No. Alaska does not recognize domestic partnerships, civil unions, or reciprocal beneficiaries.

Divorce

Grounds for divorce: Fault or no-fault grounds are allowed, or you can base your divorce on the fact that you've been separated from your spouse for at least two years.

Residency requirement: None.

How property is divided: Community property.

State laws, forms, and resources:
- Alaska state court website, www.courts.alaska.gov.
- Women's Law Initiative, www.womenslaw.org: State-by-state information on divorce, custody, and related topics.
- www.divorcenet.com, www.divorcesupport.com, www.divorceinfo.com, www.divorcecentral.com: Helpful divorce websites.

Divorce attorneys and mediators in your area:
- Nolo's Lawyer Directory, www.nolo.com: Divorce attorneys in your area.
- National Center for Lesbian Rights, www.nclrights.org, 800-528-6257: Attorneys experienced in same-sex divorces.
- www.mediate.com, 541-345-1629: Mediators in your area.

Child Custody

Child custody guidelines: Alaska courts begin with a presumption that it's best for a child to have frequent and continuing contact with both parents after a divorce. If possible, judges want to support joint custody arrangements.

State laws, forms, and resources: See list in "Divorce," above.

International custody disputes: International Parental Child Abduction Division in the Office of Children's Issues of the U.S. State Department, http://travel.state.gov/childabduction, 888-407-4747.

Alaska

Alaska

State surrogacy laws:

- Human Rights Campaign, www.hrc.org (search "surrogacy laws").
- National Infertility Association, www.resolve.org (click "Family Building Options," then "Surrogacy").

Child Support

Child support guidelines: Alaska requires all parents to support their children. The amount of child support depends primarily on each parent's income and other resources and how much time each parent spends with the children.

State laws, forms, and resources: See list in "Divorce," above.

- www.supportguidelines.com: Links to state and federal laws and agencies.

State child support enforcement agency:

- Child Support Services Division, www.csed.state.ak.us.
- National Child Support Enforcement Association, www.ncsea.org: Information about federal programs and links to state agencies.

Federal child support enforcement programs and laws: Federal Parent Locator Service, www.acf.hhs.gov/programs/cse/newhire: Links to child support enforcement programs like the passport denial program.

Child support calculators to determine state guidelines: www.alllaw.com/calculators/childsupport: Search your state.

Arizona

Statewide Legal Resources

State website:
- www.az.gov. Links and information for many state agencies and departments.
- www.azcourts.gov/familylaw. Especially relevant for state family law issues.

State and federal statutes:
- Nolo, www.nolo.com/legal-research/state-law.html.
- The Legal Information Institute at Cornell University, http://topics.law.cornell.edu/wex/table_family.
- Justia, www.justia.com/family.
- www.usa.gov: Federal government site.

State court information and family law forms:
- www.azcourts.gov: Do-it-yourself court forms and instructions, links to local court websites. Search by topic, such as divorce, adoption, or custody.
- National Center for State Courts, www.ncsc.org: Links to state courts (browse by state under "Information and Resources").

Local laws:
- www.statelocalgov.net: Links to websites of many cities and counties, where you can check local rules and ordinances, such as graffiti rules.
- www.municode.com: Municipal codes.

Marriage

Requirements: No blood test required. You must be of the age of consent, not be too closely related to your intended spouse, not be married to anyone else, and have sufficient mental capacity, meaning you understand what you are doing when you marry. You can marry immediately after your marriage license is issued, and your license is good for one year. For more details, check your county clerk's office.

Common law marriage: No.

Community property: Yes.

Same-sex marriage: No.

Marriage-equivalent relationship: No. Arizona does not recognize domestic partnerships, civil unions, or reciprocal beneficiaries.

Divorce

Grounds for divorce: No-fault. However, fault may be considered by the court as a factor in dividing property or awarding alimony.

Residency requirement: At least one spouse must be a resident of Arizona for three months or 90 days before filing for divorce.

How property is divided: Community property.

State laws, forms, and resources:
- Arizona state court website, www.azcourts.gov.
- Women's Law Initiative, www.womenslaw.org: State-by-state information on divorce, custody, and related topics.
- www.divorcenet.com, www.divorcesupport.com, www.divorceinfo.com, www.divorcecentral.com: Helpful divorce websites.

Divorce attorneys and mediators in your area:
- Nolo's Lawyer Directory, www.nolo.com: Divorce attorneys in your area.
- National Center for Lesbian Rights, www.nclrights.org, 800-528-6257: Attorneys experienced in same-sex divorces.
- www.mediate.com, 541-345-1629: Mediators in your area.

Child Custody

Child custody guidelines: Arizona courts begin with a presumption that it's best for a child to have frequent and continuing contact with both parents after a divorce. If possible, judges want to support joint custody arrangements.

State laws, forms, and resources: See list in "Divorce," above.

International custody disputes: International Parental Child Abduction Division in the Office of Children's Issues of the U.S. State Department, http://travel.state.gov/childabduction, 888-407-4747.

State surrogacy laws:
- Human Rights Campaign, www.hrc.org (search "surrogacy laws").
- National Infertility Association, www.resolve.org (click "Family Building Options," then "Surrogacy").

Child Support

Child support guidelines: Arizona requires all parents to support their children. The amount of child support depends primarily on each parent's income and other resources and how much time each parent spends with the children.

State laws, forms, and resources: See list in "Divorce," above.
- www.supportguidelines.com: Links to state and federal laws and agencies.

State child support enforcement agency:
- DES Division of Child Support Enforcement, www.azdes.gov/dcse.
- National Child Support Enforcement Association, www.ncsea.org: Information about federal programs and links to state agencies.

Federal child support enforcement programs and laws: Federal Parent Locator Service, www.acf.hhs.gov/programs/cse/newhire: Links to child support enforcement programs like the passport denial program.

Child support calculators to determine state guidelines: www.alllaw.com/calculators/childsupport: Search your state.

Arizona

Arkansas

Statewide Legal Resources

State website:

- www.arkansas.gov. Links and information for many state agencies and departments.
- www.arkansas.gov/dhs/chilnfam. Especially relevant for state family law issues.

State and federal statutes:

- Nolo, www.nolo.com/legal-research/state-law.html.
- The Legal Information Institute at Cornell University, http://topics.law.cornell.edu/wex/table_family.
- Justia, www.justia.com/family.
- www.usa.gov: Federal government site.

State court information and family law forms:

- www.courts.arkansas.gov: Do-it-yourself court forms and instructions, links to local court websites. Search by topic, such as divorce, adoption, or custody.
- National Center for State Courts, www.ncsc.org: Links to state courts (browse by state under "Information and Resources").

Local laws:

- www.statelocalgov.net: Links to websites of many cities and counties, where you can check local rules and ordinances, such as graffiti rules.
- www.municode.com: Municipal codes.

Marriage

Requirements: No blood test required. You must be of the age of consent, not be too closely related to your intended spouse, not be married to anyone else, and have sufficient mental capacity, meaning you understand what you are doing when you marry. You can marry immediately after your marriage license is issued, and your license is good for 60 days. For more details, check your county clerk's office.

Arkansas

Common law marriage: No.

Community property: No.

Same-sex marriage: No.

Marriage-equivalent relationship: No. Arkansas does not recognize domestic partnerships, civil unions, or reciprocal beneficiaries.

Divorce

Grounds for divorce: Fault or no-fault grounds are allowed.

Residency requirement: At least one spouse must be a resident of Arkansas for 60 days before filing for divorce.

How property is divided: Equitable division.

State laws, forms, and resources:
- Arkansas state court website, www.courts.arkansas.gov.
- Women's Law Initiative, www.womenslaw.org: State-by-state information on divorce, custody, and related topics.
- www.divorcenet.com, www.divorcesupport.com, www.divorceinfo.com, www.divorcecentral.com: Helpful divorce websites.

Divorce attorneys and mediators in your area:
- Nolo's Lawyer Directory, www.nolo.com: Divorce attorneys in your area.
- National Center for Lesbian Rights, www.nclrights.org, 800-528-6257: Attorneys experienced in same-sex divorces.
- www.mediate.com, 541-345-1629: Mediators in your area.

Child Custody

Child custody guidelines: Arkansas courts begin with a presumption that it's best for a child to have frequent and continuing contact with both parents after a divorce. If possible, judges want to support joint custody arrangements.

State laws, forms, and resources: See list in "Divorce," above.

International custody disputes: International Parental Child Abduction Division in the Office of Children's Issues of the U.S. State Department, http://travel.state.gov/childabduction, 888-407-4747.

State surrogacy laws:

- Human Rights Campaign, www.hrc.org (search "surrogacy laws").
- National Infertility Association, www.resolve.org (click "Family Building Options," then "Surrogacy").

Child Support

Child support guidelines: Arkansas requires all parents to support their children. The amount of child support depends primarily on each parent's income and other resources and how much time each parent spends with the children.

State laws, forms, and resources: See list in "Divorce," above.

- www.supportguidelines.com: Links to state and federal laws and agencies.

State child support enforcement agency:

- Office of Child Support Enforcement, www.dfa.arkansas.gov/offices/childsupport.
- National Child Support Enforcement Association, www.ncsea.org: Information about federal programs and links to state agencies.

Federal child support enforcement programs and laws: Federal Parent Locator Service, www.acf.hhs.gov/programs/cse/newhire: Links to child support enforcement programs like the passport denial program.

Child support calculators to determine state guidelines: www.alllaw.com/calculators/childsupport: Search your state.

California

Statewide Legal Resources

State website:

- www.ca.gov. Links and information for many state agencies and departments.
- www.ca.gov/HomeFamily/Marriage. Especially relevant for state family law issues.

State and federal statutes:

- Nolo, www.nolo.com/legal-research/state-law.html.
- The Legal Information Institute at Cornell University, http://topics.law.cornell.edu/wex/table_family.
- Justia, www.justia.com/family.
- www.usa.gov: Federal government site.

State court information and family law forms:

- www.courtinfo.ca.gov/selfhelp/family: Do-it-yourself court forms and instructions, links to local court websites. Search by topic, such as divorce, adoption, or custody.
- National Center for State Courts, www.ncsc.org: Links to state courts (browse by state under "Information and Resources").

Local laws:

- www.statelocalgov.net: Links to websites of many cities and counties, where you can check local rules and ordinances, such as graffiti rules.
- www.municode.com: Municipal codes.

Marriage

Requirements: No blood test required. You must be of the age of consent, not be too closely related to your intended spouse, not be married to anyone else, and have sufficient mental capacity, meaning you understand what you are doing when you marry. You can marry immediately after your marriage license is issued, and your license is good for 90 days. For more details, check your county clerk's office.

Common law marriage: No.

Community property: Yes.

Same-sex marriage: No. However, same-sex couples who married between June and November of 2008 are still married.

Marriage-equivalent relationship: Yes. Same-sex couples can register as domestic partners with all of the rights and responsibilities of marriage under state law.

Divorce

Grounds for divorce: No-fault. However, fault may be considered by the court as a factor in dividing property or awarding alimony.

Residency requirement: At least one spouse must be a resident of California for six months or 180 days before filing for divorce.

How property is divided: Community property.

State laws, forms, and resources:
- California state court website, www.courtinfo.ca.gov.
- Women's Law Initiative, www.womenslaw.org: State-by-state information on divorce, custody, and related topics.
- www.divorcenet.com, www.divorcesupport.com, www.divorceinfo.com, www.divorcecentral.com: Helpful divorce websites.

Divorce attorneys and mediators in your area:
- Nolo's Lawyer Directory, www.nolo.com: Divorce attorneys in your area.
- National Center for Lesbian Rights, www.nclrights.org, 800-528-6257: Attorneys experienced in same-sex divorces.
- www.mediate.com, 541-345-1629: Mediators in your area.

Child Custody

Child custody guidelines: California courts begin with a presumption that it's best for a child to have frequent and continuing contact with both parents after a divorce. If possible, judges want to support joint custody arrangements.

State laws, forms, and resources: See list in "Divorce," above.

International custody disputes: International Parental Child Abduction Division in the Office of Children's Issues of the U.S. State Department, http://travel.state.gov/childabduction, 888-407-4747.

State surrogacy laws:

- Human Rights Campaign, www.hrc.org (search "surrogacy laws").
- National Infertility Association, www.resolve.org (click "Family Building Options," then "Surrogacy").

Child Support

Child support guidelines: California requires all parents to support their children. The amount of child support depends primarily on each parent's income and other resources and how much time each parent spends with the children.

State laws, forms, and resources: See list in "Divorce," above.

- www.supportguidelines.com: Links to state and federal laws and agencies.

State child support enforcement agency:

- Department of Child Support Services, www.childsup.ca.gov, or Los Angeles County Child Support Services Department, http://childsupport.co.la.ca.us.
- National Child Support Enforcement Association, www.ncsea.org: Information about federal programs and links to state agencies.

Federal child support enforcement programs and laws: Federal Parent Locator Service, www.acf.hhs.gov/programs/cse/newhire: Links to child support enforcement programs like the passport denial program.

Child support calculators to determine state guidelines: www.alllaw.com/calculators/childsupport: Search your state.

Colorado

Statewide Legal Resources

State website:

- www.colorado.gov. Links and information for many state agencies and departments.
- www.cdhs.state.co.us. Especially relevant for state family law issues.

State and federal statutes:

- Nolo, www.nolo.com/legal-research/state-law.html.
- The Legal Information Institute at Cornell University, http://topics.law. cornell.edu/wex/table_family.
- Justia, www.justia.com/family.
- www.usa.gov: Federal government site.

State court information and family law forms:

- www.courts.state.co.us: Do-it-yourself court forms and instructions, links to local court websites. Search by topic, such as divorce, adoption, or custody.
- National Center for State Courts, www.ncsc.org: Links to state courts (browse by state under "Information and Resources").

Local laws:

- www.statelocalgov.net: Links to websites of many cities and counties, where you can check local rules and ordinances, such as graffiti rules.
- www.municode.com: Municipal codes.

Marriage

Requirements: No blood test required. You must be of the age of consent, not be too closely related to your intended spouse, not be married to anyone else, and have sufficient mental capacity, meaning you understand what you are doing when you marry. You can marry immediately after your marriage license is issued, and your license is good for 30 days. For more details, check your county clerk's office.

Common law marriage: Yes. A couple must intend to be married, live together for a significant period of time, and hold themselves out as a married couple.

Community property: No.

Same-sex marriage: No.

Marriage-equivalent relationship: No. However, same-sex couples can enter into a "designated beneficiary" relationship that allows some, but not all, of the rights of marriage.

Divorce

Grounds for divorce: No-fault. However, fault may be considered by the court as a factor in dividing property or awarding alimony.

Residency requirement: At least one spouse must be a resident of Colorado for three months or 90 days before filing for divorce.

How property is divided: Equitable division.

State laws, forms, and resources:
- Colorado state court website, www.courts.state.co.us.
- Women's Law Initiative, www.womenslaw.org: State-by-state information on divorce, custody, and related topics.
- www.divorcenet.com, www.divorcesupport.com, www.divorceinfo.com, www.divorcecentral.com: Helpful divorce websites.

Divorce attorneys and mediators in your area:
- Nolo's Lawyer Directory, www.nolo.com: Divorce attorneys in your area.
- National Center for Lesbian Rights, www.nclrights.org, 800-528-6257: Attorneys experienced in same-sex divorces.
- www.mediate.com, 541-345-1629: Mediators in your area.

Child Custody

Child custody guidelines: Colorado courts begin with a presumption that it's best for a child to have frequent and continuing contact with both parents after a divorce. If possible, judges want to support joint custody arrangements.

State laws, forms, and resources: See list in "Divorce," above.

International custody disputes: International Parental Child Abduction Division in the Office of Children's Issues of the U.S. State Department, http://travel.state.gov/childabduction, 888-407-4747.

State surrogacy laws:
- Human Rights Campaign, www.hrc.org (search "surrogacy laws").
- National Infertility Association, www.resolve.org (click "Family Building Options," then "Surrogacy").

Child Support

Child support guidelines: Colorado requires all parents to support their children. The amount of child support depends primarily on each parent's income and other resources and how much time each parent spends with the children.

State laws, forms, and resources: See list in "Divorce," above.
- www.supportguidelines.com: Links to state and federal laws and agencies.

State child support enforcement agency:
- Child Support Enforcement Program, www.childsupport.state.co.us.
- National Child Support Enforcement Association, www.ncsea.org: Information about federal programs and links to state agencies.

Federal child support enforcement programs and laws: Federal Parent Locator Service, www.acf.hhs.gov/programs/cse/newhire: Links to child support enforcement programs like the passport denial program.

Child support calculators to determine state guidelines: www.alllaw.com/calculators/childsupport: Search your state.

Connecticut

Statewide Legal Resources

State website: www.ct.gov. Links and information for many state agencies and departments.
* www.ct.gov/dss. Especially relevant for state family law issues.

State and federal statutes:
* Nolo, www.nolo.com/legal-research/state-law.html.
* The Legal Information Institute at Cornell University, http://topics.law. cornell.edu/wex/table_family.
* Justia, www.justia.com/family.
* www.usa.gov: Federal government site.

State court information and family law forms:
* www.jud.ct.gov: Do-it-yourself court forms and instructions, links to local court websites. Search by topic, such as divorce, adoption, or custody.
* National Center for State Courts, www.ncsc.org: Links to state courts (browse by state under "Information and Resources").

Local laws:
* www.statelocalgov.net: Links to websites of many cities and counties, where you can check local rules and ordinances, such as graffiti rules.
* www.municode.com: Municipal codes.

Marriage

Requirements: No blood test required. You must be of the age of consent, not be too closely related to your intended spouse, not be married to anyone else, and have sufficient mental capacity, meaning you understand what you are doing when you marry. You can marry immediately after your marriage license is issued, and your license is good for 65 days. For more details, check your county clerk's office.

Common law marriage: No.

Community property: No.

Same-sex marriage: Yes.

Marriage-equivalent relationship: No.

Divorce

Grounds for divorce: Fault or no-fault grounds are allowed, or you can base your divorce on the fact that you've been separated from your spouse for at least two years.

Residency requirement: At least one spouse must be a resident of Connecticut for 12 months before a final judgment can be entered, unless (1) one party lived in Connecticut at the time of marriage and returned with intention to stay, or (2) the cause for dissolution arose after either party moved to Connecticut.

How property is divided: Equitable division.

State laws, forms, and resources:
- Connecticut state court website, www.jud.ct.gov.
- Women's Law Initiative, www.womenslaw.org: State-by-state information on divorce, custody, and related topics.
- www.divorcenet.com, www.divorcesupport.com, www.divorceinfo.com, www.divorcecentral.com: Helpful divorce websites.

Divorce attorneys and mediators in your area:
- Nolo's Lawyer Directory, www.nolo.com: Divorce attorneys in your area.
- National Center for Lesbian Rights, www.nclrights.org, 800-528-6257: Attorneys experienced in same-sex divorces.
- www.mediate.com, 541-345-1629: Mediators in your area.

Child Custody

Child custody guidelines: Connecticut courts begin with a presumption that it's best for a child to have frequent and continuing contact with both parents after a divorce. If possible, judges want to support joint custody arrangements.

State laws, forms, and resources: See list in "Divorce," above.

International custody disputes: International Parental Child Abduction Division in the Office of Children's Issues of the U.S. State Department, http://travel.state.gov/childabduction, 888-407-4747.

State surrogacy laws:

- Human Rights Campaign, www.hrc.org (search "surrogacy laws").
- National Infertility Association, www.resolve.org (click "Family Building Options," then "Surrogacy").

Child Support

Child support guidelines: Connecticut requires all parents to support their children. The amount of child support depends primarily on each parent's income and other resources and how much time each parent spends with the children.

State laws, forms, and resources: See list in "Divorce," above.

- www.supportguidelines.com: Links to state and federal laws and agencies.

State child support enforcement agency:

- Bureau of Child Support Enforcement, www.ct.gov/dss/cwp/view. asp?a=2353&q=305182, or Support Enforcement Services, www.jud. ct.gov/childsupport/default.htm.
- National Child Support Enforcement Association, www.ncsea.org: Information about federal programs and links to state agencies.

Federal child support enforcement programs and laws: Federal Parent Locator Service, www.acf.hhs.gov/programs/cse/newhire: Links to child support enforcement programs like the passport denial program.

Child support calculators to determine state guidelines: www.alllaw.com/ calculators/childsupport: Search your state.

Delaware

Statewide Legal Resources

State website:
- www.delaware.gov. Links and information for many state agencies and departments.
- www.kids.delaware.gov. Especially relevant for state family law issues.

State and federal statutes:
- Nolo, www.nolo.com/legal-research/state-law.html.
- The Legal Information Institute at Cornell University, http://topics.law.cornell.edu/wex/table_family.
- Justia, www.justia.com/family.
- www.usa.gov: Federal government site.

State court information and family law forms:
- www.courts.delaware.gov: Do-it-yourself court forms and instructions, links to local court websites. Search by topic, such as divorce, adoption, or custody.
- National Center for State Courts, www.ncsc.org: Links to state courts (browse by state under "Information and Resources").

Local laws:
- www.statelocalgov.net: Links to websites of many cities and counties, where you can check local rules and ordinances, such as graffiti rules.
- www.municode.com: Municipal codes.

Marriage

Requirements: No blood test required. You must be of the age of consent, not be too closely related to your intended spouse, not be married to anyone else, and have sufficient mental capacity, meaning you understand what you are doing when you marry. You can marry 24 hours after your marriage license is issued, and your license is good for 30 days. For more details, check your county clerk's office.

Common law marriage: No.

Community property: No.

Same-sex marriage: No.

Marriage-equivalent relationship: No. Delaware does not recognize domestic partnerships, civil unions, or reciprocal beneficiaries.

Divorce

Grounds for divorce: Fault or no-fault grounds are allowed, or you can base your divorce on the fact that you've been separated from your spouse for at least two years.

Residency requirement: At least one spouse must be a resident of Delaware for six months before filing for divorce.

How property is divided: Equitable division.

State laws, forms, and resources:
- Delaware state court website, www.courts.delaware.gov.
- Women's Law Initiative, www.womenslaw.org: State-by-state information on divorce, custody, and related topics.
- www.divorcenet.com, www.divorcesupport.com, www.divorceinfo.com, www.divorcecentral.com: Helpful divorce websites.

Divorce attorneys and mediators in your area:
- Nolo's Lawyer Directory, www.nolo.com: Divorce attorneys in your area.
- National Center for Lesbian Rights, www.nclrights.org, 800-528-6257: Attorneys experienced in same-sex divorces.
- www.mediate.com, 541-345-1629: Mediators in your area.

Child Custody

Child custody guidelines: Delaware courts begin with a presumption that it's best for a child to have frequent and continuing contact with both parents after a divorce. If possible, judges want to support joint custody arrangements.

State laws, forms, and resources: See list in "Divorce," above.

Delaware

International custody disputes: International Parental Child Abduction Division in the Office of Children's Issues of the U.S. State Department, http://travel.state.gov/childabduction, 888-407-4747.

State surrogacy laws:
- Human Rights Campaign, www.hrc.org (search "surrogacy laws").
- National Infertility Association, www.resolve.org (click "Family Building Options," then "Surrogacy").

Child Support

Child support guidelines: Delaware requires all parents to support their children. The amount of child support depends primarily on each parent's income and other resources and how much time each parent spends with the children.

State laws, forms, and resources: See list in "Divorce," above.
- www.supportguidelines.com: Links to state and federal laws and agencies.

State child support enforcement agency:
- Division of Child Support Enforcement, www.dhss.delaware.gov/dhss/dcse.
- National Child Support Enforcement Association, www.ncsea.org: Information about federal programs and links to state agencies.

Federal child support enforcement programs and laws: Federal Parent Locator Service, www.acf.hhs.gov/programs/cse/newhire: Links to child support enforcement programs like the passport denial program.

Child support calculators to determine state guidelines: www.alllaw.com/calculators/childsupport: Search your state.

District of Columbia

Statewide Legal Resources

State website:
- www.dc.gov. Links and information for many state agencies and departments.
- www.cfsa.dc.gov/DC/CFSA. Especially relevant for state family law issues.

State and federal statutes:
- Nolo, www.nolo.com/legal-research/state-law.html.
- The Legal Information Institute at Cornell University, http://topics.law.cornell.edu/wex/table_family.
- Justia, www.justia.com/family.
- www.usa.gov: Federal government site.

State court information and family law forms:
- www.dccourts.gov: Do-it-yourself court forms and instructions, links to local court websites. Search by topic, such as divorce, adoption, or custody.
- National Center for State Courts, www.ncsc.org: Links to state courts (browse by state under "Information and Resources").

Local laws:
- www.statelocalgov.net: Links to websites of many cities and counties, where you can check local rules and ordinances, such as graffiti rules.
- www.municode.com: Municipal codes.

Marriage

Requirements: A blood test is required. You must be of the age of consent, not be too closely related to your intended spouse, not be married to anyone else, and have sufficient mental capacity, meaning you understand what you are doing when you marry. You can marry immediately after your marriage license is issued. For more details, check your county clerk's office.

Common law marriage: Yes. A couple must intend to be married, live together for a significant period of time, and hold themselves out as a married couple.

Community property: No.

Same-sex marriage: Yes.

Marriage-equivalent relationship: Yes. Unmarried same-sex and opposite-sex couples can register as domestic partners with all of the rights and responsibilities of marriage.

Divorce

Grounds for divorce: Fault or no-fault grounds are allowed.

Residency requirement: At least one spouse must be a resident of District of Columbia for six months or 180 days before filing for divorce.

How property is divided: Equitable division.

State laws, forms, and resources:
- District of Columbia state court website, www.dccourts.gov.
- Women's Law Initiative, www.womenslaw.org: State-by-state information on divorce, custody, and related topics.
- www.divorcenet.com, www.divorcesupport.com, www.divorceinfo.com, www.divorcecentral.com: Helpful divorce websites.

Divorce attorneys and mediators in your area:
- Nolo's Lawyer Directory, www.nolo.com: Divorce attorneys in your area.
- National Center for Lesbian Rights, www.nclrights.org, 800-528-6257: Attorneys experienced in same-sex divorces.
- www.mediate.com, 541-345-1629: Mediators in your area.

Child Custody

Child custody guidelines: District of Columbia courts begin with a presumption that it's best for a child to have frequent and continuing contact with both parents after a divorce. If possible, judges want to support joint custody arrangements.

State laws, forms, and resources: See list in "Divorce," above.

International custody disputes: International Parental Child Abduction Division in the Office of Children's Issues of the U.S. State Department, http://travel.state.gov/childabduction, 888-407-4747.

State surrogacy laws:
* Human Rights Campaign, www.hrc.org (search "surrogacy laws").
* National Infertility Association, www.resolve.org (click "Family Building Options," then "Surrogacy").

Child Support

Child support guidelines: District of Columbia requires all parents to support their children. The amount of child support depends primarily on each parent's income and other resources and how much time each parent spends with the children.

State laws, forms, and resources: See list in "Divorce," above.
* www.supportguidelines.com: Links to state and federal laws and agencies.

State child support enforcement agency:
* Child Support Services Division, www.csed.dc.gov/csed.
* National Child Support Enforcement Association, www.ncsea.org: Information about federal programs and links to state agencies.

Federal child support enforcement programs and laws: Federal Parent Locator Service, www.acf.hhs.gov/programs/cse/newhire: Links to child support enforcement programs like the passport denial program.

Child support calculators to determine state guidelines: www.alllaw.com/calculators/childsupport: Search your state.

Florida

Statewide Legal Resources

State website:
- www.myflorida.gov. Links and information for many state agencies and departments.
- www.dcf.state.fl.us. Especially relevant for state family law issues.

State and federal statutes:
- Nolo, www.nolo.com/legal-research/state-law.html.
- The Legal Information Institute at Cornell University, http://topics.law.cornell.edu/wex/table_family.
- Justia, www.justia.com/family.
- www.usa.gov: Federal government site.

State court information and family law forms:
- www.flcourts.org: Do-it-yourself court forms and instructions, links to local court websites. Search by topic, such as divorce, adoption, or custody.
- National Center for State Courts, www.ncsc.org: Links to state courts (browse by state under "Information and Resources").

Local laws:
- www.statelocalgov.net: Links to websites of many cities and counties, where you can check local rules and ordinances, such as graffiti rules.
- www.municode.com: Municipal codes.

Marriage

Requirements: No blood test required. You must be of the age of consent, not be too closely related to your intended spouse, not be married to anyone else, and have sufficient mental capacity, meaning you understand what you are doing when you marry. You can marry immediately after your marriage license is issued, and your license is good for 60 days. For more details, check your county clerk's office.

Common law marriage: No.

Community property: No.

Same-sex marriage: No.

Marriage-equivalent relationship: No. Florida does not recognize domestic partnerships, civil unions, or reciprocal beneficiaries.

Divorce

Grounds for divorce: No-fault. However, fault may be considered by the court as a factor in dividing property or awarding alimony.

Residency requirement: At least one spouse must be a resident of Florida for six months or 180 days before filing for divorce.

How property is divided: Equitable division.

State laws, forms, and resources:
- Florida state court website, www.flcourts.org.
- Women's Law Initiative, www.womenslaw.org: State-by-state information on divorce, custody, and related topics.
- www.divorcenet.com, www.divorcesupport.com, www.divorceinfo.com, www.divorcecentral.com: Helpful divorce websites.

Divorce attorneys and mediators in your area:
- Nolo's Lawyer Directory, www.nolo.com: Divorce attorneys in your area.
- National Center for Lesbian Rights, www.nclrights.org, 800-528-6257: Attorneys experienced in same-sex divorces.
- www.mediate.com, 541-345-1629: Mediators in your area.

Child Custody

Child custody guidelines: Florida courts begin with a presumption that it's best for a child to have frequent and continuing contact with both parents after a divorce. If possible, judges want to support joint custody arrangements.

State laws, forms, and resources: See list in "Divorce," above.

International custody disputes: International Parental Child Abduction Division in the Office of Children's Issues of the U.S. State Department, http://travel.state.gov/childabduction, 888-407-4747.

State surrogacy laws:
- Human Rights Campaign, www.hrc.org (search "surrogacy laws").
- National Infertility Association, www.resolve.org (click "Family Building Options," then "Surrogacy").

Child Support

Child support guidelines: Florida requires all parents to support their children. The amount of child support depends primarily on each parent's income and other resources and how much time each parent spends with the children.

State laws, forms, and resources: See list in "Divorce," above.
- www.supportguidelines.com: Links to state and federal laws and agencies.

State child support enforcement agency:
- Department of Revenue Child Support Enforcement, http://dor. myflorida.com/dor/childsupport.
- National Child Support Enforcement Association, www.ncsea.org: Information about federal programs and links to state agencies.

Federal child support enforcement programs and laws: Federal Parent Locator Service, www.acf.hhs.gov/programs/cse/newhire: Links to child support enforcement programs like the passport denial program.

Child support calculators to determine state guidelines: www.alllaw.com/ calculators/childsupport: Search your state.

Georgia

Statewide Legal Resources

State website:
- www.georgia.gov. Links and information for many state agencies and departments.
- www.dfcs.dhs.georgia.gov. Especially relevant for state family law issues.

State and federal statutes:
- Nolo, www.nolo.com/legal-research/state-law.html.
- The Legal Information Institute at Cornell University, http://topics.law. cornell.edu/wex/table_family.
- Justia, www.justia.com/family.
- www.usa.gov: Federal government site.

State court information and family law forms:
- www.georgiacourts.gov: Do-it-yourself court forms and instructions, links to local court websites. Search by topic, such as divorce, adoption, or custody.
- National Center for State Courts, www.ncsc.org: Links to state courts (browse by state under "Information and Resources").

Local laws:
- www.statelocalgov.net: Links to websites of many cities and counties, where you can check local rules and ordinances, such as graffiti rules.
- www.municode.com: Municipal codes.

Marriage

Requirements: No blood test required. You must be of the age of consent, not be too closely related to your intended spouse, not be married to anyone else, and have sufficient mental capacity, meaning you understand what you are doing when you marry. You can marry immediately after your marriage license is issued. For more details, check your county clerk's office.

Common law marriage: Yes. Common law marriages created before January 1, 1997 are recognized for couples who intended to be married, lived together for a significant period of time, and held themselves out as married couples.

Community property: No.

Same-sex marriage: No.

Marriage-equivalent relationship: No. Georgia does not recognize domestic partnerships, civil unions, or reciprocal beneficiaries.

Divorce

Grounds for divorce: Fault or no-fault grounds are allowed, or you can base your divorce on the fact that you've been separated from your spouse for at least two years.

Residency requirement: At least one spouse must be a resident of Georgia for six months before filing for divorce.

How property is divided: Equitable division.

State laws, forms, and resources:
- Georgia state court website, www.georgiacourts.gov.
- Women's Law Initiative, www.womenslaw.org: State-by-state information on divorce, custody, and related topics.
- www.divorcenet.com, www.divorcesupport.com, www.divorceinfo.com, www.divorcecentral.com: Helpful divorce websites.

Divorce attorneys and mediators in your area:
- Nolo's Lawyer Directory, www.nolo.com: Divorce attorneys in your area.
- National Center for Lesbian Rights, www.nclrights.org, 800-528-6257: Attorneys experienced in same-sex divorces.
- www.mediate.com, 541-345-1629: Mediators in your area.

Child Custody

Child custody guidelines: Georgia courts begin with a presumption that it's best for a child to have frequent and continuing contact with both parents after a divorce. If possible, judges want to support joint custody arrangements.

State laws, forms, and resources: See list in "Divorce," above.

International custody disputes: International Parental Child Abduction Division in the Office of Children's Issues of the U.S. State Department, http://travel.state.gov/childabduction, 888-407-4747.

State surrogacy laws:

- Human Rights Campaign, www.hrc.org (search "surrogacy laws").
- National Infertility Association, www.resolve.org (click "Family Building Options," then "Surrogacy").

Child Support

Child support guidelines: Georgia requires all parents to support their children. The amount of child support depends primarily on each parent's income and other resources and how much time each parent spends with the children.

State laws, forms, and resources: See list in "Divorce," above.

- www.supportguidelines.com: Links to state and federal laws and agencies.

State child support enforcement agency:

- Department of Human Services Division of Child Support Services, www.ocse.dhr.georgia.gov.
- National Child Support Enforcement Association, www.ncsea.org: Information about federal programs and links to state agencies.

Federal child support enforcement programs and laws: Federal Parent Locator Service, www.acf.hhs.gov/programs/cse/newhire: Links to child support enforcement programs like the passport denial program.

Child support calculators to determine state guidelines: www.alllaw.com/calculators/childsupport: Search your state.

Georgia

Hawaii

Statewide Legal Resources

State website:
- www.ehawaii.gov. Links and information for many state agencies and departments.
- www.hawaii.gov/dhs. Especially relevant for state family law issues.

State and federal statutes:
- Nolo, www.nolo.com/legal-research/state-law.html.
- The Legal Information Institute at Cornell University, http://topics.law.cornell.edu/wex/table_family.
- Justia, www.justia.com/family.
- www.usa.gov: Federal government site.

State court information and family law forms:
- www.courts.state.hi.us: Do-it-yourself court forms and instructions, links to local court websites. Search by topic, such as divorce, adoption, or custody.
- National Center for State Courts, www.ncsc.org: Links to state courts (browse by state under "Information and Resources").

Local laws:
- www.statelocalgov.net: Links to websites of many cities and counties, where you can check local rules and ordinances, such as graffiti rules.
- www.municode.com: Municipal codes.

Marriage

Requirements: No blood test required. You must be of the age of consent, not be too closely related to your intended spouse, not be married to anyone else, and have sufficient mental capacity, meaning you understand what you are doing when you marry. You can marry immediately after your marriage license is issued, and your license is good for 30 days. For more details, check your county clerk's office.

Common law marriage: No.

Community property: No.

Same-sex marriage: No.

Marriage-equivalent relationship: No. However, same-sex and opposite-sex couples may enter into reciprocal beneficiary relationships that include some, but not all, of the rights of marriage.

Divorce

Grounds for divorce: No-fault. However, fault may be considered by the court as a factor in dividing property or awarding alimony.

Residency requirement: At least one spouse must be a resident of Hawaii for six months before filing for divorce.

How property is divided: Equitable division.

State laws, forms, and resources:
- Hawaii state court website, www.courts.state.hi.us.
- Women's Law Initiative, www.womenslaw.org: State-by-state information on divorce, custody, and related topics.
- www.divorcenet.com, www.divorcesupport.com, www.divorceinfo.com, www.divorcecentral.com: Helpful divorce websites.

Divorce attorneys and mediators in your area:
- Nolo's Lawyer Directory, www.nolo.com: Divorce attorneys in your area.
- National Center for Lesbian Rights, www.nclrights.org, 800-528-6257: Attorneys experienced in same-sex divorces.
- www.mediate.com, 541-345-1629: Mediators in your area.

Child Custody

Child custody guidelines: Hawaii courts begin with a presumption that it's best for a child to have frequent and continuing contact with both parents after a divorce. If possible, judges want to support joint custody arrangements.

State laws, forms, and resources: See list in "Divorce," above.

International custody disputes: International Parental Child Abduction Division in the Office of Children's Issues of the U.S. State Department, http://travel.state.gov/childabduction, 888-407-4747.

State surrogacy laws:
- Human Rights Campaign, www.hrc.org (search "surrogacy laws").
- National Infertility Association, www.resolve.org (click "Family Building Options," then "Surrogacy").

Child Support

Child support guidelines: Hawaii requires all parents to support their children. The amount of child support depends primarily on each parent's income and other resources and how much time each parent spends with the children.

State laws, forms, and resources: See list in "Divorce," above.
- www.supportguidelines.com: Links to state and federal laws and agencies.

State child support enforcement agency:
- Child Support Enforcement Agency, www.hawaii.gov/ag/csea.
- National Child Support Enforcement Association, www.ncsea.org: Information about federal programs and links to state agencies.

Federal child support enforcement programs and laws: Federal Parent Locator Service, www.acf.hhs.gov/programs/cse/newhire: Links to child support enforcement programs like the passport denial program.

Child support calculators to determine state guidelines: www.alllaw.com/calculators/childsupport: Search your state.

Idaho

Statewide Legal Resources

State website:

- www.accessidaho.org. Links and information for many state agencies and departments.
- www.healthandwelfare.idaho.gov. Especially relevant for state family law issues.

State and federal statutes:

- Nolo, www.nolo.com/legal-research/state-law.html.
- The Legal Information Institute at Cornell University, http://topics.law.cornell.edu/wex/table_family.
- Justia, www.justia.com/family.
- www.usa.gov: Federal government site.

State court information and family law forms:

- www.isc.idaho.gov: Do-it-yourself court forms and instructions, links to local court websites. Search by topic, such as divorce, adoption, or custody.
- National Center for State Courts, www.ncsc.org: Links to state courts (browse by state under "Information and Resources").

Local laws:

- www.statelocalgov.net: Links to websites of many cities and counties, where you can check local rules and ordinances, such as graffiti rules.
- www.municode.com: Municipal codes.

Marriage

Requirements: No blood test required. You must be of the age of consent, not be too closely related to your intended spouse, not be married to anyone else, and have sufficient mental capacity, meaning you understand what you are doing when you marry. You can marry immediately after your marriage license is issued. For more details, check your county clerk's office.

Common law marriage: Yes. Common law marriages created before January 1, 1996 are recognized for couples who intended to be married, lived together for a significant period of time, and held themselves out as a married couple.

Community property: Yes.

Same-sex marriage: No.

Marriage-equivalent relationship: No. Idaho does not recognize domestic partnerships, civil unions, or reciprocal beneficiaries.

Divorce

Grounds for divorce: Fault or no-fault grounds are allowed, or you can base your divorce on the fact that you've been separated from your spouse for at least two years.

Residency requirement: At least one spouse must be a resident of Idaho for six weeks before filing for divorce.

How property is divided: Community property.

State laws, forms, and resources:
- Idaho state court website, www.isc.idaho.gov.
- Women's Law Initiative, www.womenslaw.org: State-by-state information on divorce, custody, and related topics.
- www.divorcenet.com, www.divorcesupport.com, www.divorceinfo.com, www.divorcecentral.com: Helpful divorce websites.

Divorce attorneys and mediators in your area:
- Nolo's Lawyer Directory, www.nolo.com: Divorce attorneys in your area.
- National Center for Lesbian Rights, www.nclrights.org, 800-528-6257: Attorneys experienced in same-sex divorces.
- www.mediate.com, 541-345-1629: Mediators in your area.

Child Custody

Child custody guidelines: Idaho courts begin with a presumption that it's best for a child to have frequent and continuing contact with both parents after a divorce. If possible, judges want to support joint custody arrangements.

State laws, forms, and resources: See list in "Divorce," above.

International custody disputes: International Parental Child Abduction Division in the Office of Children's Issues of the U.S. State Department, http://travel.state.gov/childabduction, 888-407-4747.

State surrogacy laws:

- Human Rights Campaign, www.hrc.org (search "surrogacy laws").
- National Infertility Association, www.resolve.org (click "Family Building Options," then "Surrogacy").

Child Support

Child support guidelines: Idaho requires all parents to support their children. The amount of child support depends primarily on each parent's income and other resources and how much time each parent spends with the children.

State laws, forms, and resources: See list in "Divorce," above.

- www.supportguidelines.com: Links to state and federal laws and agencies.

State child support enforcement agency:

- Child Support Services, www.healthandwelfare.idaho.gov/Children/ ChildSupport/tabid/76/Default.aspx.
- National Child Support Enforcement Association, www.ncsea.org: Information about federal programs and links to state agencies.

Federal child support enforcement programs and laws: Federal Parent Locator Service, www.acf.hhs.gov/programs/cse/newhire: Links to child support enforcement programs like the passport denial program.

Child support calculators to determine state guidelines: www.alllaw.com/ calculators/childsupport: Search your state.

Illinois

Statewide Legal Resources

State website:
- www.illinois.gov. Links and information for many state agencies and departments.
- www.state.il.us/dcfs. Especially relevant for state family law issues.

State and federal statutes:
- Nolo, www.nolo.com/legal-research/state-law.html.
- The Legal Information Institute at Cornell University, http://topics.law. cornell.edu/wex/table_family.
- Justia, www.justia.com/family.
- www.usa.gov: Federal government site.

State court information and family law forms:
- www.state.il.us/court: Do-it-yourself court forms and instructions, links to local court websites. Search by topic, such as divorce, adoption, or custody.
- National Center for State Courts, www.ncsc.org: Links to state courts (browse by state under "Information and Resources").

Local laws:
- www.statelocalgov.net: Links to websites of many cities and counties, where you can check local rules and ordinances, such as graffiti rules.
- www.municode.com: Municipal codes.

Marriage

Requirements: No blood test required. You must be of the age of consent, not be too closely related to your intended spouse, not be married to anyone else, and have sufficient mental capacity, meaning you understand what you are doing when you marry. You can marry one day after your marriage license is issued, and your license is good for 60 days. For more details, check your county clerk's office.

Common law marriage: No.

Community property: No.

Same-sex marriage: No.

Marriage-equivalent relationship: Yes. As of July 1, 2011, both same-sex and opposite-sex couples in Illinois can enter into civil unions with all of the rights and responsibilities of marriage under state law.

Divorce

Grounds for divorce: Fault or no-fault grounds are allowed.

Residency requirement: At least one spouse must be a resident of Illinois for three months or 90 days before filing for divorce.

How property is divided: Equitable division.

State laws, forms, and resources:
- Illinois state court website, www.state.il.us/court.
- Women's Law Initiative, www.womenslaw.org: State-by-state information on divorce, custody, and related topics.
- www.divorcenet.com, www.divorcesupport.com, www.divorceinfo.com, www.divorcecentral.com: Helpful divorce websites.

Divorce attorneys and mediators in your area:
- Nolo's Lawyer Directory, www.nolo.com: Divorce attorneys in your area.
- National Center for Lesbian Rights, www.nclrights.org, 800-528-6257: Attorneys experienced in same-sex divorces.
- www.mediate.com, 541-345-1629: Mediators in your area.

Child Custody

Child custody guidelines: Illinois courts begin with a presumption that it's best for a child to have frequent and continuing contact with both parents after a divorce. If possible, judges want to support joint custody arrangements.

State laws, forms, and resources: See list in "Divorce," above.

International custody disputes: International Parental Child Abduction Division in the Office of Children's Issues of the U.S. State Department, http://travel.state.gov/childabduction, 888-407-4747.

State surrogacy laws:
- Human Rights Campaign, www.hrc.org (search "surrogacy laws").
- National Infertility Association, www.resolve.org (click "Family Building Options," then "Surrogacy").

Child Support

Child support guidelines: Illinois requires all parents to support their children. The amount of child support depends primarily on each parent's income and other resources and how much time each parent spends with the children.

State laws, forms, and resources: See list in "Divorce," above.
- www.supportguidelines.com: Links to state and federal laws and agencies.

State child support enforcement agency:
- Child Support Services, www.childsupportillinois.com.
- National Child Support Enforcement Association, www.ncsea.org: Information about federal programs and links to state agencies.

Federal child support enforcement programs and laws: Federal Parent Locator Service, www.acf.hhs.gov/programs/cse/newhire: Links to child support enforcement programs like the passport denial program.

Child support calculators to determine state guidelines: www.alllaw.com/calculators/childsupport: Search your state.

Indiana

Statewide Legal Resources

State website:
- www.in.gov. Links and information for many state agencies and departments.
- www.in.gov/fssa. Especially relevant for state family law issues.

State and federal statutes:
- Nolo, www.nolo.com/legal-research/state-law.html.
- The Legal Information Institute at Cornell University, http://topics.law.cornell.edu/wex/table_family.
- Justia, www.justia.com/family.
- www.usa.gov: Federal government site.

State court information and family law forms:
- www.in.gov/judiciary: Do-it-yourself court forms and instructions, links to local court websites. Search by topic, such as divorce, adoption, or custody.
- National Center for State Courts, www.ncsc.org: Links to state courts (browse by state under "Information and Resources").

Local laws:
- www.statelocalgov.net: Links to websites of many cities and counties, where you can check local rules and ordinances, such as graffiti rules.
- www.municode.com: Municipal codes.

Marriage

Requirements: No blood test required. You must be of the age of consent, not be too closely related to your intended spouse, not be married to anyone else, and have sufficient mental capacity, meaning you understand what you are doing when you marry. You can marry immediately after your marriage license is issued, and your license is good for 60 days. For more details, check your county clerk's office.

Common law marriage: No.

Community property: No.

Same-sex marriage: No.

Marriage-equivalent relationship: No. Indiana does not recognize domestic partnerships, civil unions, or reciprocal beneficiaries.

Divorce

Grounds for divorce: Fault or no-fault grounds are allowed, or you can base your divorce on the fact that you've been separated from your spouse for at least two years.

Residency requirement: At least one spouse must be a resident of Indiana for six months before filing for divorce.

How property is divided: Equitable division.

State laws, forms, and resources:
- Indiana state court website, www.in.gov/judiciary.
- Women's Law Initiative, www.womenslaw.org: State-by-state information on divorce, custody, and related topics.
- www.divorcenet.com, www.divorcesupport.com, www.divorceinfo.com, www.divorcecentral.com: Helpful divorce websites.

Divorce attorneys and mediators in your area:
- Nolo's Lawyer Directory, www.nolo.com: Divorce attorneys in your area.
- National Center for Lesbian Rights, www.nclrights.org, 800-528-6257: Attorneys experienced in same-sex divorces.
- www.mediate.com, 541-345-1629: Mediators in your area.

Child Custody

Child custody guidelines: Indiana courts begin with a presumption that it's best for a child to have frequent and continuing contact with both parents after a divorce. If possible, judges want to support joint custody arrangements.

State laws, forms, and resources: See list in "Divorce," above.

International custody disputes: International Parental Child Abduction Division in the Office of Children's Issues of the U.S. State Department, http://travel.state.gov/childabduction, 888-407-4747.

State surrogacy laws:

- Human Rights Campaign, www.hrc.org (search "surrogacy laws").
- National Infertility Association, www.resolve.org (click "Family Building Options," then "Surrogacy").

Child Support

Child support guidelines: Indiana requires all parents to support their children. The amount of child support depends primarily on each parent's income and other resources and how much time each parent spends with the children.

State laws, forms, and resources: See list in "Divorce," above.

- www.supportguidelines.com: Links to state and federal laws and agencies.

State child support enforcement agency:

- Child Support Bureau, www.in.gov/dcs/support.htm.
- National Child Support Enforcement Association, www.ncsea.org: Information about federal programs and links to state agencies.

Federal child support enforcement programs and laws: Federal Parent Locator Service, www.acf.hhs.gov/programs/cse/newhire: Links to child support enforcement programs like the passport denial program.

Child support calculators to determine state guidelines: www.alllaw.com/calculators/childsupport: Search your state.

Iowa

Statewide Legal Resources

State website:
- www.iowa.gov. Links and information for many state agencies and departments.
- www.dhs.state.ia.us. Especially relevant for state family law issues.

State and federal statutes:
- Nolo, www.nolo.com/legal-research/state-law.html.
- The Legal Information Institute at Cornell University, http://topics.law.cornell.edu/wex/table_family.
- Justia, www.justia.com/family.
- www.usa.gov: Federal government site.

State court information and family law forms:
- www.iowacourts.gov: Do-it-yourself court forms and instructions, links to local court websites. Search by topic, such as divorce, adoption, or custody.
- National Center for State Courts, www.ncsc.org: Links to state courts (browse by state under "Information and Resources").

Local laws:
- www.statelocalgov.net: Links to websites of many cities and counties, where you can check local rules and ordinances, such as graffiti rules.
- www.municode.com: Municipal codes.

Marriage

Requirements: No blood test required. You must be of the age of consent, not be too closely related to your intended spouse, not be married to anyone else, and have sufficient mental capacity, meaning you understand what you are doing when you marry. You can marry three days after your marriage license is issued, and your license is good for six months. For more details, check your county clerk's office.

Iowa

Common law marriage: Yes. A couple must intend to be married, live together for a significant period of time, and hold themselves out as a married couple.

Community property: No.

Same-sex marriage: Yes.

Marriage-equivalent relationship: No. Same-sex marriages, domestic partnerships, and civil unions from other states are recognized in Iowa.

Divorce

Grounds for divorce: No-fault. However, fault may be considered by the court as a factor in dividing property or awarding alimony.

Residency requirement: At least one spouse must be a resident of Iowa for 12 months or one year before filing for divorce.

How property is divided: Equitable division.

State laws, forms, and resources:
- Iowa state court website, www.iowacourts.gov.
- Women's Law Initiative, www.womenslaw.org: State-by-state information on divorce, custody, and related topics.
- www.divorcenet.com, www.divorcesupport.com, www.divorceinfo.com, www.divorcecentral.com: Helpful divorce websites.

Divorce attorneys and mediators in your area:
- Nolo's Lawyer Directory, www.nolo.com: Divorce attorneys in your area.
- National Center for Lesbian Rights, www.nclrights.org, 800-528-6257: Attorneys experienced in same-sex divorces.
- www.mediate.com, 541-345-1629: Mediators in your area.

Child Custody

Child custody guidelines: Iowa courts begin with a presumption that it's best for a child to have frequent and continuing contact with both parents after a divorce. If possible, judges want to support joint custody arrangements.

State laws, forms, and resources: See list in "Divorce," above.

International custody disputes: International Parental Child Abduction Division in the Office of Children's Issues of the U.S. State Department, http://travel.state.gov/childabduction, 888-407-4747.

State surrogacy laws:
- Human Rights Campaign, www.hrc.org (search "surrogacy laws").
- National Infertility Association, www.resolve.org (click "Family Building Options," then "Surrogacy").

Child Support

Child support guidelines: Iowa requires all parents to support their children. The amount of child support depends primarily on each parent's income and other resources and how much time each parent spends with the children.

State laws, forms, and resources: See list in "Divorce," above.
- www.supportguidelines.com: Links to state and federal laws and agencies.

State child support enforcement agency:
- Child Support Enforcement, https://secureapp.dhs.state.ia.us/childsupport/welcome.asp.
- National Child Support Enforcement Association, www.ncsea.org: Information about federal programs and links to state agencies.

Federal child support enforcement programs and laws: Federal Parent Locator Service, www.acf.hhs.gov/programs/cse/newhire: Links to child support enforcement programs like the passport denial program.

Child support calculators to determine state guidelines: www.alllaw.com/calculators/childsupport: Search your state.

Kansas

Statewide Legal Resources

State website:
- www.kansas.gov. Links and information for many state agencies and departments.
- www.srs.ks.gov. Especially relevant for state family law issues.

State and federal statutes:
- Nolo, www.nolo.com/legal-research/state-law.html.
- The Legal Information Institute at Cornell University, http://topics.law.cornell.edu/wex/table_family.
- Justia, www.justia.com/family.
- www.usa.gov: Federal government site.

State court information and family law forms:
- www.kscourts.org: Do-it-yourself court forms and instructions, links to local court websites. Search by topic, such as divorce, adoption, or custody.
- National Center for State Courts, www.ncsc.org: Links to state courts (browse by state under "Information and Resources").

Local laws:
- www.statelocalgov.net: Links to websites of many cities and counties, where you can check local rules and ordinances, such as graffiti rules.
- www.municode.com: Municipal codes.

Marriage

Requirements: No blood test required. You must be of the age of consent, not be too closely related to your intended spouse, not be married to anyone else, and have sufficient mental capacity, meaning you understand what you are doing when you marry. You can marry immediately after your marriage license is issued, and your license is good for six months. For more details, check your county clerk's office.

Common law marriage: Yes. A couple must intend to be married, live together for a significant period of time, and hold themselves out as a married couple.

Community property: No.

Same-sex marriage: No.

Marriage-equivalent relationship: No. Kansas does not recognize same-sex marriages, domestic partnerships, or civil unions from other jurisdictions.

Divorce

Grounds for divorce: Fault or no-fault grounds are allowed, or you can base your divorce on the fact that you've been separated from your spouse for at least two years.

Residency requirement: At least one spouse must be a resident of Kansas for 60 days before filing for divorce.

How property is divided: Equitable division.

State laws, forms, and resources:
- Kansas state court website, www.kscourts.org.
- Women's Law Initiative, www.womenslaw.org: State-by-state information on divorce, custody, and related topics.
- www.divorcenet.com, www.divorcesupport.com, www.divorceinfo.com, www.divorcecentral.com: Helpful divorce websites.

Divorce attorneys and mediators in your area:
- Nolo's Lawyer Directory, www.nolo.com: Divorce attorneys in your area.
- National Center for Lesbian Rights, www.nclrights.org, 800-528-6257: Attorneys experienced in same-sex divorces.
- www.mediate.com, 541-345-1629: Mediators in your area.

Child Custody

Child custody guidelines: Kansas courts begin with a presumption that it's best for a child to have frequent and continuing contact with both parents after a divorce. If possible, judges want to support joint custody arrangements.

State laws, forms, and resources: See list in "Divorce," above.

International custody disputes: International Parental Child Abduction Division in the Office of Children's Issues of the U.S. State Department, http://travel.state.gov/childabduction, 888-407-4747.

State surrogacy laws:

- Human Rights Campaign, www.hrc.org (search "surrogacy laws").
- National Infertility Association, www.resolve.org (click "Family Building Options," then "Surrogacy").

Child Support

Child support guidelines: Kansas requires all parents to support their children. The amount of child support depends primarily on each parent's income and other resources and how much time each parent spends with the children.

State laws, forms, and resources: See list in "Divorce," above.

- www.supportguidelines.com: Links to state and federal laws and agencies.

State child support enforcement agency:

- Child Support Enforcement, www.srs.ks.gov/agency/cse.
- National Child Support Enforcement Association, www.ncsea.org: Information about federal programs and links to state agencies.

Federal child support enforcement programs and laws: Federal Parent Locator Service, www.acf.hhs.gov/programs/cse/newhire: Links to child support enforcement programs like the passport denial program.

Child support calculators to determine state guidelines: www.alllaw.com/calculators/childsupport: Search your state.

Kentucky

Statewide Legal Resources

State website:
- www.kentucky.gov. Links and information for many state agencies and departments.
- www.chfs.ky.gov. Especially relevant for state family law issues.

State and federal statutes:
- Nolo, www.nolo.com/legal-research/state-law.html.
- The Legal Information Institute at Cornell University, http://topics.law.cornell.edu/wex/table_family.
- Justia, www.justia.com/family.
- www.usa.gov: Federal government site.

State court information and family law forms:
- www.courts.ky.gov: Do-it-yourself court forms and instructions, links to local court websites. Search by topic, such as divorce, adoption, or custody.
- National Center for State Courts, www.ncsc.org: Links to state courts (browse by state under "Information and Resources").

Local laws:
- www.statelocalgov.net: Links to websites of many cities and counties, where you can check local rules and ordinances, such as graffiti rules.
- www.municode.com: Municipal codes.

Marriage

Requirements: No blood test required. You must be of the age of consent, not be too closely related to your intended spouse, not be married to anyone else, and have sufficient mental capacity, meaning you understand what you are doing when you marry. You can marry immediately after your marriage license is issued, and your license is good for 30 days. For more details, check your county clerk's office.

Common law marriage: No.

Community property: No.

Same-sex marriage: No.

Marriage-equivalent relationship: No. Kentucky does not recognize same-sex marriages, domestic partnerships, or civil unions from other jurisdictions.

Divorce

Grounds for divorce: No-fault. However, fault may be considered by the court as a factor in dividing property or awarding alimony.

Residency requirement: At least one spouse must be a resident of Kentucky for six months or 180 days before filing for divorce.

How property is divided: Equitable division.

State laws, forms, and resources:
- Kentucky state court website, www.courts.ky.gov.
- Women's Law Initiative, www.womenslaw.org: State-by-state information on divorce, custody, and related topics.
- www.divorcenet.com, www.divorcesupport.com, www.divorceinfo.com, www.divorcecentral.com: Helpful divorce websites.

Divorce attorneys and mediators in your area:
- Nolo's Lawyer Directory, www.nolo.com: Divorce attorneys in your area.
- National Center for Lesbian Rights, www.nclrights.org, 800-528-6257: Attorneys experienced in same-sex divorces.
- www.mediate.com, 541-345-1629: Mediators in your area.

Child Custody

Child custody guidelines: Kentucky courts begin with a presumption that it's best for a child to have frequent and continuing contact with both parents after a divorce. If possible, judges want to support joint custody arrangements.

State laws, forms, and resources: See list in "Divorce," above.

International custody disputes: International Parental Child Abduction Division in the Office of Children's Issues of the U.S. State Department, http://travel.state.gov/childabduction, 888-407-4747.

State surrogacy laws:
- Human Rights Campaign, www.hrc.org (search "surrogacy laws").
- National Infertility Association, www.resolve.org (click "Family Building Options," then "Surrogacy").

Child Support

Child support guidelines: Kentucky requires all parents to support their children. The amount of child support depends primarily on each parent's income and other resources and how much time each parent spends with the children.

State laws, forms, and resources: See list in "Divorce," above.
- www.supportguidelines.com: Links to state and federal laws and agencies.

State child support enforcement agency:
- Child Support Enforcement, www.chfs.ky.gov/dis/cse.htm.
- National Child Support Enforcement Association, www.ncsea.org: Information about federal programs and links to state agencies.

Federal child support enforcement programs and laws: Federal Parent Locator Service, www.acf.hhs.gov/programs/cse/newhire: Links to child support enforcement programs like the passport denial program.

Child support calculators to determine state guidelines: www.alllaw.com/calculators/childsupport: Search your state.

Louisiana

Statewide Legal Resources

State website:
- www.louisiana.gov. Links and information for many state agencies and departments.
- www.dcfs.louisiana.gov. Especially relevant for state family law issues.

State and federal statutes:
- Nolo, www.nolo.com/legal-research/state-law.html.
- The Legal Information Institute at Cornell University, http://topics.law. cornell.edu/wex/table_family.
- Justia, www.justia.com/family.
- www.usa.gov: Federal government site.

State court information and family law forms:
- www.louisiana.gov/Government/Judicial_Branch: Do-it-yourself court forms and instructions, links to local court websites. Search by topic, such as divorce, adoption, or custody.
- National Center for State Courts, www.ncsc.org: Links to state courts (browse by state under "Information and Resources").

Local laws:
- www.statelocalgov.net: Links to websites of many cities and counties, where you can check local rules and ordinances, such as graffiti rules.
- www.municode.com: Municipal codes.

Marriage

Requirements: No blood test required. You must be of the age of consent, not be too closely related to your intended spouse, not be married to anyone else, and have sufficient mental capacity, meaning you understand what you are doing when you marry. You can marry three days after your marriage license is issued, and your license is good for 30 days. For more details, check your county clerk's office.

Common law marriage: No.

Community property: Yes.

Same-sex marriage: No.

Marriage-equivalent relationship: No. Louisiana does not recognize same-sex marriages, domestic partnerships, or civil unions from other jurisdictions.

Divorce

Grounds for divorce: Fault or no-fault grounds are allowed.

Residency requirement: At least one spouse must be a resident of Louisiana for six months or 180 days before filing for divorce.

How property is divided: Community property.

State laws, forms, and resources:

- Louisiana state court website, www.louisiana.gov/Government/Judicial_ Branch.
- Women's Law Initiative, www.womenslaw.org: State-by-state information on divorce, custody, and related topics.
- www.divorcenet.com, www.divorcesupport.com, www.divorceinfo.com, www.divorcecentral.com: Helpful divorce websites.

Divorce attorneys and mediators in your area:

- Nolo's Lawyer Directory, www.nolo.com: Divorce attorneys in your area.
- National Center for Lesbian Rights, www.nclrights.org, 800-528-6257: Attorneys experienced in same-sex divorces.
- www.mediate.com, 541-345-1629: Mediators in your area.

Child Custody

Child custody guidelines: Louisiana courts begin with a presumption that it's best for a child to have frequent and continuing contact with both parents after a divorce. If possible, judges want to support joint custody arrangements.

State laws, forms, and resources: See list in "Divorce," above.

International custody disputes: International Parental Child Abduction Division in the Office of Children's Issues of the U.S. State Department, http://travel.state.gov/childabduction, 888-407-4747.

State surrogacy laws:

- Human Rights Campaign, www.hrc.org (search "surrogacy laws").
- National Infertility Association, www.resolve.org (click "Family Building Options," then "Surrogacy").

Child Support

Child support guidelines: Louisiana requires all parents to support their children. The amount of child support depends primarily on each parent's income and other resources and how much time each parent spends with the children.

State laws, forms, and resources: See list in "Divorce," above.

- www.supportguidelines.com: Links to state and federal laws and agencies.

State child support enforcement agency:

- Child Support Enforcement, www.dss.louisiana.gov.
- National Child Support Enforcement Association, www.ncsea.org: Information about federal programs and links to state agencies.

Federal child support enforcement programs and laws: Federal Parent Locator Service, www.acf.hhs.gov/programs/cse/newhire: Links to child support enforcement programs like the passport denial program.

Child support calculators to determine state guidelines: www.alllaw.com/calculators/childsupport: Search your state.

Maine

Statewide Legal Resources

State website:
- www.maine.gov. Links and information for many state agencies and departments.
- www.maine.gov/dhhs. Especially relevant for state family law issues.

State and federal statutes:
- Nolo, www.nolo.com/legal-research/state-law.html.
- The Legal Information Institute at Cornell University, http://topics.law. cornell.edu/wex/table_family.
- Justia, www.justia.com/family.
- www.usa.gov: Federal government site.

State court information and family law forms:
- www.courts.state.me.us: Do-it-yourself court forms and instructions, links to local court websites. Search by topic, such as divorce, adoption, or custody.
- National Center for State Courts, www.ncsc.org: Links to state courts (browse by state under "Information and Resources").

Local laws:
- www.statelocalgov.net: Links to websites of many cities and counties, where you can check local rules and ordinances, such as graffiti rules.
- www.municode.com: Municipal codes.

Marriage

Requirements: No blood test required. You must be of the age of consent, not be too closely related to your intended spouse, not be married to anyone else, and have sufficient mental capacity, meaning you understand what you are doing when you marry. You can marry immediately after your marriage license is issued, and your license is good for 90 days. For more details, check your county clerk's office.

Common law marriage: No.

Maine

Community property: No.

Same-sex marriage: No.

Marriage-equivalent relationship: No. However, same-sex partners in Maine can register as domestic partners and acquire some, but not nearly all, of the rights of marriage.

Divorce

Grounds for divorce: Fault or no-fault grounds are allowed, or you can base your divorce on the fact that you've been separated from your spouse for at least two years.

Residency requirement: At least one spouse must be a resident of Maine for six months before filing for divorce.

How property is divided: Equitable division.

State laws, forms, and resources:
- Maine state court website, www.courts.state.me.us.
- Women's Law Initiative, www.womenslaw.org: State-by-state information on divorce, custody, and related topics.
- www.divorcenet.com, www.divorcesupport.com, www.divorceinfo.com, www.divorcecentral.com: Helpful divorce websites.

Divorce attorneys and mediators in your area:
- Nolo's Lawyer Directory, www.nolo.com: Divorce attorneys in your area.
- National Center for Lesbian Rights, www.nclrights.org, 800-528-6257: Attorneys experienced in same-sex divorces.
- www.mediate.com, 541-345-1629: Mediators in your area.

Child Custody

Child custody guidelines: Maine courts begin with a presumption that it's best for a child to have frequent and continuing contact with both parents after a divorce. If possible, judges want to support joint custody arrangements.

State laws, forms, and resources: See list in "Divorce," above.

International custody disputes: International Parental Child Abduction Division in the Office of Children's Issues of the U.S. State Department, http://travel.state.gov/childabduction, 888-407-4747.

State surrogacy laws:

- Human Rights Campaign, www.hrc.org (search "surrogacy laws").
- National Infertility Association, www.resolve.org (click "Family Building Options," then "Surrogacy").

Child Support

Child support guidelines: Maine requires all parents to support their children. The amount of child support depends primarily on each parent's income and other resources and how much time each parent spends with the children.

State laws, forms, and resources: See list in "Divorce," above.

- www.supportguidelines.com: Links to state and federal laws and agencies.

State child support enforcement agency:

- Child Support: Division of Support Enforcement & Recovery, www.maine.gov/dhhs/OIAS/dser.
- National Child Support Enforcement Association, www.ncsea.org: Information about federal programs and links to state agencies.

Federal child support enforcement programs and laws: Federal Parent Locator Service, www.acf.hhs.gov/programs/cse/newhire: Links to child support enforcement programs like the passport denial program.

Child support calculators to determine state guidelines: www.alllaw.com/calculators/childsupport: Search your state.

Maryland

Statewide Legal Resources

State website:
- www.maryland.gov. Links and information for many state agencies and departments.
- www.ocyf.state.md.us. Especially relevant for state family law issues.

State and federal statutes:
- Nolo, www.nolo.com/legal-research/state-law.html.
- The Legal Information Institute at Cornell University, http://topics.law.cornell.edu/wex/table_family.
- Justia, www.justia.com/family.
- www.usa.gov: Federal government site.

State court information and family law forms:
- www.courts.state.md.us: Do-it-yourself court forms and instructions, links to local court websites. Search by topic, such as divorce, adoption, or custody.
- National Center for State Courts, www.ncsc.org: Links to state courts (browse by state under "Information and Resources").

Local laws:
- www.statelocalgov.net: Links to websites of many cities and counties, where you can check local rules and ordinances, such as graffiti rules.
- www.municode.com: Municipal codes.

Marriage

Requirements: No blood test required. You must be of the age of consent, not be too closely related to your intended spouse, not be married to anyone else, and have sufficient mental capacity, meaning you understand what you are doing when you marry. You can marry two days after your marriage license is issued, and your license is good for six months. For more details, check your county clerk's office.

Common law marriage: No.

Community property: No.

Same-sex marriage: No.

Marriage-equivalent relationship: No. However, same-sex couples can gain some, but not all, state marital rights by registering as domestic partners. In addition, it's likely that Maryland will recognize same-sex marriages entered into in places where same-sex marriage is legal.

Divorce

Grounds for divorce: Fault or no-fault grounds are allowed.

Residency requirement: At least one spouse must be a resident of Maryland for 12 months or one year before filing for divorce.

How property is divided: Equitable division.

State laws, forms, and resources:
- Maryland state court website, www.courts.state.md.us.
- Women's Law Initiative, www.womenslaw.org: State-by-state information on divorce, custody, and related topics.
- www.divorcenet.com, www.divorcesupport.com, www.divorceinfo.com, www.divorcecentral.com: Helpful divorce websites.

Divorce attorneys and mediators in your area:
- Nolo's Lawyer Directory, www.nolo.com: Divorce attorneys in your area.
- National Center for Lesbian Rights, www.nclrights.org, 800-528-6257: Attorneys experienced in same-sex divorces.
- www.mediate.com, 541-345-1629: Mediators in your area.

Child Custody

Child custody guidelines: Maryland courts begin with a presumption that it's best for a child to have frequent and continuing contact with both parents after a divorce. If possible, judges want to support joint custody arrangements.

State laws, forms, and resources: See list in "Divorce," above.

International custody disputes: International Parental Child Abduction Division in the Office of Children's Issues of the U.S. State Department, http://travel.state.gov/childabduction, 888-407-4747.

State surrogacy laws:
- Human Rights Campaign, www.hrc.org (search "surrogacy laws").
- National Infertility Association, www.resolve.org (click "Family Building Options," then "Surrogacy").

Child Support

Child support guidelines: Maryland requires all parents to support their children. The amount of child support depends primarily on each parent's income and other resources and how much time each parent spends with the children.

State laws, forms, and resources: See list in "Divorce," above.
- www.supportguidelines.com: Links to state and federal laws and agencies.

State child support enforcement agency:
- Child Support Enforcement Program, www.dhr.state.md.us/csea/index. htm.
- National Child Support Enforcement Association, www.ncsea.org: Information about federal programs and links to state agencies.

Federal child support enforcement programs and laws: Federal Parent Locator Service, www.acf.hhs.gov/programs/cse/newhire: Links to child support enforcement programs like the passport denial program.

Child support calculators to determine state guidelines: www.alllaw.com/ calculators/childsupport: Search your state.

Massachusetts

Statewide Legal Resources

State website:
- www.mass.gov. Links and information for many state agencies and departments.
- www.mass.gov/eohhs. Especially relevant for state family law issues.

State and federal statutes:
- Nolo, www.nolo.com/legal-research/state-law.html.
- The Legal Information Institute at Cornell University, http://topics.law.cornell.edu/wex/table_family.
- Justia, www.justia.com/family.
- www.usa.gov: Federal government site.

State court information and family law forms:
- www.mass.gov/courts: Do-it-yourself court forms and instructions, links to local court websites. Search by topic, such as divorce, adoption, or custody.
- National Center for State Courts, www.ncsc.org: Links to state courts (browse by state under "Information and Resources").

Local laws:
- www.statelocalgov.net: Links to websites of many cities and counties, where you can check local rules and ordinances, such as graffiti rules.
- www.municode.com: Municipal codes.

Marriage

Requirements: No blood test required. You must be of the age of consent, not be too closely related to your intended spouse, not be married to anyone else, and have sufficient mental capacity, meaning you understand what you are doing when you marry. You can marry immediately after your marriage license is issued, and your license is good for 60 days. For more details, check your county clerk's office.

Common law marriage: No.

Community property: No.

Same-sex marriage: Yes.

Marriage-equivalent relationship: No.

Divorce

Grounds for divorce: Fault or no-fault grounds are allowed, or you can base your divorce on the fact that you've been separated from your spouse for at least two years.

Residency requirement: At least one spouse must be a resident of Massachusetts for one year before filing for divorce. However, if the cause of the divorce occurred in the state, then the requirement is waived.

How property is divided: Equitable division.

State laws, forms, and resources:
- Massachusetts state court website, www.mass.gov/courts.
- Women's Law Initiative, www.womenslaw.org: State-by-state information on divorce, custody, and related topics.
- www.divorcenet.com, www.divorcesupport.com, www.divorceinfo.com, www.divorcecentral.com: Helpful divorce websites.

Divorce attorneys and mediators in your area:
- Nolo's Lawyer Directory, www.nolo.com: Divorce attorneys in your area.
- National Center for Lesbian Rights, www.nclrights.org, 800-528-6257: Attorneys experienced in same-sex divorces.
- www.mediate.com, 541-345-1629: Mediators in your area.

Child Custody

Child custody guidelines: Massachusetts courts begin with a presumption that it's best for a child to have frequent and continuing contact with both parents after a divorce. If possible, judges want to support joint custody arrangements.

State laws, forms, and resources: See list in "Divorce," above.

International custody disputes: International Parental Child Abduction Division in the Office of Children's Issues of the U.S. State Department, http://travel.state.gov/childabduction, 888-407-4747.

State surrogacy laws:

- Human Rights Campaign, www.hrc.org (search "surrogacy laws").
- National Infertility Association, www.resolve.org (click "Family Building Options," then "Surrogacy").

Child Support

Child support guidelines: Massachusetts requires all parents to support their children. The amount of child support depends primarily on each parent's income and other resources and how much time each parent spends with the children.

State laws, forms, and resources: See list in "Divorce," above.

- www.supportguidelines.com: Links to state and federal laws and agencies.

State child support enforcement agency:

- Child Support Enforcement, www.mass.gov/dor.
- National Child Support Enforcement Association, www.ncsea.org: Information about federal programs and links to state agencies.

Federal child support enforcement programs and laws: Federal Parent Locator Service, www.acf.hhs.gov/programs/cse/newhire: Links to child support enforcement programs like the passport denial program.

Child support calculators to determine state guidelines: www.alllaw.com/calculators/childsupport: Search your state.

Michigan

Statewide Legal Resources

State website:
- www.michigan.gov. Links and information for many state agencies and departments.
- www.michigan.gov/dhs. Especially relevant for state family law issues.

State and federal statutes:
- Nolo, www.nolo.com/legal-research/state-law.html.
- The Legal Information Institute at Cornell University, http://topics.law.cornell.edu/wex/table_family.
- Justia, www.justia.com/family.
- www.usa.gov: Federal government site.

State court information and family law forms:
- www.courts.michigan.gov: Do-it-yourself court forms and instructions, links to local court websites. Search by topic, such as divorce, adoption, or custody.
- National Center for State Courts, www.ncsc.org: Links to state courts (browse by state under "Information and Resources").

Local laws:
- www.statelocalgov.net: Links to websites of many cities and counties, where you can check local rules and ordinances, such as graffiti rules.
- www.municode.com: Municipal codes.

Marriage

Requirements: No blood test required. You must be of the age of consent, not be too closely related to your intended spouse, not be married to anyone else, and have sufficient mental capacity, meaning you understand what you are doing when you marry. You can marry immediately after your marriage license is issued, and your license is good for 33 days. For more details, check your county clerk's office.

Common law marriage: No.

Community property: No.

Same-sex marriage: No.

Marriage-equivalent relationship: No. Michigan does not recognize domestic partnerships, civil unions, or reciprocal beneficiaries.

Divorce

Grounds for divorce: No-fault. However, fault may be considered by the court as a factor in dividing property or awarding alimony.

Residency requirement: At least one spouse must be a resident of Michigan for six months or 180 days before filing for divorce.

How property is divided: Equitable division.

State laws, forms, and resources:
- Michigan state court website, www.courts.michigan.gov.
- Women's Law Initiative, www.womenslaw.org: State-by-state information on divorce, custody, and related topics.
- www.divorcenet.com, www.divorcesupport.com, www.divorceinfo.com, www.divorcecentral.com: Helpful divorce websites.

Divorce attorneys and mediators in your area:
- Nolo's Lawyer Directory, www.nolo.com: Divorce attorneys in your area.
- National Center for Lesbian Rights, www.nclrights.org, 800-528-6257: Attorneys experienced in same-sex divorces.
- www.mediate.com, 541-345-1629: Mediators in your area.

Child Custody

Child custody guidelines: Michigan courts begin with a presumption that it's best for a child to have frequent and continuing contact with both parents after a divorce. If possible, judges want to support joint custody arrangements.

State laws, forms, and resources: See list in "Divorce," above.

International custody disputes: International Parental Child Abduction Division in the Office of Children's Issues of the U.S. State Department, http://travel.state.gov/childabduction, 888-407-4747.

State surrogacy laws:
- Human Rights Campaign, www.hrc.org (search "surrogacy laws").
- National Infertility Association, www.resolve.org (click "Family Building Options," then "Surrogacy").

Child Support

Child support guidelines: Michigan requires all parents to support their children. The amount of child support depends primarily on each parent's income and other resources and how much time each parent spends with the children.

State laws, forms, and resources: See list in "Divorce," above.
- www.supportguidelines.com: Links to state and federal laws and agencies.

State child support enforcement agency:
- Department of Human Services, Child Support and Enforcement of Support webpages, www.michigan.gov/dhs.
- National Child Support Enforcement Association, www.ncsea.org: Information about federal programs and links to state agencies.

Federal child support enforcement programs and laws: Federal Parent Locator Service, www.acf.hhs.gov/programs/cse/newhire: Links to child support enforcement programs like the passport denial program.

Child support calculators to determine state guidelines: www.alllaw.com/calculators/childsupport: Search your state.

Minnesota

Statewide Legal Resources

State website:
- www.state.mn.us. Links and information for many state agencies and departments.
- www.dhs.state.mn.us. Especially relevant for state family law issues.

State and federal statutes:
- Nolo, www.nolo.com/legal-research/state-law.html.
- The Legal Information Institute at Cornell University, http://topics.law.cornell.edu/wex/table_family.
- Justia, www.justia.com/family.
- www.usa.gov: Federal government site.

State court information and family law forms:
- www.mncourts.gov: Do-it-yourself court forms and instructions, links to local court websites. Search by topic, such as divorce, adoption, or custody.
- National Center for State Courts, www.ncsc.org: Links to state courts (browse by state under "Information and Resources").

Local laws:
- www.statelocalgov.net: Links to websites of many cities and counties, where you can check local rules and ordinances, such as graffiti rules.
- www.municode.com: Municipal codes.

Marriage

Requirements: No blood test required. You must be of the age of consent, not be too closely related to your intended spouse, not be married to anyone else, and have sufficient mental capacity, meaning you understand what you are doing when you marry. You can marry immediately after your marriage license is issued, and your license is good for six months. For more details, check your county clerk's office.

Common law marriage: No.

Community property: No.

Same-sex marriage: No.

Marriage-equivalent relationship: No. Minnesota does not recognize domestic partnerships, civil unions, or reciprocal beneficiaries.

Divorce

Grounds for divorce: No-fault. However, fault may be considered by the court as a factor in dividing property or awarding alimony.

Residency requirement: At least one spouse must be a resident of Minnesota for six months or 180 days before filing for divorce.

How property is divided: Equitable division.

State laws, forms, and resources:
- Minnesota state court website, www.mncourts.gov.
- Women's Law Initiative, www.womenslaw.org: State-by-state information on divorce, custody, and related topics.
- www.divorcenet.com, www.divorcesupport.com, www.divorceinfo.com, www.divorcecentral.com: Helpful divorce websites.

Divorce attorneys and mediators in your area:
- Nolo's Lawyer Directory, www.nolo.com: Divorce attorneys in your area.
- National Center for Lesbian Rights, www.nclrights.org, 800-528-6257: Attorneys experienced in same-sex divorces.
- www.mediate.com, 541-345-1629: Mediators in your area.

Child Custody

Child custody guidelines: Minnesota courts begin with a presumption that it's best for a child to have frequent and continuing contact with both parents after a divorce. If possible, judges want to support joint custody arrangements.

State laws, forms, and resources: See list in "Divorce," above.

International custody disputes: International Parental Child Abduction Division in the Office of Children's Issues of the U.S. State Department, http://travel.state.gov/childabduction, 888-407-4747.

State surrogacy laws:

- Human Rights Campaign, www.hrc.org (search "surrogacy laws").
- National Infertility Association, www.resolve.org (click "Family Building Options," then "Surrogacy").

Child Support

Child support guidelines: Minnesota requires all parents to support their children. The amount of child support depends primarily on each parent's income and other resources and how much time each parent spends with the children.

State laws, forms, and resources: See list in "Divorce," above.

- www.supportguidelines.com: Links to state and federal laws and agencies.

State child support enforcement agency:

- Department of Human Services, Child Support and Child Support Services webpages, www.dhs.state.mn.us.
- National Child Support Enforcement Association, www.ncsea.org: Information about federal programs and links to state agencies.

Federal child support enforcement programs and laws: Federal Parent Locator Service, www.acf.hhs.gov/programs/cse/newhire: Links to child support enforcement programs like the passport denial program.

Child support calculators to determine state guidelines: www.alllaw.com/calculators/childsupport: Search your state.

Mississippi

Statewide Legal Resources

State website:
- www.ms.gov. Links and information for many state agencies and departments.
- www.mdhs.state.ms.us/fcs.html. Especially relevant for state family law issues.

State and federal statutes:
- Nolo, www.nolo.com/legal-research/state-law.html.
- The Legal Information Institute at Cornell University, http://topics.law. cornell.edu/wex/table_family.
- Justia, www.justia.com/family.
- www.usa.gov: Federal government site.

State court information and family law forms:
- www.mississippi.gov/ms_sub_sub_template.jsp?Category_ID=13: Do-it-yourself court forms and instructions, links to local court websites. Search by topic, such as divorce, adoption, or custody.
- National Center for State Courts, www.ncsc.org: Links to state courts (browse by state under "Information and Resources").

Local laws:
- www.statelocalgov.net: Links to websites of many cities and counties, where you can check local rules and ordinances, such as graffiti rules.
- www.municode.com: Municipal codes.

Marriage

Requirements: A blood test is required. You must be of the age of consent, not be too closely related to your intended spouse, not be married to anyone else, and have sufficient mental capacity, meaning you understand what you are doing when you marry. You can marry immediately after your marriage license is issued. For more details, check your county clerk's office.

Common law marriage: No.

Community property: No.

Same-sex marriage: No.

Marriage-equivalent relationship: No. Mississippi does not recognize domestic partnerships, civil unions, or reciprocal beneficiaries.

Divorce

Grounds for divorce: Fault or no-fault grounds are allowed, or you can base your divorce on the fact that you've been separated from your spouse for at least two years.

Residency requirement: At least one spouse must be a resident of Mississippi for six months before filing for divorce.

How property is divided: Equitable division.

State laws, forms, and resources:
- Mississippi state court website, www.mississippi.gov/ms_sub_sub_template.jsp?Category_ID=13.
- Women's Law Initiative, www.womenslaw.org: State-by-state information on divorce, custody, and related topics.
- www.divorcenet.com, www.divorcesupport.com, www.divorceinfo.com, www.divorcecentral.com: Helpful divorce websites.

Divorce attorneys and mediators in your area:
- Nolo's Lawyer Directory, www.nolo.com: Divorce attorneys in your area.
- National Center for Lesbian Rights, www.nclrights.org, 800-528-6257: Attorneys experienced in same-sex divorces.
- www.mediate.com, 541-345-1629: Mediators in your area.

Child Custody

Child custody guidelines: Mississippi courts begin with a presumption that it's best for a child to have frequent and continuing contact with both parents after a divorce. If possible, judges want to support joint custody arrangements.

State laws, forms, and resources: See list in "Divorce," above.

International custody disputes: International Parental Child Abduction Division in the Office of Children's Issues of the U.S. State Department, http://travel.state.gov/childabduction, 888-407-4747.

State surrogacy laws:

* Human Rights Campaign, www.hrc.org (search "surrogacy laws").
* National Infertility Association, www.resolve.org (click "Family Building Options," then "Surrogacy").

Child Support

Child support guidelines: Mississippi requires all parents to support their children. The amount of child support depends primarily on each parent's income and other resources and how much time each parent spends with the children.

State laws, forms, and resources: See list in "Divorce," above.

* www.supportguidelines.com: Links to state and federal laws and agencies.

State child support enforcement agency:

* Division of Child Support Enforcement, www.mdhs.state.ms.us/cse.html.
* National Child Support Enforcement Association, www.ncsea.org: Information about federal programs and links to state agencies.

Federal child support enforcement programs and laws: Federal Parent Locator Service, www.acf.hhs.gov/programs/cse/newhire: Links to child support enforcement programs like the passport denial program.

Child support calculators to determine state guidelines: www.alllaw.com/calculators/childsupport: Search your state.

Mississippi

Missouri

Statewide Legal Resources

State website:
- www.mo.gov. Links and information for many state agencies and departments.
- www.mo.gov/living-in-missouri/marriagedivorce. Especially relevant for state family law issues.

State and federal statutes:
- Nolo, www.nolo.com/legal-research/state-law.html.
- The Legal Information Institute at Cornell University, http://topics.law.cornell.edu/wex/table_family.
- Justia, www.justia.com/family.
- www.usa.gov: Federal government site.

State court information and family law forms:
- www.courts.mo.gov: Do-it-yourself court forms and instructions, links to local court websites. Search by topic, such as divorce, adoption, or custody.
- National Center for State Courts, www.ncsc.org: Links to state courts (browse by state under "Information and Resources").

Local laws:
- www.statelocalgov.net: Links to websites of many cities and counties, where you can check local rules and ordinances, such as graffiti rules.
- www.municode.com: Municipal codes.

Marriage

Requirements: No blood test required. You must be of the age of consent, not be too closely related to your intended spouse, not be married to anyone else, and have sufficient mental capacity, meaning you understand what you are doing when you marry. You can marry immediately after your marriage license is issued, and your license is good for 30 days. For more details, check your county clerk's office.

Common law marriage: No.

Community property: No.

Same-sex marriage: No.

Marriage-equivalent relationship: No. Missouri does not recognize domestic partnerships, civil unions, or reciprocal beneficiaries.

Divorce

Grounds for divorce: Fault or no-fault grounds are allowed, or you can base your divorce on the fact that you've been separated from your spouse for at least two years.

Residency requirement: At least one spouse must be a resident of Missouri for three months or 90 days before filing for divorce.

How property is divided: Equitable division.

State laws, forms, and resources:
- Missouri state court website, www.courts.mo.gov.
- Women's Law Initiative, www.womenslaw.org: State-by-state information on divorce, custody, and related topics.
- www.divorcenet.com, www.divorcesupport.com, www.divorceinfo.com, www.divorcecentral.com: Helpful divorce websites.

Divorce attorneys and mediators in your area:
- Nolo's Lawyer Directory, www.nolo.com: Divorce attorneys in your area.
- National Center for Lesbian Rights, www.nclrights.org, 800-528-6257: Attorneys experienced in same-sex divorces.
- www.mediate.com, 541-345-1629: Mediators in your area.

Child Custody

Child custody guidelines: Missouri courts begin with a presumption that it's best for a child to have frequent and continuing contact with both parents after a divorce. If possible, judges want to support joint custody arrangements.

State laws, forms, and resources: See list in "Divorce," above.

International custody disputes: International Parental Child Abduction Division in the Office of Children's Issues of the U.S. State Department, http://travel.state.gov/childabduction, 888-407-4747.

State surrogacy laws:
- Human Rights Campaign, www.hrc.org (search "surrogacy laws").
- National Infertility Association, www.resolve.org (click "Family Building Options," then "Surrogacy").

Child Support

Child support guidelines: Missouri requires all parents to support their children. The amount of child support depends primarily on each parent's income and other resources and how much time each parent spends with the children.

State laws, forms, and resources: See list in "Divorce," above.
- www.supportguidelines.com: Links to state and federal laws and agencies.

State child support enforcement agency:
- Child Support Enforcement, www.dss.mo.gov/cse.
- National Child Support Enforcement Association, www.ncsea.org: Information about federal programs and links to state agencies.

Federal child support enforcement programs and laws: Federal Parent Locator Service, www.acf.hhs.gov/programs/cse/newhire: Links to child support enforcement programs like the passport denial program.

Child support calculators to determine state guidelines: www.alllaw.com/calculators/childsupport: Search your state.

Montana

Statewide Legal Resources

State website:

- www.mt.gov. Links and information for many state agencies and departments.
- www.dphhs.mt.gov/cfsd. Especially relevant for state family law issues.

State and federal statutes:

- Nolo, www.nolo.com/legal-research/state-law.html.
- The Legal Information Institute at Cornell University, http://topics.law. cornell.edu/wex/table_family.
- Justia, www.justia.com/family.
- www.usa.gov: Federal government site.

State court information and family law forms:

- www.courts.mt.gov: Do-it-yourself court forms and instructions, links to local court websites. Search by topic, such as divorce, adoption, or custody.
- National Center for State Courts, www.ncsc.org: Links to state courts (browse by state under "Information and Resources").

Local laws:

- www.statelocalgov.net: Links to websites of many cities and counties, where you can check local rules and ordinances, such as graffiti rules.
- www.municode.com: Municipal codes.

Marriage

Requirements: A blood test is required. You must be of the age of consent, not be too closely related to your intended spouse, not be married to anyone else, and have sufficient mental capacity, meaning you understand what you are doing when you marry. You can marry immediately after your marriage license is issued, and your license is good for 180 days. For more details, check your county clerk's office.

Common law marriage: Yes. A couple must intend to be married, live together for a significant period of time, and hold themselves out as a married couple.

Community property: No.

Same-sex marriage: No.

Marriage-equivalent relationship: No. Montana does not recognize domestic partnerships, civil unions, or reciprocal beneficiaries.

Divorce

Grounds for divorce: No-fault. However, fault may be considered by the court as a factor in dividing property or awarding alimony.

Residency requirement: At least one spouse must be a resident of Montana for 90 days before filing for divorce.

How property is divided: Equitable division.

State laws, forms, and resources:
- Montana state court website, www.courts.mt.gov.
- Women's Law Initiative, www.womenslaw.org: State-by-state information on divorce, custody, and related topics.
- www.divorcenet.com, www.divorcesupport.com, www.divorceinfo.com, www.divorcecentral.com: Helpful divorce websites.

Divorce attorneys and mediators in your area:
- Nolo's Lawyer Directory, www.nolo.com: Divorce attorneys in your area.
- National Center for Lesbian Rights, www.nclrights.org, 800-528-6257: Attorneys experienced in same-sex divorces.
- www.mediate.com, 541-345-1629: Mediators in your area.

Child Custody

Child custody guidelines: Montana courts begin with a presumption that it's best for a child to have frequent and continuing contact with both parents after a divorce. If possible, judges want to support joint custody arrangements.

State laws, forms, and resources: See list in "Divorce," above.

International custody disputes: International Parental Child Abduction Division in the Office of Children's Issues of the U.S. State Department, http://travel.state.gov/childabduction, 888-407-4747.

State surrogacy laws:
- Human Rights Campaign, www.hrc.org (search "surrogacy laws").
- National Infertility Association, www.resolve.org (click "Family Building Options," then "Surrogacy").

Child Support

Child support guidelines: Montana requires all parents to support their children. The amount of child support depends primarily on each parent's income and other resources and how much time each parent spends with the children.

State laws, forms, and resources: See list in "Divorce," above.
- www.supportguidelines.com: Links to state and federal laws and agencies.

State child support enforcement agency:
- Child Support Enforcement Division, www.dphhs.mt.gov/csed/index. shtml.
- National Child Support Enforcement Association, www.ncsea.org: Information about federal programs and links to state agencies.

Federal child support enforcement programs and laws: Federal Parent Locator Service, www.acf.hhs.gov/programs/cse/newhire: Links to child support enforcement programs like the passport denial program.

Child support calculators to determine state guidelines: www.alllaw.com/calculators/childsupport: Search your state.

Nebraska

Statewide Legal Resources

State website:
- www.nebraska.gov. Links and information for many state agencies and departments.
- www.hhs.state.ne.us/children_families.htm. Especially relevant for state family law issues.

State and federal statutes:
- Nolo, www.nolo.com/legal-research/state-law.html.
- The Legal Information Institute at Cornell University, http://topics.law.cornell.edu/wex/table_family.
- Justia, www.justia.com/family.
- www.usa.gov: Federal government site.

State court information and family law forms:
- www.supremecourt.ne.gov: Do-it-yourself court forms and instructions, links to local court websites. Search by topic, such as divorce, adoption, or custody.
- National Center for State Courts, www.ncsc.org: Links to state courts (browse by state under "Information and Resources").

Local laws:
- www.statelocalgov.net: Links to websites of many cities and counties, where you can check local rules and ordinances, such as graffiti rules.
- www.municode.com: Municipal codes.

Marriage

Requirements: No blood test required. You must be of the age of consent, not be too closely related to your intended spouse, not be married to anyone else, and have sufficient mental capacity, meaning you understand what you are doing when you marry. You can marry immediately after your marriage license is issued, and your license is good for one year. For more details, check your county clerk's office.

Common law marriage: No.

Community property: No.

Same-sex marriage: No.

Marriage-equivalent relationship: No. Nebraska does not recognize domestic partnerships, civil unions, or reciprocal beneficiaries.

Divorce

Grounds for divorce: No-fault. However, fault may be considered by the court as a factor in dividing property or awarding alimony.

Residency requirement: At least one spouse must be a resident of Nebraska for 12 months or one year before filing for divorce.

How property is divided: Equitable division.

State laws, forms, and resources:
- Nebraska state court website, www.supremecourt.ne.gov.
- Women's Law Initiative, www.womenslaw.org: State-by-state information on divorce, custody, and related topics.
- www.divorcenet.com, www.divorcesupport.com, www.divorceinfo.com, www.divorcecentral.com: Helpful divorce websites.

Divorce attorneys and mediators in your area:
- Nolo's Lawyer Directory, www.nolo.com: Divorce attorneys in your area.
- National Center for Lesbian Rights, www.nclrights.org, 800-528-6257: Attorneys experienced in same-sex divorces.
- www.mediate.com, 541-345-1629: Mediators in your area.

Child Custody

Child custody guidelines: Nebraska courts begin with a presumption that it's best for a child to have frequent and continuing contact with both parents after a divorce. If possible, judges want to support joint custody arrangements.

State laws, forms, and resources: See list in "Divorce," above.

International custody disputes: International Parental Child Abduction Division in the Office of Children's Issues of the U.S. State Department, http://travel.state.gov/childabduction, 888-407-4747.

State surrogacy laws:
- Human Rights Campaign, www.hrc.org (search "surrogacy laws").
- National Infertility Association, www.resolve.org (click "Family Building Options," then "Surrogacy").

Child Support

Child support guidelines: Nebraska requires all parents to support their children. The amount of child support depends primarily on each parent's income and other resources and how much time each parent spends with the children.

State laws, forms, and resources: See list in "Divorce," above.
- www.supportguidelines.com: Links to state and federal laws and agencies.

State child support enforcement agency:
- Child Support Enforcement, www.hhs.state.ne.us/cse/cseindex.htm.
- National Child Support Enforcement Association, www.ncsea.org: Information about federal programs and links to state agencies.

Federal child support enforcement programs and laws: Federal Parent Locator Service, www.acf.hhs.gov/programs/cse/newhire: Links to child support enforcement programs like the passport denial program.

Child support calculators to determine state guidelines: www.alllaw.com/calculators/childsupport: Search your state.

Nevada

Statewide Legal Resources

State website:

* www.nv.gov. Links and information for many state agencies and departments.
* www.dcfs.state.nv.us. Especially relevant for state family law issues.

State and federal statutes:

* Nolo, www.nolo.com/legal-research/state-law.html.
* The Legal Information Institute at Cornell University, http://topics.law. cornell.edu/wex/table_family.
* Justia, www.justia.com/family.
* www.usa.gov: Federal government site.

State court information and family law forms:

* www.nevadajudiciary.us: Do-it-yourself court forms and instructions, links to local court websites. Search by topic, such as divorce, adoption, or custody.
* National Center for State Courts, www.ncsc.org: Links to state courts (browse by state under "Information and Resources").

Local laws:

* www.statelocalgov.net: Links to websites of many cities and counties, where you can check local rules and ordinances, such as graffiti rules.
* www.municode.com: Municipal codes.

Marriage

Requirements: No blood test required. You must be of the age of consent, not be too closely related to your intended spouse, not be married to anyone else, and have sufficient mental capacity, meaning you understand what you are doing when you marry. You can marry immediately after your marriage license is issued, and your license is good for one year. For more details, check your county clerk's office.

Common law marriage: No.

Nevada

Community property: Yes.

Same-sex marriage: No.

Marriage-equivalent relationship: Yes. Same-sex couples can register as domestic partners in Nevada and registered partners have all of the rights and responsibilities of marriage under state law.

Divorce

Grounds for divorce: No-fault. However, fault may be considered by the court as a factor in dividing property or awarding alimony.

Residency requirement: At least one spouse must be a resident of Nevada for six weeks before filing for divorce.

How property is divided: Community property.

State laws, forms, and resources:
- Nevada state court website, www.nevadajudiciary.us.
- Women's Law Initiative, www.womenslaw.org: State-by-state information on divorce, custody, and related topics.
- www.divorcenet.com, www.divorcesupport.com, www.divorceinfo.com, www.divorcecentral.com: Helpful divorce websites.

Divorce attorneys and mediators in your area:
- Nolo's Lawyer Directory, www.nolo.com: Divorce attorneys in your area.
- National Center for Lesbian Rights, www.nclrights.org, 800-528-6257: Attorneys experienced in same-sex divorces.
- www.mediate.com, 541-345-1629: Mediators in your area.

Child Custody

Child custody guidelines: Nevada courts begin with a presumption that it's best for a child to have frequent and continuing contact with both parents after a divorce. If possible, judges want to support joint custody arrangements.

State laws, forms, and resources: See list in "Divorce," above.

International custody disputes: International Parental Child Abduction Division in the Office of Children's Issues of the U.S. State Department, http://travel.state.gov/childabduction, 888-407-4747.

State surrogacy laws:
- Human Rights Campaign, www.hrc.org (search "surrogacy laws").
- National Infertility Association, www.resolve.org (click "Family Building Options," then "Surrogacy").

Child Support

Child support guidelines: Nevada requires all parents to support their children. The amount of child support depends primarily on each parent's income and other resources and how much time each parent spends with the children.

State laws, forms, and resources: See list in "Divorce," above.
- www.supportguidelines.com: Links to state and federal laws and agencies.

State child support enforcement agency:
- Division of Welfare and Supportive Services, visit the Child Support Enforcement Program, https://dwss.nv.gov.
- National Child Support Enforcement Association, www.ncsea.org: Information about federal programs and links to state agencies.

Federal child support enforcement programs and laws: Federal Parent Locator Service, www.acf.hhs.gov/programs/cse/newhire: Links to child support enforcement programs like the passport denial program.

Child support calculators to determine state guidelines: www.alllaw.com/calculators/childsupport: Search your state.

Nevada

New Hampshire

Statewide Legal Resources

State website:

- www.nh.gov. Links and information for many state agencies and departments.
- www.dhhs.state.nh.us/foryou/families.htm. Especially relevant for state family law issues.

State and federal statutes:

- Nolo, www.nolo.com/legal-research/state-law.html.
- The Legal Information Institute at Cornell University, http://topics.law. cornell.edu/wex/table_family.
- Justia, www.justia.com/family.
- www.usa.gov: Federal government site.

State court information and family law forms:

- www.courts.state.nh.us: Do-it-yourself court forms and instructions, links to local court websites. Search by topic, such as divorce, adoption, or custody.
- National Center for State Courts, www.ncsc.org: Links to state courts (browse by state under "Information and Resources").

Local laws:

- www.statelocalgov.net: Links to websites of many cities and counties, where you can check local rules and ordinances, such as graffiti rules.
- www.municode.com: Municipal codes.

Marriage

Requirements: No blood test required. You must be of the age of consent, not be too closely related to your intended spouse, not be married to anyone else, and have sufficient mental capacity, meaning you understand what you are doing when you marry. You can marry immediately after your marriage license is issued, and your license is good for 90 days. For more details, check your county clerk's office.

Common law marriage: No.

Community property: No.

Same-sex marriage: Yes.

Marriage-equivalent relationship: No.

Divorce

Grounds for divorce: Fault or no-fault grounds are allowed, or you can base your divorce on the fact that you've been separated from your spouse for at least two years.

Residency requirement: At least one spouse must be a resident of New Hampshire for one year before filing for divorce.

How property is divided: Equitable division.

State laws, forms, and resources:
- New Hampshire state court website, www.courts.state.nh.us.
- Women's Law Initiative, www.womenslaw.org: State-by-state information on divorce, custody, and related topics.
- www.divorcenet.com, www.divorcesupport.com, www.divorceinfo.com, www.divorcecentral.com: Helpful divorce websites.

Divorce attorneys and mediators in your area:
- Nolo's Lawyer Directory, www.nolo.com: Divorce attorneys in your area.
- National Center for Lesbian Rights, www.nclrights.org, 800-528-6257: Attorneys experienced in same-sex divorces.
- www.mediate.com, 541-345-1629: Mediators in your area.

Child Custody

Child custody guidelines: New Hampshire courts begin with a presumption that it's best for a child to have frequent and continuing contact with both parents after a divorce. If possible, judges want to support joint custody arrangements.

State laws, forms, and resources: See list in "Divorce," above.

International custody disputes: International Parental Child Abduction Division in the Office of Children's Issues of the U.S. State Department, http://travel.state.gov/childabduction, 888-407-4747.

State surrogacy laws:
- Human Rights Campaign, www.hrc.org (search "surrogacy laws").
- National Infertility Association, www.resolve.org (click "Family Building Options," then "Surrogacy").

Child Support

Child support guidelines: New Hampshire requires all parents to support their children. The amount of child support depends primarily on each parent's income and other resources and how much time each parent spends with the children.

State laws, forms, and resources: See list in "Divorce," above.
- www.supportguidelines.com: Links to state and federal laws and agencies.

State child support enforcement agency:
- Division of Child Support Services, www.dhhs.nh.gov/dcss/index.htm.
- National Child Support Enforcement Association, www.ncsea.org: Information about federal programs and links to state agencies.

Federal child support enforcement programs and laws: Federal Parent Locator Service, www.acf.hhs.gov/programs/cse/newhire: Links to child support enforcement programs like the passport denial program.

Child support calculators to determine state guidelines: www.alllaw.com/calculators/childsupport: Search your state.

New Jersey

Statewide Legal Resources

State website:

- www.state.nj.us. Links and information for many state agencies and departments.
- www.state.nj.us/humanservices/clients/family. Especially relevant for state family law issues.

State and federal statutes:

- Nolo, www.nolo.com/legal-research/state-law.html.
- The Legal Information Institute at Cornell University, http://topics.law. cornell.edu/wex/table_family.
- Justia, www.justia.com/family.
- www.usa.gov: Federal government site.

State court information and family law forms:

- www.judiciary.state.nj.us: Do-it-yourself court forms and instructions, links to local court websites. Search by topic, such as divorce, adoption, or custody.
- National Center for State Courts, www.ncsc.org: Links to state courts (browse by state under "Information and Resources").

Local laws:

- www.statelocalgov.net: Links to websites of many cities and counties, where you can check local rules and ordinances, such as graffiti rules.
- www.municode.com: Municipal codes.

Marriage

Requirements: N/A for blood test requirement. You must be of the age of consent, not be too closely related to your intended spouse, not be married to anyone else, and have sufficient mental capacity, meaning you understand what you are doing when you marry. For more details, check your county clerk's office.

Common law marriage: No.

Community property: No.

Same-sex marriage: No.

Marriage-equivalent relationship: Yes. Same-sex couples in New Jersey can enter into civil unions that come with all of the rights and responsibilities of marriage under state law.

Divorce

Grounds for divorce: Fault or no-fault grounds are allowed, or you can base your divorce on the fact that you've been separated from your spouse for at least two years.

Residency requirement: At least one spouse must be a resident of New Jersey for one year before filing for divorce.

How property is divided: Equitable division.

State laws, forms, and resources:
- New Jersey state court website, www.judiciary.state.nj.us.
- Women's Law Initiative, www.womenslaw.org: State-by-state information on divorce, custody, and related topics.
- www.divorcenet.com, www.divorcesupport.com, www.divorceinfo.com, www.divorcecentral.com: Helpful divorce websites.

Divorce attorneys and mediators in your area:
- Nolo's Lawyer Directory, www.nolo.com: Divorce attorneys in your area.
- National Center for Lesbian Rights, www.nclrights.org, 800-528-6257: Attorneys experienced in same-sex divorces.
- www.mediate.com, 541-345-1629: Mediators in your area.

Child Custody

Child custody guidelines: New Jersey courts begin with a presumption that it's best for a child to have frequent and continuing contact with both parents after a divorce. If possible, judges want to support joint custody arrangements.

State laws, forms, and resources: See list in "Divorce," above.

International custody disputes: International Parental Child Abduction Division in the Office of Children's Issues of the U.S. State Department, http://travel.state.gov/childabduction, 888-407-4747.

State surrogacy laws:

- Human Rights Campaign, www.hrc.org (search "surrogacy laws").
- National Infertility Association, www.resolve.org (click "Family Building Options," then "Surrogacy").

Child Support

Child support guidelines: New Jersey requires all parents to support their children. The amount of child support depends primarily on each parent's income and other resources and how much time each parent spends with the children.

State laws, forms, and resources: See list in "Divorce," above.

- www.supportguidelines.com: Links to state and federal laws and agencies.

State child support enforcement agency:

- Child Support Program, www.njchildsupport.org.
- National Child Support Enforcement Association, www.ncsea.org: Information about federal programs and links to state agencies.

Federal child support enforcement programs and laws: Federal Parent Locator Service, www.acf.hhs.gov/programs/cse/newhire: Links to child support enforcement programs like the passport denial program.

Child support calculators to determine state guidelines: www.alllaw.com/calculators/childsupport: Search your state.

New Mexico

Statewide Legal Resources

State website:

- www.newmexico.gov. Links and information for many state agencies and departments.
- www.cyfd.org. Especially relevant for state family law issues.

State and federal statutes:

- Nolo, www.nolo.com/legal-research/state-law.html.
- The Legal Information Institute at Cornell University, http://topics.law.cornell.edu/wex/table_family.
- Justia, www.justia.com/family.
- www.usa.gov: Federal government site.

State court information and family law forms:

- www.nmcourts.gov: Do-it-yourself court forms and instructions, links to local court websites. Search by topic, such as divorce, adoption, or custody.
- National Center for State Courts, www.ncsc.org: Links to state courts (browse by state under "Information and Resources").

Local laws:

- www.statelocalgov.net: Links to websites of many cities and counties, where you can check local rules and ordinances, such as graffiti rules.
- www.municode.com: Municipal codes.

Marriage

Requirements: No blood test required. You must be of the age of consent, not be too closely related to your intended spouse, not be married to anyone else, and have sufficient mental capacity, meaning you understand what you are doing when you marry. You can marry immediately after your marriage license is issued. For more details, check your county clerk's office.

Common law marriage: No.

New Mexico

Community property: Yes.

Same-sex marriage: No.

Marriage-equivalent relationship: No. New Mexico does not recognize domestic partnerships, civil unions, or reciprocal beneficiaries.

Divorce

Grounds for divorce: Fault or no-fault grounds are allowed, or you can base your divorce on the fact that you've been separated from your spouse for at least two years.

Residency requirement: At least one spouse must be a resident of New Mexico for six months before filing for divorce.

How property is divided: Community property.

State laws, forms, and resources:
- New Mexico state court website, www.nmcourts.gov.
- Women's Law Initiative, www.womenslaw.org: State-by-state information on divorce, custody, and related topics.
- www.divorcenet.com, www.divorcesupport.com, www.divorceinfo.com, www.divorcecentral.com: Helpful divorce websites.

Divorce attorneys and mediators in your area:
- Nolo's Lawyer Directory, www.nolo.com: Divorce attorneys in your area.
- National Center for Lesbian Rights, www.nclrights.org, 800-528-6257: Attorneys experienced in same-sex divorces.
- www.mediate.com, 541-345-1629: Mediators in your area.

Child Custody

Child custody guidelines: New Mexico courts begin with a presumption that it's best for a child to have frequent and continuing contact with both parents after a divorce. If possible, judges want to support joint custody arrangements.

State laws, forms, and resources: See list in "Divorce," above.

International custody disputes: International Parental Child Abduction Division in the Office of Children's Issues of the U.S. State Department, http://travel.state.gov/childabduction, 888-407-4747.

State surrogacy laws:

- Human Rights Campaign, www.hrc.org (search "surrogacy laws").
- National Infertility Association, www.resolve.org (click "Family Building Options," then "Surrogacy").

Child Support

Child support guidelines: New Mexico requires all parents to support their children. The amount of child support depends primarily on each parent's income and other resources and how much time each parent spends with the children.

State laws, forms, and resources: See list in "Divorce," above.

- www.supportguidelines.com: Links to state and federal laws and agencies.

State child support enforcement agency:

- Child Support Enforcement Division, www.hsd.state.nm.us/csed.html.
- National Child Support Enforcement Association, www.ncsea.org: Information about federal programs and links to state agencies.

Federal child support enforcement programs and laws: Federal Parent Locator Service, www.acf.hhs.gov/programs/cse/newhire: Links to child support enforcement programs like the passport denial program.

Child support calculators to determine state guidelines: www.alllaw.com/calculators/childsupport: Search your state.

New York

Statewide Legal Resources

State website:
- www.state.ny.us. Links and information for many state agencies and departments.
- www.ocfs.state.ny.us/main. Especially relevant for state family law issues.

State and federal statutes:
- Nolo, www.nolo.com/legal-research/state-law.html.
- The Legal Information Institute at Cornell University, http://topics.law.cornell.edu/wex/table_family.
- Justia, www.justia.com/family.
- www.usa.gov: Federal government site.

State court information and family law forms:
- www.courts.state.ny.us: Do-it-yourself court forms and instructions, links to local court websites. Search by topic, such as divorce, adoption, or custody.
- National Center for State Courts, www.ncsc.org: Links to state courts (browse by state under "Information and Resources").

Local laws:
- www.statelocalgov.net: Links to websites of many cities and counties, where you can check local rules and ordinances, such as graffiti rules.
- www.municode.com: Municipal codes.

Marriage

Requirements: A blood test is generally not required, but African American and Hispanic applicants are required to take a sickle cell test. You must be of the age of consent, not be too closely related to your intended spouse, not be married to anyone else, and have sufficient mental capacity, meaning you understand what you are doing when you marry. You can marry 24 hours after your marriage license is issued, and your license is good for 60 days. For more details, check your county clerk's office.

Common law marriage: No.

Community property: No.

Same-sex marriage: No.

Marriage-equivalent relationship: No. However, New York courts and state agencies generally recognize same-sex marriages from places where same-sex marriage is legal.

Divorce

Grounds for divorce: Fault or no-fault grounds are allowed.

Residency requirement: At least one spouse must be a resident of New York for one year before filing for divorce.

How property is divided: Equitable division.

State laws, forms, and resources:
- New York state court website, www.courts.state.ny.us.
- Women's Law Initiative, www.womenslaw.org: State-by-state information on divorce, custody, and related topics.
- www.divorcenet.com, www.divorcesupport.com, www.divorceinfo.com, www.divorcecentral.com: Helpful divorce websites.

Divorce attorneys and mediators in your area:
- Nolo's Lawyer Directory, www.nolo.com: Divorce attorneys in your area.
- National Center for Lesbian Rights, www.nclrights.org, 800-528-6257: Attorneys experienced in same-sex divorces.
- www.mediate.com, 541-345-1629: Mediators in your area.

Child Custody

Child custody guidelines: New York courts begin with a presumption that it's best for a child to have frequent and continuing contact with both parents after a divorce. If possible, judges want to support joint custody arrangements.

State laws, forms, and resources: See list in "Divorce," above.

International custody disputes: International Parental Child Abduction Division in the Office of Children's Issues of the U.S. State Department, http://travel.state.gov/childabduction, 888-407-4747.

State surrogacy laws:

* Human Rights Campaign, www.hrc.org (search "surrogacy laws").
* National Infertility Association, www.resolve.org (click "Family Building Options," then "Surrogacy").

Child Support

Child support guidelines: New York requires all parents to support their children. The amount of child support depends primarily on each parent's income and other resources and how much time each parent spends with the children.

State laws, forms, and resources: See list in "Divorce," above.

* www.supportguidelines.com: Links to state and federal laws and agencies.

State child support enforcement agency:

* Division of Child Support Enforcement, www.newyorkchildsupport.com.
* National Child Support Enforcement Association, www.ncsea.org: Information about federal programs and links to state agencies.

Federal child support enforcement programs and laws: Federal Parent Locator Service, www.acf.hhs.gov/programs/cse/newhire: Links to child support enforcement programs like the passport denial program.

Child support calculators to determine state guidelines: www.alllaw.com/calculators/childsupport: Search your state.

North Carolina

Statewide Legal Resources

State website:
- www.ncgov.com. Links and information for many state agencies and departments.
- www.ncdhhs.gov/residents. Especially relevant for state family law issues.

State and federal statutes:
- Nolo, www.nolo.com/legal-research/state-law.html.
- The Legal Information Institute at Cornell University, http://topics.law.cornell.edu/wex/table_family.
- Justia, www.justia.com/family.
- www.usa.gov: Federal government site.

State court information and family law forms:
- www.nccourts.org: Do-it-yourself court forms and instructions, links to local court websites. Search by topic, such as divorce, adoption, or custody.
- National Center for State Courts, www.ncsc.org: Links to state courts (browse by state under "Information and Resources").

Local laws:
- www.statelocalgov.net: Links to websites of many cities and counties, where you can check local rules and ordinances, such as graffiti rules.
- www.municode.com: Municipal codes.

Marriage

Requirements: No blood test required. You must be of the age of consent, not be too closely related to your intended spouse, not be married to anyone else, and have sufficient mental capacity, meaning you understand what you are doing when you marry. You can marry immediately after your marriage license is issued, and your license is good for 60 days. For more details, check your county clerk's office.

Common law marriage: No.

Community property: No.

Same-sex marriage: No.

Marriage-equivalent relationship: No. North Carolina does not recognize domestic partnerships, civil unions, or reciprocal beneficiaries.

Divorce

Grounds for divorce: Fault or no-fault grounds are allowed.

Residency requirement: At least one spouse must be a resident of North Carolina for six months or 180 days before filing for divorce.

How property is divided: Equitable division.

State laws, forms, and resources:
- North Carolina state court website, www.nccourts.org.
- Women's Law Initiative, www.womenslaw.org: State-by-state information on divorce, custody, and related topics.
- www.divorcenet.com, www.divorcesupport.com, www.divorceinfo.com, www.divorcecentral.com: Helpful divorce websites.

Divorce attorneys and mediators in your area:
- Nolo's Lawyer Directory, www.nolo.com: Divorce attorneys in your area.
- National Center for Lesbian Rights, www.nclrights.org, 800-528-6257: Attorneys experienced in same-sex divorces.
- www.mediate.com, 541-345-1629: Mediators in your area.

Child Custody

Child custody guidelines: North Carolina courts begin with a presumption that it's best for a child to have frequent and continuing contact with both parents after a divorce. If possible, judges want to support joint custody arrangements.

State laws, forms, and resources: See list in "Divorce," above.

International custody disputes: International Parental Child Abduction Division in the Office of Children's Issues of the U.S. State Department, http://travel.state.gov/childabduction, 888-407-4747.

State surrogacy laws:
- Human Rights Campaign, www.hrc.org (search "surrogacy laws").
- National Infertility Association, www.resolve.org (click "Family Building Options," then "Surrogacy").

Child Support

Child support guidelines: North Carolina requires all parents to support their children. The amount of child support depends primarily on each parent's income and other resources and how much time each parent spends with the children.

State laws, forms, and resources: See list in "Divorce," above.
- www.supportguidelines.com: Links to state and federal laws and agencies.

State child support enforcement agency:
- Child Support Enforcement, www.ncdhhs.gov/dss/cse/index.htm.
- National Child Support Enforcement Association, www.ncsea.org: Information about federal programs and links to state agencies.

Federal child support enforcement programs and laws: Federal Parent Locator Service, www.acf.hhs.gov/programs/cse/newhire: Links to child support enforcement programs like the passport denial program.

Child support calculators to determine state guidelines: www.alllaw.com/calculators/childsupport: Search your state.

North Dakota

Statewide Legal Resources

State website:

- www.nd.gov. Links and information for many state agencies and departments.
- www.nd.gov/dhs/services/childfamily. Especially relevant for state family law issues.

State and federal statutes:

- Nolo, www.nolo.com/legal-research/state-law.html.
- The Legal Information Institute at Cornell University, http://topics.law.cornell.edu/wex/table_family.
- Justia, www.justia.com/family.
- www.usa.gov: Federal government site.

State court information and family law forms:

- www.ndcourts.com/Court/Courts.htm: Do-it-yourself court forms and instructions, links to local court websites. Search by topic, such as divorce, adoption, or custody.
- National Center for State Courts, www.ncsc.org: Links to state courts (browse by state under "Information and Resources").

Local laws:

- www.statelocalgov.net: Links to websites of many cities and counties, where you can check local rules and ordinances, such as graffiti rules.
- www.municode.com: Municipal codes.

Marriage

Requirements: No blood test required. You must be of the age of consent, not be too closely related to your intended spouse, not be married to anyone else, and have sufficient mental capacity, meaning you understand what you are doing when you marry. You can marry immediately after your marriage license is issued, and your license is good for 60 days. For more details, check your county clerk's office.

Common law marriage: No.

Community property: No.

Same-sex marriage: No.

Marriage-equivalent relationship: No. North Dakota does not recognize domestic partnerships, civil unions, or reciprocal beneficiaries.

Divorce

Grounds for divorce: Fault or no-fault grounds are allowed.

Residency requirement: At least one spouse must be a resident of North Dakota for six months before filing for divorce.

How property is divided: Equitable division.

State laws, forms, and resources:
- North Dakota state court website, www.ndcourts.com/Court/Courts. htm.
- Women's Law Initiative, www.womenslaw.org: State-by-state information on divorce, custody, and related topics.
- www.divorcenet.com, www.divorcesupport.com, www.divorceinfo.com, www.divorcecentral.com: Helpful divorce websites.

Divorce attorneys and mediators in your area:
- Nolo's Lawyer Directory, www.nolo.com: Divorce attorneys in your area.
- National Center for Lesbian Rights, www.nclrights.org, 800-528-6257: Attorneys experienced in same-sex divorces.
- www.mediate.com, 541-345-1629: Mediators in your area.

Child Custody

Child custody guidelines: North Dakota courts begin with a presumption that it's best for a child to have frequent and continuing contact with both parents after a divorce. If possible, judges want to support joint custody arrangements.

State laws, forms, and resources: See list in "Divorce," above.

International custody disputes: International Parental Child Abduction Division in the Office of Children's Issues of the U.S. State Department, http://travel.state.gov/childabduction, 888-407-4747.

State surrogacy laws:

- Human Rights Campaign, www.hrc.org (search "surrogacy laws").
- National Infertility Association, www.resolve.org (click "Family Building Options," then "Surrogacy").

Child Support

Child support guidelines: North Dakota requires all parents to support their children. The amount of child support depends primarily on each parent's income and other resources and how much time each parent spends with the children.

State laws, forms, and resources: See list in "Divorce," above.

- www.supportguidelines.com: Links to state and federal laws and agencies.

State child support enforcement agency:

- Child Support Enforcement, www.nd.gov/dhs/services/childsupport.
- National Child Support Enforcement Association, www.ncsea.org: Information about federal programs and links to state agencies.

Federal child support enforcement programs and laws: Federal Parent Locator Service, www.acf.hhs.gov/programs/cse/newhire: Links to child support enforcement programs like the passport denial program.

Child support calculators to determine state guidelines: www.alllaw.com/calculators/childsupport: Search your state.

Ohio

Ohio

Statewide Legal Resources

State website:
- www.ohio.gov. Links and information for many state agencies and departments.
- www.jfs.ohio.gov/families. Especially relevant for state family law issues.

State and federal statutes:
- Nolo, www.nolo.com/legal-research/state-law.html.
- The Legal Information Institute at Cornell University, http://topics.law.cornell.edu/wex/table_family.
- Justia, www.justia.com/family.
- www.usa.gov: Federal government site.

State court information and family law forms:
- www.supremecourt.ohio.gov: Do-it-yourself court forms and instructions, links to local court websites. Search by topic, such as divorce, adoption, or custody.
- National Center for State Courts, www.ncsc.org: Links to state courts (browse by state under "Information and Resources").

Local laws:
- www.statelocalgov.net: Links to websites of many cities and counties, where you can check local rules and ordinances, such as graffiti rules.
- www.municode.com: Municipal codes.

Marriage

Requirements: No blood test required. You must be of the age of consent, not be too closely related to your intended spouse, not be married to anyone else, and have sufficient mental capacity, meaning you understand what you are doing when you marry. You can marry immediately after your marriage license is issued, and your license is good for 60 days. For more details, check your county clerk's office.

Common law marriage: Yes. A couple must intend to be married, live together for a significant period of time, and hold themselves out as a married couple.

Community property: No.

Same-sex marriage: No.

Marriage-equivalent relationship: No. Ohio does not recognize domestic partnerships, civil unions, or reciprocal beneficiaries.

Divorce

Grounds for divorce: Fault or no-fault grounds are allowed, or you can base your divorce on the fact that you've been separated from your spouse for at least two years.

Residency requirement: At least one spouse must be a resident of Ohio for six months before filing for divorce.

How property is divided: Equitable division.

State laws, forms, and resources:
- Ohio state court website, www.supremecourt.ohio.gov.
- Women's Law Initiative, www.womenslaw.org: State-by-state information on divorce, custody, and related topics.
- www.divorcenet.com, www.divorcesupport.com, www.divorceinfo.com, www.divorcecentral.com: Helpful divorce websites.

Divorce attorneys and mediators in your area:
- Nolo's Lawyer Directory, www.nolo.com: Divorce attorneys in your area.
- National Center for Lesbian Rights, www.nclrights.org, 800-528-6257: Attorneys experienced in same-sex divorces.
- www.mediate.com, 541-345-1629: Mediators in your area.

Child Custody

Child custody guidelines: Ohio courts begin with a presumption that it's best for a child to have frequent and continuing contact with both parents after a divorce. If possible, judges want to support joint custody arrangements.

State laws, forms, and resources: See list in "Divorce," above.

Ohio

International custody disputes: International Parental Child Abduction Division in the Office of Children's Issues of the U.S. State Department, http://travel.state.gov/childabduction, 888-407-4747.

State surrogacy laws:
- Human Rights Campaign, www.hrc.org (search "surrogacy laws").
- National Infertility Association, www.resolve.org (click "Family Building Options," then "Surrogacy").

Child Support

Child support guidelines: Ohio requires all parents to support their children. The amount of child support depends primarily on each parent's income and other resources and how much time each parent spends with the children.

State laws, forms, and resources: See list in "Divorce," above.
- www.supportguidelines.com: Links to state and federal laws and agencies.

State child support enforcement agency:
- Office of Child Support, www.jfs.ohio.gov/Ocs/index.stm.
- National Child Support Enforcement Association, www.ncsea.org: Information about federal programs and links to state agencies.

Federal child support enforcement programs and laws: Federal Parent Locator Service, www.acf.hhs.gov/programs/cse/newhire: Links to child support enforcement programs like the passport denial program.

Child support calculators to determine state guidelines: www.alllaw.com/calculators/childsupport: Search your state.

Oklahoma

Statewide Legal Resources

State website:
- www.ok.gov. Links and information for many state agencies and departments.
- www.okdhs.org/divisionsoffices/hsc/cfsd. Especially relevant for state family law issues.

State and federal statutes:
- Nolo, www.nolo.com/legal-research/state-law.html.
- The Legal Information Institute at Cornell University, http://topics.law. cornell.edu/wex/table_family.
- Justia, www.justia.com/family.
- www.usa.gov: Federal government site.

State court information and family law forms:
- www.oscn.net/applications/oscn: Do-it-yourself court forms and instructions, links to local court websites. Search by topic, such as divorce, adoption, or custody.
- National Center for State Courts, www.ncsc.org: Links to state courts (browse by state under "Information and Resources").

Local laws:
- www.statelocalgov.net: Links to websites of many cities and counties, where you can check local rules and ordinances, such as graffiti rules.
- www.municode.com: Municipal codes.

Marriage

Requirements: No blood test required. You must be of the age of consent, not be too closely related to your intended spouse, not be married to anyone else, and have sufficient mental capacity, meaning you understand what you are doing when you marry. You can marry immediately after your marriage license is issued, and your license is good for 30 days. For more details, check your county clerk's office.

Common law marriage: Yes. A couple must intend to be married, live together for a significant period of time, and hold themselves out as a married couple.

Community property: No.

Same-sex marriage: No.

Marriage-equivalent relationship: No. Oklahoma does not recognize domestic partnerships, civil unions, or reciprocal beneficiaries.

Divorce

Grounds for divorce: Fault or no-fault grounds are allowed, or you can base your divorce on the fact that you've been separated from your spouse for at least two years.

Residency requirement: At least one spouse must be a resident of Oklahoma for six months before filing for divorce.

How property is divided: Equitable division.

State laws, forms, and resources:
- Oklahoma state court website, www.oscn.net/applications/oscn.
- Women's Law Initiative, www.womenslaw.org: State-by-state information on divorce, custody, and related topics.
- www.divorcenet.com, www.divorcesupport.com, www.divorceinfo.com, www.divorcecentral.com: Helpful divorce websites.

Divorce attorneys and mediators in your area:
- Nolo's Lawyer Directory, www.nolo.com: Divorce attorneys in your area.
- National Center for Lesbian Rights, www.nclrights.org, 800-528-6257: Attorneys experienced in same-sex divorces.
- www.mediate.com, 541-345-1629: Mediators in your area.

Child Custody

Child custody guidelines: Oklahoma courts begin with a presumption that it's best for a child to have frequent and continuing contact with both parents after a divorce. If possible, judges want to support joint custody arrangements.

State laws, forms, and resources: See list in "Divorce," above.

International custody disputes: International Parental Child Abduction Division in the Office of Children's Issues of the U.S. State Department, http://travel.state.gov/childabduction, 888-407-4747.

State surrogacy laws:

- Human Rights Campaign, www.hrc.org (search "surrogacy laws").
- National Infertility Association, www.resolve.org (click "Family Building Options," then "Surrogacy").

Child Support

Child support guidelines: Oklahoma requires all parents to support their children. The amount of child support depends primarily on each parent's income and other resources and how much time each parent spends with the children.

State laws, forms, and resources: See list in "Divorce," above.

- www.supportguidelines.com: Links to state and federal laws and agencies.

State child support enforcement agency:

- Child Support Services, www.okdhs.org/programsandservices/ocss.
- National Child Support Enforcement Association, www.ncsea.org: Information about federal programs and links to state agencies.

Federal child support enforcement programs and laws: Federal Parent Locator Service, www.acf.hhs.gov/programs/cse/newhire: Links to child support enforcement programs like the passport denial program.

Child support calculators to determine state guidelines: www.alllaw.com/calculators/childsupport: Search your state.

Oregon

Statewide Legal Resources

State website:
- www.oregon.gov. Links and information for many state agencies and departments.
- www.oregon.gov/DHS/aboutdhs/structure/caf.shtml. Especially relevant for state family law issues.

State and federal statutes:
- Nolo, www.nolo.com/legal-research/state-law.html.
- The Legal Information Institute at Cornell University, http://topics.law.cornell.edu/wex/table_family.
- Justia, www.justia.com/family.
- www.usa.gov: Federal government site.

State court information and family law forms:
- www.courts.oregon.gov: Do-it-yourself court forms and instructions, links to local court websites. Search by topic, such as divorce, adoption, or custody.
- National Center for State Courts, www.ncsc.org: Links to state courts (browse by state under "Information and Resources").

Local laws:
- www.statelocalgov.net: Links to websites of many cities and counties, where you can check local rules and ordinances, such as graffiti rules.
- www.municode.com: Municipal codes.

Marriage

Requirements: No blood test required. You must be of the age of consent, not be too closely related to your intended spouse, not be married to anyone else, and have sufficient mental capacity, meaning you understand what you are doing when you marry. You can marry three days after your marriage license is issued, and your license is good for 60 days. For more details, check your county clerk's office.

Oregon

Common law marriage: No.

Community property: No.

Same-sex marriage: No.

Marriage-equivalent relationship: Yes. Same-sex couples can register as domestic partners, creating a relationship with all of the rights and responsibilities of marriage under state law.

Divorce

Grounds for divorce: No-fault. However, fault may be considered by the court as a factor in dividing property or awarding alimony.

Residency requirement: At least one spouse must be a resident of Oregon for six months or 180 days before filing for divorce.

How property is divided: Equitable division.

State laws, forms, and resources:
- Oregon state court website, www.courts.oregon.gov.
- Women's Law Initiative, www.womenslaw.org: State-by-state information on divorce, custody, and related topics.
- www.divorcenet.com, www.divorcesupport.com, www.divorceinfo.com, www.divorcecentral.com: Helpful divorce websites.

Divorce attorneys and mediators in your area:
- Nolo's Lawyer Directory, www.nolo.com: Divorce attorneys in your area.
- National Center for Lesbian Rights, www.nclrights.org, 800-528-6257: Attorneys experienced in same-sex divorces.
- www.mediate.com, 541-345-1629: Mediators in your area.

Child Custody

Child custody guidelines: Oregon courts begin with a presumption that it's best for a child to have frequent and continuing contact with both parents after a divorce. If possible, judges want to support joint custody arrangements.

State laws, forms, and resources: See list in "Divorce," above.

International custody disputes: International Parental Child Abduction Division in the Office of Children's Issues of the U.S. State Department, http://travel.state.gov/childabduction, 888-407-4747.

State surrogacy laws:
- Human Rights Campaign, www.hrc.org (search "surrogacy laws").
- National Infertility Association, www.resolve.org (click "Family Building Options," then "Surrogacy").

Child Support

Child support guidelines: Oregon requires all parents to support their children. The amount of child support depends primarily on each parent's income and other resources and how much time each parent spends with the children.

State laws, forms, and resources: See list in "Divorce," above.
- www.supportguidelines.com: Links to state and federal laws and agencies.

State child support enforcement agency:
- Division of Child Support, www.doj.state.or.us/dcs/index.shtml.
- National Child Support Enforcement Association, www.ncsea.org: Information about federal programs and links to state agencies.

Federal child support enforcement programs and laws: Federal Parent Locator Service, www.acf.hhs.gov/programs/cse/newhire: Links to child support enforcement programs like the passport denial program.

Child support calculators to determine state guidelines: www.alllaw.com/calculators/childsupport: Search your state.

Pennsylvania

Statewide Legal Resources

State website:
- www.state.pa.us. Links and information for many state agencies and departments.
- www.pachildren.state.pa.us. Especially relevant for state family law issues.

State and federal statutes:
- Nolo, www.nolo.com/legal-research/state-law.html.
- The Legal Information Institute at Cornell University, http://topics.law.cornell.edu/wex/table_family.
- Justia, www.justia.com/family.
- www.usa.gov: Federal government site.

State court information and family law forms:
- www.aopc.org: Do-it-yourself court forms and instructions, links to local court websites. Search by topic, such as divorce, adoption, or custody.
- National Center for State Courts, www.ncsc.org: Links to state courts (browse by state under "Information and Resources").

Local laws:
- www.statelocalgov.net: Links to websites of many cities and counties, where you can check local rules and ordinances, such as graffiti rules.
- www.municode.com: Municipal codes.

Marriage

Requirements: No blood test required. You must be of the age of consent, not be too closely related to your intended spouse, not be married to anyone else, and have sufficient mental capacity, meaning you understand what you are doing when you marry. You can marry immediately after your marriage license is issued, and your license is good for 60 days. For more details, check your county clerk's office.

Common law marriage: Yes. Common law marriages created before January 1, 2005 are recognized when the couple intended to be married, lived together for a significant period of time, and held themselves out as a married couple.

Community property: No.

Same-sex marriage: No.

Marriage-equivalent relationship: No. Pennsylvania does not recognize domestic partnerships, civil unions, or reciprocal beneficiaries.

Divorce

Grounds for divorce: Fault or no-fault grounds are allowed.

Residency requirement: At least one spouse must be a resident of Pennsylvania for six months before filing for divorce.

How property is divided: Equitable division.

State laws, forms, and resources:
- Pennsylvania state court website, www.aopc.org.
- Women's Law Initiative, www.womenslaw.org: State-by-state information on divorce, custody, and related topics.
- www.divorcenet.com, www.divorcesupport.com, www.divorceinfo.com, www.divorcecentral.com: Helpful divorce websites.

Divorce attorneys and mediators in your area:
- Nolo's Lawyer Directory, www.nolo.com: Divorce attorneys in your area.
- National Center for Lesbian Rights, www.nclrights.org, 800-528-6257: Attorneys experienced in same-sex divorces.
- www.mediate.com, 541-345-1629: Mediators in your area.

Child Custody

Child custody guidelines: Pennsylvania courts begin with a presumption that it's best for a child to have frequent and continuing contact with both parents after a divorce. If possible, judges want to support joint custody arrangements.

State laws, forms, and resources: See list in "Divorce," above.

International custody disputes: International Parental Child Abduction Division in the Office of Children's Issues of the U.S. State Department, http://travel.state.gov/childabduction, 888-407-4747.

State surrogacy laws:

* Human Rights Campaign, www.hrc.org (search "surrogacy laws").
* National Infertility Association, www.resolve.org (click "Family Building Options," then "Surrogacy").

Child Support

Child support guidelines: Pennsylvania requires all parents to support their children. The amount of child support depends primarily on each parent's income and other resources and how much time each parent spends with the children.

State laws, forms, and resources: See list in "Divorce," above.

* www.supportguidelines.com: Links to state and federal laws and agencies.

State child support enforcement agency:

* Bureau of Child Support Enforcement, www.humanservices.state.pa.us/csws/index.aspx.
* National Child Support Enforcement Association, www.ncsea.org: Information about federal programs and links to state agencies.

Federal child support enforcement programs and laws: Federal Parent Locator Service, www.acf.hhs.gov/programs/cse/newhire: Links to child support enforcement programs like the passport denial program.

Child support calculators to determine state guidelines: www.alllaw.com/calculators/childsupport: Search your state.

Rhode Island

Statewide Legal Resources

State website:

* www.ri.gov. Links and information for many state agencies and departments.
* www.dcyf.ri.gov. Especially relevant for state family law issues.

State and federal statutes:

* Nolo, www.nolo.com/legal-research/state-law.html.
* The Legal Information Institute at Cornell University, http://topics.law. cornell.edu/wex/table_family.
* Justia, www.justia.com/family.
* www.usa.gov: Federal government site.

State court information and family law forms:

* www.courts.ri.gov: Do-it-yourself court forms and instructions, links to local court websites. Search by topic, such as divorce, adoption, or custody.
* National Center for State Courts, www.ncsc.org: Links to state courts (browse by state under "Information and Resources").

Local laws:

* www.statelocalgov.net: Links to websites of many cities and counties, where you can check local rules and ordinances, such as graffiti rules.
* www.municode.com: Municipal codes.

Marriage

Requirements: No blood test required. You must be of the age of consent, not be too closely related to your intended spouse, not be married to anyone else, and have sufficient mental capacity, meaning you understand what you are doing when you marry. You can marry immediately after your marriage license is issued, and your license is good for three months. For more details, check your county clerk's office.

Common law marriage: Yes. A couple must intend to be married, live together for a significant period of time, and hold themselves out as a married couple.

Community property: No.

Same-sex marriage: No.

Marriage-equivalent relationship: No. Rhode Island does not recognize domestic partnerships, civil unions, or reciprocal beneficiaries.

Divorce

Grounds for divorce: Fault or no-fault grounds are allowed, or you can base your divorce on the fact that you've been separated from your spouse for at least two years.

Residency requirement: At least one spouse must be a resident of Rhode Island for 12 months or one year before filing for divorce.

How property is divided: Equitable division.

State laws, forms, and resources:
- Rhode Island state court website, www.courts.ri.gov.
- Women's Law Initiative, www.womenslaw.org: State-by-state information on divorce, custody, and related topics.
- www.divorcenet.com, www.divorcesupport.com, www.divorceinfo.com, www.divorcecentral.com: Helpful divorce websites.

Divorce attorneys and mediators in your area:
- Nolo's Lawyer Directory, www.nolo.com: Divorce attorneys in your area.
- National Center for Lesbian Rights, www.nclrights.org, 800-528-6257: Attorneys experienced in same-sex divorces.
- www.mediate.com, 541-345-1629: Mediators in your area.

Child Custody

Child custody guidelines: Rhode Island courts begin with a presumption that it's best for a child to have frequent and continuing contact with both parents after a divorce. If possible, judges want to support joint custody arrangements.

State laws, forms, and resources: See list in "Divorce," above.

International custody disputes: International Parental Child Abduction Division in the Office of Children's Issues of the U.S. State Department, http://travel.state.gov/childabduction, 888-407-4747.

State surrogacy laws:

- Human Rights Campaign, www.hrc.org (search "surrogacy laws").
- National Infertility Association, www.resolve.org (click "Family Building Options," then "Surrogacy").

Child Support

Child support guidelines: Rhode Island requires all parents to support their children. The amount of child support depends primarily on each parent's income and other resources and how much time each parent spends with the children.

State laws, forms, and resources: See list in "Divorce," above.

- www.supportguidelines.com: Links to state and federal laws and agencies.

State child support enforcement agency:

- Office of Child Support Services, www.cse.ri.gov.
- National Child Support Enforcement Association, www.ncsea.org: Information about federal programs and links to state agencies.

Federal child support enforcement programs and laws: Federal Parent Locator Service, www.acf.hhs.gov/programs/cse/newhire: Links to child support enforcement programs like the passport denial program.

Child support calculators to determine state guidelines: www.alllaw.com/calculators/childsupport: Search your state.

South Carolina

Statewide Legal Resources

State website:
- www.sc.gov. Links and information for many state agencies and departments.
- www.dss.sc.gov/content/customers/index.aspx. Especially relevant for state family law issues.

State and federal statutes:
- Nolo, www.nolo.com/legal-research/state-law.html.
- The Legal Information Institute at Cornell University, http://topics.law.cornell.edu/wex/table_family.
- Justia, www.justia.com/family.
- www.usa.gov: Federal government site.

State court information and family law forms:
- www.sccourts.org: Do-it-yourself court forms and instructions, links to local court websites. Search by topic, such as divorce, adoption, or custody.
- National Center for State Courts, www.ncsc.org: Links to state courts (browse by state under "Information and Resources").

Local laws:
- www.statelocalgov.net: Links to websites of many cities and counties, where you can check local rules and ordinances, such as graffiti rules.
- www.municode.com: Municipal codes.

Marriage

Requirements: No blood test required. You must be of the age of consent, not be too closely related to your intended spouse, not be married to anyone else, and have sufficient mental capacity, meaning you understand what you are doing when you marry. You can marry immediately after your marriage license is issued. For more details, check your county clerk's office.

Common law marriage: Yes. A couple must intend to be married, live together for a significant period of time, and hold themselves out as a married couple.

Community property: No.

Same-sex marriage: No.

Marriage-equivalent relationship: No. South Carolina does not recognize domestic partnerships, civil unions, or reciprocal beneficiaries.

Divorce

Grounds for divorce: Fault or no-fault grounds are allowed.

Residency requirement: At least one spouse must be a resident of South Carolina for three months or 90 days (unless only one spouse is resident, then one year) before filing for divorce.

How property is divided: Equitable division.

State laws, forms, and resources:
- South Carolina state court website, www.sccourts.org.
- Women's Law Initiative, www.womenslaw.org: State-by-state information on divorce, custody, and related topics.
- www.divorcenet.com, www.divorcesupport.com, www.divorceinfo.com, www.divorcecentral.com: Helpful divorce websites.

Divorce attorneys and mediators in your area:
- Nolo's Lawyer Directory, www.nolo.com: Divorce attorneys in your area.
- National Center for Lesbian Rights, www.nclrights.org, 800-528-6257: Attorneys experienced in same-sex divorces.
- www.mediate.com, 541-345-1629: Mediators in your area.

Child Custody

Child custody guidelines: South Carolina courts begin with a presumption that it's best for a child to have frequent and continuing contact with both parents after a divorce. If possible, judges want to support joint custody arrangements.

State laws, forms, and resources: See list in "Divorce," above.

International custody disputes: International Parental Child Abduction Division in the Office of Children's Issues of the U.S. State Department, http://travel.state.gov/childabduction, 888-407-4747.

State surrogacy laws:

- Human Rights Campaign, www.hrc.org (search "surrogacy laws").
- National Infertility Association, www.resolve.org (click "Family Building Options," then "Surrogacy").

Child Support

Child support guidelines: South Carolina requires all parents to support their children. The amount of child support depends primarily on each parent's income and other resources and how much time each parent spends with the children.

State laws, forms, and resources: See list in "Divorce," above.

- www.supportguidelines.com: Links to state and federal laws and agencies.

State child support enforcement agency:

- Child Support Enforcement, www.state.sc.us/dss/csed.
- National Child Support Enforcement Association, www.ncsea.org: Information about federal programs and links to state agencies.

Federal child support enforcement programs and laws: Federal Parent Locator Service, www.acf.hhs.gov/programs/cse/newhire: Links to child support enforcement programs like the passport denial program.

Child support calculators to determine state guidelines: www.alllaw.com/calculators/childsupport: Search your state.

South Dakota

Statewide Legal Resources

State website:

- www.sd.gov. Links and information for many state agencies and departments.
- www.dss.sd.gov/divisions. Especially relevant for state family law issues.

State and federal statutes:

- Nolo, www.nolo.com/legal-research/state-law.html.
- The Legal Information Institute at Cornell University, http://topics.law.cornell.edu/wex/table_family.
- Justia, www.justia.com/family.
- www.usa.gov: Federal government site.

State court information and family law forms:

- www.sdjudicial.com: Do-it-yourself court forms and instructions, links to local court websites. Search by topic, such as divorce, adoption, or custody.
- National Center for State Courts, www.ncsc.org: Links to state courts (browse by state under "Information and Resources").

Local laws:

- www.statelocalgov.net: Links to websites of many cities and counties, where you can check local rules and ordinances, such as graffiti rules.
- www.municode.com: Municipal codes.

Marriage

Requirements: No blood test required. You must be of the age of consent, not be too closely related to your intended spouse, not be married to anyone else, and have sufficient mental capacity, meaning you understand what you are doing when you marry. You can marry immediately after your marriage license is issued, and your license is good for 20 days. For more details, check your county clerk's office.

Common law marriage: No.

Community property: No.

Same-sex marriage: No.

Marriage-equivalent relationship: No. South Dakota does not recognize domestic partnerships, civil unions, or reciprocal beneficiaries.

Divorce

Grounds for divorce: No-fault. However, fault may be considered by the court as a factor in dividing property or awarding alimony.

Residency requirement: N/A

How property is divided: Equitable division.

State laws, forms, and resources:
- South Dakota state court website, www.sdjudicial.com.
- Women's Law Initiative, www.womenslaw.org: State-by-state information on divorce, custody, and related topics.
- www.divorcenet.com, www.divorcesupport.com, www.divorceinfo.com, www.divorcecentral.com: Helpful divorce websites.

Divorce attorneys and mediators in your area:
- Nolo's Lawyer Directory, www.nolo.com: Divorce attorneys in your area.
- National Center for Lesbian Rights, www.nclrights.org, 800-528-6257: Attorneys experienced in same-sex divorces.
- www.mediate.com, 541-345-1629: Mediators in your area.

Child Custody

Child custody guidelines: South Dakota courts begin with a presumption that it's best for a child to have frequent and continuing contact with both parents after a divorce. If possible, judges want to support joint custody arrangements.

State laws, forms, and resources: See list in "Divorce," above.

International custody disputes: International Parental Child Abduction Division in the Office of Children's Issues of the U.S. State Department, http://travel.state.gov/childabduction, 888-407-4747.

State surrogacy laws:

- Human Rights Campaign, www.hrc.org (search "surrogacy laws").
- National Infertility Association, www.resolve.org (click "Family Building Options," then "Surrogacy").

Child Support

Child support guidelines: South Dakota requires all parents to support their children. The amount of child support depends primarily on each parent's income and other resources and how much time each parent spends with the children.

State laws, forms, and resources: See list in "Divorce," above.

- www.supportguidelines.com: Links to state and federal laws and agencies.

State child support enforcement agency:

- Division of Child Support, www.dss.sd.gov/childsupport.
- National Child Support Enforcement Association, www.ncsea.org: Information about federal programs and links to state agencies.

Federal child support enforcement programs and laws: Federal Parent Locator Service, www.acf.hhs.gov/programs/cse/newhire: Links to child support enforcement programs like the passport denial program.

Child support calculators to determine state guidelines: www.alllaw.com/calculators/childsupport: Search your state.

Tennessee

Statewide Legal Resources

State website:

- www.tn.gov. Links and information for many state agencies and departments.
- www.state.tn.us/humanserv/adfam/afs_index.html. Especially relevant for state family law issues.

State and federal statutes:

- Nolo, www.nolo.com/legal-research/state-law.html.
- The Legal Information Institute at Cornell University, http://topics.law.cornell.edu/wex/table_family.
- Justia, www.justia.com/family.
- www.usa.gov: Federal government site.

State court information and family law forms:

- www.tsc.state.tn.us: Do-it-yourself court forms and instructions, links to local court websites. Search by topic, such as divorce, adoption, or custody.
- National Center for State Courts, www.ncsc.org: Links to state courts (browse by state under "Information and Resources").

Local laws:

- www.statelocalgov.net: Links to websites of many cities and counties, where you can check local rules and ordinances, such as graffiti rules.
- www.municode.com: Municipal codes.

Marriage

Requirements: No blood test required. You must be of the age of consent, not be too closely related to your intended spouse, not be married to anyone else, and have sufficient mental capacity, meaning you understand what you are doing when you marry. You can marry immediately after your marriage license is issued, and your license is good for 30 days. For more details, check your county clerk's office.

Common law marriage: No.

Community property: No.

Same-sex marriage: No.

Marriage-equivalent relationship: No. Tennessee does not recognize domestic partnerships, civil unions, or reciprocal beneficiaries.

Divorce

Grounds for divorce: Fault or no-fault grounds are allowed, or you can base your divorce on the fact that you've been separated from your spouse for at least two years.

Residency requirement: At least one spouse must be a resident of Tennessee for six months or 180 days before filing for divorce.

How property is divided: Equitable division.

State laws, forms, and resources:
* Tennessee state court website, www.tsc.state.tn.us.
* Women's Law Initiative, www.womenslaw.org: State-by-state information on divorce, custody, and related topics.
* www.divorcenet.com, www.divorcesupport.com, www.divorceinfo.com, www.divorcecentral.com: Helpful divorce websites.

Divorce attorneys and mediators in your area:
* Nolo's Lawyer Directory, www.nolo.com: Divorce attorneys in your area.
* National Center for Lesbian Rights, www.nclrights.org, 800-528-6257: Attorneys experienced in same-sex divorces.
* www.mediate.com, 541-345-1629: Mediators in your area.

Child Custody

Child custody guidelines: Tennessee courts begin with a presumption that it's best for a child to have frequent and continuing contact with both parents after a divorce. If possible, judges want to support joint custody arrangements.

State laws, forms, and resources: See list in "Divorce," above.

International custody disputes: International Parental Child Abduction Division in the Office of Children's Issues of the U.S. State Department, http://travel.state.gov/childabduction, 888-407-4747.

State surrogacy laws:
- Human Rights Campaign, www.hrc.org (search "surrogacy laws").
- National Infertility Association, www.resolve.org (click "Family Building Options," then "Surrogacy").

Child Support

Child support guidelines: Tennessee requires all parents to support their children. The amount of child support depends primarily on each parent's income and other resources and how much time each parent spends with the children.

State laws, forms, and resources: See list in "Divorce," above.
- www.supportguidelines.com: Links to state and federal laws and agencies.

State child support enforcement agency:
- Department of Human Services—Child Support Services, http://state.tn.us/humanserv/cs/cs_main.html.
- National Child Support Enforcement Association, www.ncsea.org: Information about federal programs and links to state agencies.

Federal child support enforcement programs and laws: Federal Parent Locator Service, www.acf.hhs.gov/programs/cse/newhire: Links to child support enforcement programs like the passport denial program.

Child support calculators to determine state guidelines: www.alllaw.com/calculators/childsupport: Search your state.

Texas

Statewide Legal Resources

State website:
- www.texas.gov. Links and information for many state agencies and departments.
- www.dfps.state.tx.us/Site_Map/parents.asp. Especially relevant for state family law issues.

State and federal statutes:
- Nolo, www.nolo.com/legal-research/state-law.html.
- The Legal Information Institute at Cornell University, http://topics.law. cornell.edu/wex/table_family.
- Justia, www.justia.com/family.
- www.usa.gov: Federal government site.

State court information and family law forms:
- www.courts.state.tx.us: Do-it-yourself court forms and instructions, links to local court websites. Search by topic, such as divorce, adoption, or custody.
- National Center for State Courts, www.ncsc.org: Links to state courts (browse by state under "Information and Resources").

Local laws:
- www.statelocalgov.net: Links to websites of many cities and counties, where you can check local rules and ordinances, such as graffiti rules.
- www.municode.com: Municipal codes.

Marriage

Requirements: No blood test required. You must be of the age of consent, not be too closely related to your intended spouse, not be married to anyone else, and have sufficient mental capacity, meaning you understand what you are doing when you marry. You can marry three days after your marriage license is issued, and your license is good for 30 days. For more details, check your county clerk's office.

Common law marriage: Yes. A couple must intend to be married, live together for a significant period of time, and hold themselves out as a married couple.

Community property: Yes.

Same-sex marriage: No.

Marriage-equivalent relationship: No. Texas does not recognize domestic partnerships, civil unions, or reciprocal beneficiaries.

Divorce

Grounds for divorce: Fault or no-fault grounds are allowed, or you can base your divorce on the fact that you've been separated from your spouse for at least two years.

Residency requirement: At least one spouse must be a resident of Texas for six months before filing for divorce.

How property is divided: Community property.

State laws, forms, and resources:
- Texas state court website, www.courts.state.tx.us.
- Women's Law Initiative, www.womenslaw.org: State-by-state information on divorce, custody, and related topics.
- www.divorcenet.com, www.divorcesupport.com, www.divorceinfo.com, www.divorcecentral.com: Helpful divorce websites.

Divorce attorneys and mediators in your area:
- Nolo's Lawyer Directory, www.nolo.com: Divorce attorneys in your area.
- National Center for Lesbian Rights, www.nclrights.org, 800-528-6257: Attorneys experienced in same-sex divorces.
- www.mediate.com, 541-345-1629: Mediators in your area.

Child Custody

Child custody guidelines: Texas courts begin with a presumption that it's best for a child to have frequent and continuing contact with both parents after a divorce. If possible, judges want to support joint custody arrangements.

State laws, forms, and resources: See list in "Divorce," above.

International custody disputes: International Parental Child Abduction Division in the Office of Children's Issues of the U.S. State Department, http://travel.state.gov/childabduction, 888-407-4747.

State surrogacy laws:

- Human Rights Campaign, www.hrc.org (search "surrogacy laws").
- National Infertility Association, www.resolve.org (click "Family Building Options," then "Surrogacy").

Child Support

Child support guidelines: Texas requires all parents to support their children. The amount of child support depends primarily on each parent's income and other resources and how much time each parent spends with the children.

State laws, forms, and resources: See list in "Divorce," above.

- www.supportguidelines.com: Links to state and federal laws and agencies.

State child support enforcement agency:

- Child Support Division, Office of the Attorney General, www.oag.state.tx.us/cs/index.shtml.
- National Child Support Enforcement Association, www.ncsea.org: Information about federal programs and links to state agencies.

Federal child support enforcement programs and laws: Federal Parent Locator Service, www.acf.hhs.gov/programs/cse/newhire: Links to child support enforcement programs like the passport denial program.

Child support calculators to determine state guidelines: www.alllaw.com/calculators/childsupport: Search your state.

Utah

Statewide Legal Resources

State website:
- www.utah.gov. Links and information for many state agencies and departments.
- www.dhs.utah.gov/service_childrenfamilies.htm. Especially relevant for state family law issues.

State and federal statutes:
- Nolo, www.nolo.com/legal-research/state-law.html.
- The Legal Information Institute at Cornell University, http://topics.law.cornell.edu/wex/table_family.
- Justia, www.justia.com/family.
- www.usa.gov: Federal government site.

State court information and family law forms:
- www.utcourts.gov: Do-it-yourself court forms and instructions, links to local court websites. Search by topic, such as divorce, adoption, or custody.
- National Center for State Courts, www.ncsc.org: Links to state courts (browse by state under "Information and Resources").

Local laws:
- www.statelocalgov.net: Links to websites of many cities and counties, where you can check local rules and ordinances, such as graffiti rules.
- www.municode.com: Municipal codes.

Marriage

Requirements: No blood test required. You must be of the age of consent, not be too closely related to your intended spouse, not be married to anyone else, and have sufficient mental capacity, meaning you understand what you are doing when you marry. You can marry immediately after your marriage license is issued, and your license is good for 30 days. For more details, check your county clerk's office.

Utah

Common law marriage: No.

Community property: No.

Same-sex marriage: No.

Marriage-equivalent relationship: No. Utah does not recognize domestic partnerships, civil unions, or reciprocal beneficiaries.

Divorce

Grounds for divorce: Fault or no-fault grounds are allowed, or you can base your divorce on the fact that you've been separated from your spouse for at least two years.

Residency requirement: At least one spouse must be a resident of Utah for three months or 90 days before filing for divorce.

How property is divided: Equitable division.

State laws, forms, and resources:
- Utah state court website, www.utcourts.gov.
- Women's Law Initiative, www.womenslaw.org: State-by-state information on divorce, custody, and related topics.
- www.divorcenet.com, www.divorcesupport.com, www.divorceinfo.com, www.divorcecentral.com: Helpful divorce websites.

Divorce attorneys and mediators in your area:
- Nolo's Lawyer Directory, www.nolo.com: Divorce attorneys in your area.
- National Center for Lesbian Rights, www.nclrights.org, 800-528-6257: Attorneys experienced in same-sex divorces.
- www.mediate.com, 541-345-1629: Mediators in your area.

Child Custody

Child custody guidelines: Utah courts begin with a presumption that it's best for a child to have frequent and continuing contact with both parents after a divorce. If possible, judges want to support joint custody arrangements.

State laws, forms, and resources: See list in "Divorce," above.

International custody disputes: International Parental Child Abduction Division in the Office of Children's Issues of the U.S. State Department, http://travel.state.gov/childabduction, 888-407-4747.

State surrogacy laws:

- Human Rights Campaign, www.hrc.org (search "surrogacy laws").
- National Infertility Association, www.resolve.org (click "Family Building Options," then "Surrogacy").

Child Support

Child support guidelines: Utah requires all parents to support their children. The amount of child support depends primarily on each parent's income and other resources and how much time each parent spends with the children.

State laws, forms, and resources: See list in "Divorce," above.

- www.supportguidelines.com: Links to state and federal laws and agencies.

State child support enforcement agency:

- Child Support Services, Office of Recovery Services, www.ors.utah.gov/child_support_services.htm.
- National Child Support Enforcement Association, www.ncsea.org: Information about federal programs and links to state agencies.

Federal child support enforcement programs and laws: Federal Parent Locator Service, www.acf.hhs.gov/programs/cse/newhire: Links to child support enforcement programs like the passport denial program.

Child support calculators to determine state guidelines: www.alllaw.com/calculators/childsupport: Search your state.

Vermont

Statewide Legal Resources

State website:

- www.vermont.gov. Links and information for many state agencies and departments.
- www.dcf.vermont.gov Especially relevant for state family law issues.

State and federal statutes:

- Nolo, www.nolo.com/legal-research/state-law.html.
- The Legal Information Institute at Cornell University, http://topics.law.cornell.edu/wex/table_family.
- Justia, www.justia.com/family.
- www.usa.gov: Federal government site.

State court information and family law forms:

- www.vermontjudiciary.org: Do-it-yourself court forms and instructions, links to local court websites. Search by topic, such as divorce, adoption, or custody.
- National Center for State Courts, www.ncsc.org: Links to state courts (browse by state under "Information and Resources").

Local laws:

- www.statelocalgov.net: Links to websites of many cities and counties, where you can check local rules and ordinances, such as graffiti rules.
- www.municode.com: Municipal codes.

Marriage

Requirements: No blood test required. You must be of the age of consent, not be too closely related to your intended spouse, not be married to anyone else, and have sufficient mental capacity, meaning you understand what you are doing when you marry. You can marry immediately after your marriage license is issued, and your license is good for 60 days. For more details, check your county clerk's office.

Common law marriage: No.

Vermont

Community property: No.

Same-sex marriage: Yes.

Marriage-equivalent relationship: No.

Divorce

Grounds for divorce: Fault or no-fault grounds are allowed.

Residency requirement: At least one spouse must be a resident of Vermont for six months or 180 days before filing for divorce.

How property is divided: Equitable division.

State laws, forms, and resources:
- Vermont state court website, www.vermontjudiciary.org.
- Women's Law Initiative, www.womenslaw.org: State-by-state information on divorce, custody, and related topics.
- www.divorcenet.com, www.divorcesupport.com, www.divorceinfo.com, www.divorcecentral.com: Helpful divorce websites.

Divorce attorneys and mediators in your area:
- Nolo's Lawyer Directory, www.nolo.com: Divorce attorneys in your area.
- National Center for Lesbian Rights, www.nclrights.org, 800-528-6257: Attorneys experienced in same-sex divorces.
- www.mediate.com, 541-345-1629: Mediators in your area.

Child Custody

Child custody guidelines: Vermont courts begin with a presumption that it's best for a child to have frequent and continuing contact with both parents after a divorce. If possible, judges want to support joint custody arrangements.

State laws, forms, and resources: See list in "Divorce," above.

International custody disputes: International Parental Child Abduction Division in the Office of Children's Issues of the U.S. State Department, http://travel.state.gov/childabduction, 888-407-4747.

State surrogacy laws:

- Human Rights Campaign, www.hrc.org (search "surrogacy laws").
- National Infertility Association, www.resolve.org (click "Family Building Options," then "Surrogacy").

Child Support

Child support guidelines: Vermont requires all parents to support their children. The amount of child support depends primarily on each parent's income and other resources and how much time each parent spends with the children.

State laws, forms, and resources: See list in "Divorce," above.

- www.supportguidelines.com: Links to state and federal laws and agencies.
- **State child support enforcement agency:** Office of Child Support, www.dcf. vermont.gov/ocs/services/enforce_support.
- National Child Support Enforcement Association, www.ncsea.org: Information about federal programs and links to state agencies.

Federal child support enforcement programs and laws: Federal Parent Locator Service, www.acf.hhs.gov/programs/cse/newhire: Links to child support enforcement programs like the passport denial program.

Child support calculators to determine state guidelines: www.alllaw.com/ calculators/childsupport: Search your state.

Virginia

Statewide Legal Resources

State website:
- www.virginia.gov. Links and information for many state agencies and departments.
- www.dss.virginia.gov/family/children.html. Especially relevant for state family law issues.

State and federal statutes:
- Nolo, www.nolo.com/legal-research/state-law.html.
- The Legal Information Institute at Cornell University, http://topics.law.cornell.edu/wex/table_family.
- Justia, www.justia.com/family.
- www.usa.gov: Federal government site.

State court information and family law forms:
- www.courts.state.va.us: Do-it-yourself court forms and instructions, links to local court websites. Search by topic, such as divorce, adoption, or custody.
- National Center for State Courts, www.ncsc.org: Links to state courts (browse by state under "Information and Resources").

Local laws:
- www.statelocalgov.net: Links to websites of many cities and counties, where you can check local rules and ordinances, such as graffiti rules.
- www.municode.com: Municipal codes.

Marriage

Requirements: No blood test required. You must be of the age of consent, not be too closely related to your intended spouse, not be married to anyone else, and have sufficient mental capacity, meaning you understand what you are doing when you marry. You can marry immediately after your marriage license is issued, and your license is good for 60 days. For more details, check your county clerk's office.

Common law marriage: No.

Community property: No.

Same-sex marriage: No.

Marriage-equivalent relationship: No. Virginia does not recognize domestic partnerships, civil unions, or reciprocal beneficiaries.

Divorce

Grounds for divorce: Fault or no-fault grounds are allowed.

Residency requirement: At least one spouse must be a resident of Virginia for six months or 180 days before filing for divorce.

How property is divided: Equitable division.

State laws, forms, and resources:
- Virginia state court website, www.courts.state.va.us.
- Women's Law Initiative, www.womenslaw.org: State-by-state information on divorce, custody, and related topics.
- www.divorcenet.com, www.divorcesupport.com, www.divorceinfo.com, www.divorcecentral.com: Helpful divorce websites.

Divorce attorneys and mediators in your area:
- Nolo's Lawyer Directory, www.nolo.com: Divorce attorneys in your area.
- National Center for Lesbian Rights, www.nclrights.org, 800-528-6257: Attorneys experienced in same-sex divorces.
- www.mediate.com, 541-345-1629: Mediators in your area.

Child Custody

Child custody guidelines: Virginia courts begin with a presumption that it's best for a child to have frequent and continuing contact with both parents after a divorce. If possible, judges want to support joint custody arrangements.

State laws, forms, and resources: See list in "Divorce," above.

International custody disputes: International Parental Child Abduction Division in the Office of Children's Issues of the U.S. State Department, http://travel.state.gov/childabduction, 888-407-4747.

State surrogacy laws:

- Human Rights Campaign, www.hrc.org (search "surrogacy laws").
- National Infertility Association, www.resolve.org (click "Family Building Options," then "Surrogacy").

Child Support

Child support guidelines: Virginia requires all parents to support their children. The amount of child support depends primarily on each parent's income and other resources and how much time each parent spends with the children.

State laws, forms, and resources: See list in "Divorce," above.

- www.supportguidelines.com: Links to state and federal laws and agencies.

State child support enforcement agency:

- Division of Child Support Enforcement, www.dss.virginia.gov/division/dcse/index.html.
- National Child Support Enforcement Association, www.ncsea.org: Information about federal programs and links to state agencies.

Federal child support enforcement programs and laws: Federal Parent Locator Service, www.acf.hhs.gov/programs/cse/newhire: Links to child support enforcement programs like the passport denial program.

Child support calculators to determine state guidelines: www.alllaw.com/calculators/childsupport: Search your state.

Washington

Statewide Legal Resources

State website:
- www.access.wa.gov. Links and information for many state agencies and departments.
- www.dshs.wa.gov/children.shtml. Especially relevant for state family law issues.

State and federal statutes:
- Nolo, www.nolo.com/legal-research/state-law.html.
- The Legal Information Institute at Cornell University, http://topics.law.cornell.edu/wex/table_family.
- Justia, www.justia.com/family.
- www.usa.gov: Federal government site.

State court information and family law forms:
- www.courts.wa.gov: Do-it-yourself court forms and instructions, links to local court websites. Search by topic, such as divorce, adoption, or custody.
- National Center for State Courts, www.ncsc.org: Links to state courts (browse by state under "Information and Resources").

Local laws:
- www.statelocalgov.net: Links to websites of many cities and counties, where you can check local rules and ordinances, such as graffiti rules.
- www.municode.com: Municipal codes.

Marriage

Requirements: No blood test required. You must be of the age of consent, not be too closely related to your intended spouse, not be married to anyone else, and have sufficient mental capacity, meaning you understand what you are doing when you marry. You can marry three days after your marriage license is issued, and your license is good for 60 days. For more details, check your county clerk's office.

Common law marriage: No.

Community property: Yes.

Same-sex marriage: No.

Marriage-equivalent relationship: Yes. Same-sex couples can register as domestic partners and have the same rights and responsibilities as a married couple under state law.

Divorce

Grounds for divorce: No-fault. However, fault may be considered by the court as a factor in dividing property or awarding alimony.

Residency requirement: None

How property is divided: Community property.

State laws, forms, and resources:
* Washington state court website, www.courts.wa.gov.
* Women's Law Initiative, www.womenslaw.org: State-by-state information on divorce, custody, and related topics.
* www.divorcenet.com, www.divorcesupport.com, www.divorceinfo.com, www.divorcecentral.com: Helpful divorce websites.

Divorce attorneys and mediators in your area:
* Nolo's Lawyer Directory, www.nolo.com: Divorce attorneys in your area.
* National Center for Lesbian Rights, www.nclrights.org, 800-528-6257: Attorneys experienced in same-sex divorces.
* www.mediate.com, 541-345-1629: Mediators in your area.

Child Custody

Child custody guidelines: Washington courts begin with a presumption that it's best for a child to have frequent and continuing contact with both parents after a divorce. If possible, judges want to support joint custody arrangements.

State laws, forms, and resources: See list in "Divorce," above.

International custody disputes: International Parental Child Abduction Division in the Office of Children's Issues of the U.S. State Department, http://travel.state.gov/childabduction, 888-407-4747.

State surrogacy laws:

- Human Rights Campaign, www.hrc.org (search "surrogacy laws").
- National Infertility Association, www.resolve.org (click "Family Building Options," then "Surrogacy").

Child Support

Child support guidelines: Washington requires all parents to support their children. The amount of child support depends primarily on each parent's income and other resources and how much time each parent spends with the children.

State laws, forms, and resources: See list in "Divorce," above.

- www.supportguidelines.com: Links to state and federal laws and agencies.

State child support enforcement agency:

- State Division of Child Support, www.dshs.wa.gov/dcs.
- National Child Support Enforcement Association, www.ncsea.org: Information about federal programs and links to state agencies.

Federal child support enforcement programs and laws: Federal Parent Locator Service, www.acf.hhs.gov/programs/cse/newhire: Links to child support enforcement programs like the passport denial program.

Child support calculators to determine state guidelines: www.alllaw.com/calculators/childsupport: Search your state.

West Virginia

Statewide Legal Resources

State website:

- www.wv.gov. Links and information for many state agencies and departments.
- www.wvdhhr.org/bcf. Especially relevant for state family law issues.

State and federal statutes:

- Nolo, www.nolo.com/legal-research/state-law.html.
- The Legal Information Institute at Cornell University, http://topics.law.cornell.edu/wex/table_family.
- Justia, www.justia.com/family.
- www.usa.gov: Federal government site.

State court information and family law forms:

- www.state.wv.us/wvsca/wvsystem.htm: Do-it-yourself court forms and instructions, links to local court websites. Search by topic, such as divorce, adoption, or custody.
- National Center for State Courts, www.ncsc.org: Links to state courts (browse by state under "Information and Resources").

Local laws:

- www.statelocalgov.net: Links to websites of many cities and counties, where you can check local rules and ordinances, such as graffiti rules.
- www.municode.com: Municipal codes.

Marriage

Requirements: No blood test required. You must be of the age of consent, not be too closely related to your intended spouse, not be married to anyone else, and have sufficient mental capacity, meaning you understand what you are doing when you marry. You can marry immediately after your marriage license is issued, and your license is good for 60 days. For more details, check your county clerk's office.

Common law marriage: No.

Community property: No.

Same-sex marriage: No.

Marriage-equivalent relationship: No. West Virginia does not recognize domestic partnerships, civil unions, or reciprocal beneficiaries.

Divorce

Grounds for divorce: Fault or no-fault grounds are allowed, or you can base your divorce on the fact that you've been separated from your spouse for at least two years.

Residency requirement: At least one spouse must be a resident of West Virginia for 12 months if marriage was out of state (none if marriage was in West Virginia) before filing for divorce.

How property is divided: Equitable division.

State laws, forms, and resources:
- West Virginia state court website, www.state.wv.us/wvsca/wvsystem.htm.
- Women's Law Initiative, www.womenslaw.org: State-by-state information on divorce, custody, and related topics.
- www.divorcenet.com, www.divorcesupport.com, www.divorceinfo.com, www.divorcecentral.com: Helpful divorce websites.

Divorce attorneys and mediators in your area:
- Nolo's Lawyer Directory, www.nolo.com: Divorce attorneys in your area.
- National Center for Lesbian Rights, www.nclrights.org, 800-528-6257: Attorneys experienced in same-sex divorces.
- www.mediate.com, 541-345-1629: Mediators in your area.

Child Custody

Child custody guidelines: West Virginia courts begin with a presumption that it's best for a child to have frequent and continuing contact with both parents after a divorce. If possible, judges want to support joint custody arrangements.

State laws, forms, and resources: See list in "Divorce," above.

International custody disputes: International Parental Child Abduction Division in the Office of Children's Issues of the U.S. State Department, http://travel.state.gov/childabduction, 888-407-4747.

State surrogacy laws:
- Human Rights Campaign, www.hrc.org (search "surrogacy laws").
- National Infertility Association, www.resolve.org (click "Family Building Options," then "Surrogacy").

Child Support

Child support guidelines: West Virginia requires all parents to support their children. The amount of child support depends primarily on each parent's income and other resources and how much time each parent spends with the children.

State laws, forms, and resources: See list in "Divorce," above.
- www.supportguidelines.com: Links to state and federal laws and agencies.

State child support enforcement agency:
- Bureau for Child Support Enforcement, www.wvdhhr.org/bcse.
- National Child Support Enforcement Association, www.ncsea.org: Information about federal programs and links to state agencies.

Federal child support enforcement programs and laws: Federal Parent Locator Service, www.acf.hhs.gov/programs/cse/newhire: Links to child support enforcement programs like the passport denial program.

Child support calculators to determine state guidelines: www.alllaw.com/calculators/childsupport: Search your state.

Wisconsin

Statewide Legal Resources

State website:
* www.wisconsin.gov. Links and information for many state agencies and departments.
* www.dcf.wisconsin.gov. Especially relevant for state family law issues.

State and federal statutes:
* Nolo, www.nolo.com/legal-research/state-law.html.
* The Legal Information Institute at Cornell University, http://topics.law.cornell.edu/wex/table_family.
* Justia, www.justia.com/family.
* www.usa.gov: Federal government site.

State court information and family law forms:
* www.wicourts.gov: Do-it-yourself court forms and instructions, links to local court websites. Search by topic, such as divorce, adoption, or custody.
* National Center for State Courts, www.ncsc.org: Links to state courts (browse by state under "Information and Resources").

Local laws:
* www.statelocalgov.net: Links to websites of many cities and counties, where you can check local rules and ordinances, such as graffiti rules.
* www.municode.com: Municipal codes.

Marriage

Requirements: No blood test required. You must be of the age of consent, not be too closely related to your intended spouse, not be married to anyone else, and have sufficient mental capacity, meaning you understand what you are doing when you marry. You can marry immediately after your marriage license is issued, and your license is good for 30 days. For more details, check your county clerk's office.

Common law marriage: No.

Community property: Yes.

Same-sex marriage: No.

Marriage-equivalent relationship: No. However, same-sex couples in Wisconsin can register as domestic partnerships and receive some, but not all, of the rights of marriage.

Divorce

Grounds for divorce: No-fault. However, fault may be considered by the court as a factor in dividing property or awarding alimony.

Residency requirement: At least one spouse must be a resident of Wisconsin for six months before filing for divorce.

How property is divided: Community property.

State laws, forms, and resources:
* Wisconsin state court website, www.wicourts.gov.
* Women's Law Initiative, www.womenslaw.org: State-by-state information on divorce, custody, and related topics.
* www.divorcenet.com, www.divorcesupport.com, www.divorceinfo.com, www.divorcecentral.com: Helpful divorce websites.

Divorce attorneys and mediators in your area:
* Nolo's Lawyer Directory, www.nolo.com: Divorce attorneys in your area.
* National Center for Lesbian Rights, www.nclrights.org, 800-528-6257: Attorneys experienced in same-sex divorces.
* www.mediate.com, 541-345-1629: Mediators in your area.

Child Custody

Child custody guidelines: Wisconsin courts begin with a presumption that it's best for a child to have frequent and continuing contact with both parents after a divorce. If possible, judges want to support joint custody arrangements.

State laws, forms, and resources: See list in "Divorce," above.

International custody disputes: International Parental Child Abduction Division in the Office of Children's Issues of the U.S. State Department, http://travel.state.gov/childabduction, 888-407-4747.

State surrogacy laws:
- Human Rights Campaign, www.hrc.org (search "surrogacy laws").
- National Infertility Association, www.resolve.org (click "Family Building Options," then "Surrogacy").

Child Support

Child support guidelines: Wisconsin requires all parents to support their children. The amount of child support depends primarily on each parent's income and other resources and how much time each parent spends with the children.

State laws, forms, and resources: See list in "Divorce," above.
- www.supportguidelines.com: Links to state and federal laws and agencies.

State child support enforcement agency:
- Case Management Services, Wisconsin Child Support Program, www.dcf.wisconsin.gov/bcs/enforcement.htm.
- National Child Support Enforcement Association, www.ncsea.org: Information about federal programs and links to state agencies.

Federal child support enforcement programs and laws: Federal Parent Locator Service, www.acf.hhs.gov/programs/cse/newhire: Links to child support enforcement programs like the passport denial program.

Child support calculators to determine state guidelines: www.alllaw.com/calculators/childsupport: Search your state.

Wyoming

Statewide Legal Resources

State website:

- www.wyoming.gov. Links and information for many state agencies and departments.
- http://dfsweb.state.wy.us. Especially relevant for state family law issues.

State and federal statutes:

- Nolo, www.nolo.com/legal-research/state-law.html.
- The Legal Information Institute at Cornell University, http://topics.law.cornell.edu/wex/table_family.
- Justia, www.justia.com/family.
- www.usa.gov: Federal government site.

State court information and family law forms:

- www.courts.state.wy.us: Do-it-yourself court forms and instructions, links to local court websites. Search by topic, such as divorce, adoption, or custody.
- National Center for State Courts, www.ncsc.org: Links to state courts (browse by state under "Information and Resources").

Local laws:

- www.statelocalgov.net: Links to websites of many cities and counties, where you can check local rules and ordinances, such as graffiti rules.
- www.municode.com: Municipal codes.

Marriage

Requirements: No blood test required. You must be of the age of consent, not be too closely related to your intended spouse, not be married to anyone else, and have sufficient mental capacity, meaning you understand what you are doing when you marry. You can marry immediately after your marriage license is issued. For more details, check your county clerk's office.

Common law marriage: No.

Wyoming

Community property: No.

Same-sex marriage: No.

Marriage-equivalent relationship: No. Wyoming does not recognize domestic partnerships, civil unions, or reciprocal beneficiaries.

Divorce

Grounds for divorce: No-fault. However, fault may be considered by the court as a factor in dividing property or awarding alimony.

Residency requirement: At least one spouse must be a resident of Wyoming for 60 days before filing for divorce.

How property is divided: Equitable division.

State laws, forms, and resources:
- Wyoming state court website, www.courts.state.wy.us.
- Women's Law Initiative, www.womenslaw.org: State-by-state information on divorce, custody, and related topics.
- www.divorcenet.com, www.divorcesupport.com, www.divorceinfo.com, www.divorcecentral.com: Helpful divorce websites.

Divorce attorneys and mediators in your area:
- Nolo's Lawyer Directory, www.nolo.com: Divorce attorneys in your area.
- National Center for Lesbian Rights, www.nclrights.org, 800-528-6257: Attorneys experienced in same-sex divorces.
- www.mediate.com, 541-345-1629: Mediators in your area.

Child Custody

Child custody guidelines: Wyoming courts begin with a presumption that it's best for a child to have frequent and continuing contact with both parents after a divorce. If possible, judges want to support joint custody arrangements.

State laws, forms, and resources: See list in "Divorce," above.

International custody disputes: International Parental Child Abduction Division in the Office of Children's Issues of the U.S. State Department, http://travel.state.gov/childabduction, 888-407-4747.

State surrogacy laws:
- Human Rights Campaign, www.hrc.org (search "surrogacy laws").
- National Infertility Association, www.resolve.org (click "Family Building Options," then "Surrogacy").

Child Support

Child support guidelines: Wyoming requires all parents to support their children. The amount of child support depends primarily on each parent's income and other resources and how much time each parent spends with the children.

State laws, forms, and resources: See list in "Divorce," above.
- www.supportguidelines.com: Links to state and federal laws and agencies.

State child support enforcement agency:
- Child Support Enforcement Division, http://dfsweb.state.wy.us/child-support-enforcement/index.html.
- National Child Support Enforcement Association, www.ncsea.org: Information about federal programs and links to state agencies.

Federal child support enforcement programs and laws: Federal Parent Locator Service, www.acf.hhs.gov/programs/cse/newhire: Links to child support enforcement programs like the passport denial program.

Child support calculators to determine state guidelines: www.alllaw.com/calculators/childsupport: Search your state.

Adoption, Children, and Elder Care Resources

Th"his appendix provides resources and links to websites that provide state-by-state information on topics covered in the Adoption, Children, and Elder Care chapters. See Appendix A for state-by-state details on the topics covered in the Marriage, Divorce, Child Custody, and Child Support chapters.

> ### TIP
> **Keep up to date.** Be aware that contact information may change, and that the law itself is not static. Always make sure you have the most up-to-date information by checking for legal updates at www.nolo.com.

Adoption

State adoption laws, forms, and resources: See list in "Divorce," in Appendix A. Useful websites for state-by-state information include the following:

- The National Adoption Information Clearinghouse, www.adoption.com: State-by-state information on consent to adoption, regulation of adoption expenses, use of advertising, post-adoption contact agreements, access to adoption records, and extensive information on all aspects of adoption. See http://laws.adoption.com/statutes/state-adoption-laws.html for state rules and federal laws related to adoption, such as the Indian Child Welfare Act, and international adoption laws, such as the Hague Convention on Protection of Children.

- Adoption and Child Welfare Lawsite (National Center for Adoption Law and Policy), www.adoptionchildwelfarelaw.org: Summaries of state laws and court cases on various adoption issues.

- Child Welfare Information Gateway, www.childwelfare.gov.adoption: Details on state laws, such as who may adopt, be adopted, or place a child for adoption; links to state statutes; and fact sheets on topics such as stepparent adoptions and home studies. Includes National Foster Care & Adoption Directory (www.childwelfare.gov/nfcad) which lists licensed state and local adoption agencies, support groups, and links to state child welfare agency websites.

State laws on minors' consent to adoption: www.guttmacher.org (search "minors' rights as parents").

State associations for foster parents: National Foster Parent Association, www.nfpainc.org, 800-557-5238: Contact information for state and local associations and other foster care resources.

Independent adoptions: Independent Adoption Center, www.adoption.help. org, 800-877-6736: National nonprofit that specializes in open adoptions.

International adoption:
- U.S. State Department, http://travel.state.gov/family/adoption/adoption_485.html.
- U.S. Citizenship and Immigration Services, www.uscis.gov (click "Resources" then "Adoption-Based Resource").

State laws on same-sex adoptions, including second parent adoptions:
- National Center for Lesbian Rights, www.nclrights.org.
- Human Rights Campaign, www.hrc.org.
- Lambda Legal, www.lambdalegal.org.

Children

State laws, forms, and resources: See lists in "Divorce" and "Statewide Legal Resources" in Appendix A.

State agency that issues birth certificates: Centers for Disease Control and Prevention, www.cdc.gov/nchs/w2w.htm: Copies of birth certificates (see "Where to Write for Vital Records"); information on getting other records (such as marriage and divorce) in your state.

Local Social Security office (for birth registration forms and Social Security numbers): Social Security Administration's Office Locator www.ssa.gov/locator, 800-772-1213.

Information and forms on tax breaks for parents:
- www.irs.gov: Information and forms for the dependent exemption, child tax credit, adoption tax credit, child care credit, and dependent care accounts.
- www.irs.gov/taxpros/article/0,,id=100236,00.html, 800-829-1040: State tax agencies.

State tobacco control laws, including youth access to cigarettes and penalties for sales to minors:

- American Lung Association, http://slati.lungusa.org: Links to state rules and articles on smoking by children.
- Your state department of health website (available at www.cdc.gov/mmwr/international/relres.html) will also have articles and resources.

State alcohol laws and agencies: Mothers Against Drunk Driving, www.madd.org, 800-438-6233: Extensive information on underage drinking.

Drug laws and enforcement agencies:

- www.justice.gov/dea/agency/domestic.htm: Local offices of the U.S. Drug Enforcement Administration; articles on drug prevention and education and resources for parents.
- National Alliance of State Drug Enforcement Agencies, www.nasdea.org/members.html: Links to state drug enforcement agencies.
- National Organization for the Reform of Marijuana Laws, http://norml.org/index.cfm?Group_ID=4516: State marijuana laws.

State department of motor vehicles: Search your state page, listed in Appendix A.

State rules on tattoos and piercing:

- National Conference of State Legislatures, www.ncsl.org/default.aspx?tabid=14393: State laws and age of consent for tattoos and body piercing.
- Also check the state department of health and tattoo websites, such as www.everytattoo.com.

Children's Internet use and online privacy:

- www.onguardonline.gov: Articles on Internet safety.
- www.ftc.gov/bcp/edu/pubs/consumer/tech/tec08.shtm: Information on federal privacy rules under the Children's Online Privacy Act.
- National Center for Missing and Exploited Children, www.cybertipline.com, 800-843-5678: Report unsolicited obscene material sent to a child.

State laws on bullying:

- Stop Bullying Now, stopbullyingnow.hrsa.gov, 888-ASK-HRSA: State anti-bullying laws and advice on how to stop bullying.
- Gay, Lesbian and Straight Education Network, www.glsen.org/bullying.
- Anti-Defamation League, www.adl.org/combatbullying.

State child welfare laws and child protective services agencies: Child Welfare Information Gateway, www.childwelfare.gov/systemwide/laws_policies/state, 800-394-3366: Links to state laws on child abuse and neglect, infant "safe haven" laws, and other child welfare rules and resources.

State laws on minors' access to healthcare without parental consent:

- Guttmacher Institute, www.guttmacher.org/statecenter/spibs/index.html: State-by-state information on laws affecting sexual and reproductive rights, including abortion laws.
- State department of health (available at www.cdc.gov/mmwr/international/relres.html): Information on this and other topics, such as immunization requirements for minors.

Health insurance rules:

- U.S. Department of Health and Human Services, www.healthcare.gov: Details on federal health care reform and health insurance options by state.
- Your state department of health or insurance (search your state page, listed in Appendix A) should also have information.

Federal, state, and local school rules:

- U.S. Department of Education, www.ed.gov, 800-872-5327: Federal laws such as No Child Left Behind or the Individuals with Disabilities Education Act, and state departments of education, contacts, and information.
- National School Boards Association, www.nsba.org/MainMenu/SchoolLaw.aspx, 703-838-6722: Legal updates on topics such as school safety and student rights (see "School Law").
- www.wrightslaw.com: State and federal special education law and programs.
- LD Online, www.ldonline.com: Resources about learning disabilities and ADHD.

Child labor laws:

- U.S. Department of Labor, www.dol.gov: Federal labor laws affecting minors (see www.dol.gov/compliance/audience/youth.htm or call 866-487-2365).
- www.dol.gov/whd/state/certification.htm: State rules on work permits (employment certificates) for minors.
- www.dol.gov/whd/state/state.htm: Labor laws and agencies by state.

Federal and state resources on juvenile crime:

- U.S. Department of Justice Office of Juvenile Justice and Delinquency Prevention, www.ojjdp.gov/statecontacts/resourcelist.asp, 202-307-5911: State resources.
- National Center for Juvenile Justice, www.ncjj.org/stateprofiles: State Juvenile Justice Profiles; http://70.89.227.250:8080/stateprofiles/asp/slinksAL_CA.asp: "State Links" page links to Youth Services Boards, Divisions of Juvenile Justice, Department of Juvenile Corrections, and many state information centers.

Elder Care

State laws, forms, and resources: See lists in "Divorce" and "Statewide Legal Resources" in Appendix A.

State healthcare directive forms: Contact a local hospital or the U.S. Living Will Registry, http://uslwr.com/formslist.shtm.

State help with insurance: State Health Insurance Assistance Program (SHIP), www.shiptalk.org (search "Find a State SHIP"): State programs that provide counselors who can review seniors' existing coverage and find government programs that may help with health insurance and long-term care expenses.

Federal, state, and local programs and services for seniors:

- National Association of the Area Agencies on Aging Elder Care Locator, www.eldercare.gov, 800-677-1116: Information on eldercare services and local programs.
- Administration on Aging, www.aoa.gov, 202-619-0724. State and area offices on aging.

Medicare and Medicaid benefits and rules:

- Centers for Medicare & Medicaid Services, www.cms.gov.
- www.medicare.gov: Official Medicare site.

State adult protective services offices: National Center on Elder Abuse, www.ncea.aoa.gov, 302-831-3525. www.dhr.state.al.us/page.asp?pageid=274: Federal and state agencies charged with investigating reports of elder financial abuse and helping victims; state laws, hotlines, and other resources.

Index

⚖️ NOLO *Online Legal Forms*

Nolo offers a large library of legal solutions and forms, created by Nolo's in-house legal staff. These reliable documents can be prepared in minutes.

Create a Document

- **Incorporation.** Incorporate your business in any state.
- **LLC Formations.** Gain asset protection and pass-through tax status in any state.
- **Wills.** Nolo has helped people make over 2 million wills. Is it time to make or revise yours?
- **Living Trust (avoid probate).** Plan now to save your family the cost, delays, and hassle of probate.
- **Trademark.** Protect the name of your business or product.
- **Provisional Patent.** Preserve your rights under patent law and claim "patent pending" status.

Download a Legal Form

Nolo.com has hundreds of top quality legal forms available for download—bills of sale, promissory notes, nondisclosure agreements, LLC operating agreements, corporate minutes, commercial lease and sublease, motor vehicle bill of sale, consignment agreements and many, many more.

Review Your Documents

Many lawyers in Nolo's consumer-friendly lawyer directory will review Nolo documents for a very reasonable fee. Check their detailed profiles at **Nolo.com/lawyers**.

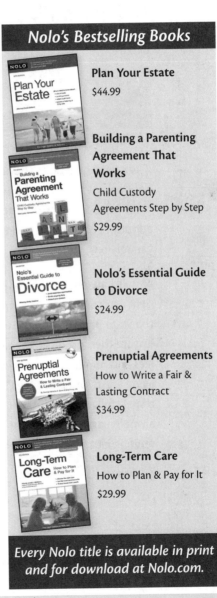

3 1901 04965 9685